Microsoft® Works 4 Projects for Windows® 95

Carl A. Scharpf
University of Southern California

The Benjamin/Cummings Publishing Company, Inc.
Menlo Park, California • Reading, Massachusetts
New York • Don Mills, Ontario • Harlow, U.K. • Amsterdam
Bonn • Paris • Milan • Madrid • Sydney • Singapore • Tokyo
Seoul • Taipei • Mexico City • San Juan, Puerto Rico

ISBN 0-8053-1268-4   bundled version
ISBN 0-8053-7260-1   stand alone version
1 2 3 4 5 6 7 8 9 10—DOW—00 99 98 97 96

Senior Editor: *Maureen A. Allaire*
Project Manager: *Adam Ray*
Project Editor: *Kathy G. Yankton*
Assistant Editor: *Heide Chavez*
Executive Editor: *Michael Payne*
Production Editor: *Sue Purdy Pelosi*
Marketing Manager: *Melissa Baumwald*
Custom Publishing Operations Specialist: *Michael Smith*
Senior Manufacturing Coordinator: *Janet Weaver*

Ordering from the SELECT System

For more information on ordering and pricing policies for the SELECT System of microcomputer applications texts and their supplements, please contact your Addison-Wesley • Benjamin/Cummings sales representative or call our SELECT Hotline at 800/854-2595.

The Benjamin/Cummings Publishing Company, Inc.
2725 Sand Hill Road
Menlo Park, CA 94025
http://www.aw.com/bc/is
bc.is@aw.com

Getting Started

Welcome to the *SELECT Lab Series.* We invite you to explore how you can take advantage of the newest Windows 95 features of the most popular software applications using this up-to-date learning package.

Greater access to ideas and information is changing the way people work. With Windows 95 applications you have greater integration capabilities and access to Internet resources than ever before. The *SELECT Lab Series* helps you take advantage of these valuable resources with special assignments devoted to the Internet and additional connectivity resources which can be accessed through our web site, **http://www.aw.com/bc/is.**

The key to using software is making the software work for you. The *SELECT Lab Series* will help you learn to use software as a productivity tool by guiding you step-by-step through case-based projects similar to those you will encounter at school, work, or home. When you are finished with this learning package, you will be fully prepared to use the resources this software offers. Your success is our success.

A GUIDED TOUR

To facilitate the learning process, we have developed a consistent organizational structure for each module in the *SELECT Lab Series.*

You begin using the software almost immediately. A brief **Overview** introduces the software package and the basic application functions. **Getting Help** covers the on-line Help feature in each package. **A Note to the Student** explains any special conventions or system configurations observed in a particular module.

Each module contains six to eight **Projects,** an **Operations Reference** of all the operations covered in each module, an extensive **Glossary** of **key terms,** and an **Index.**

The following figures introduce the elements you will encounter as you use each SELECT module.

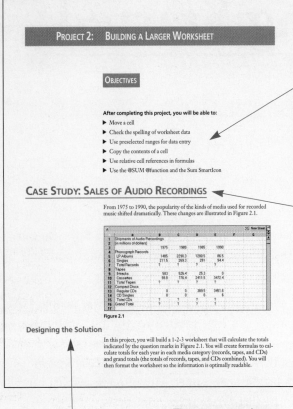

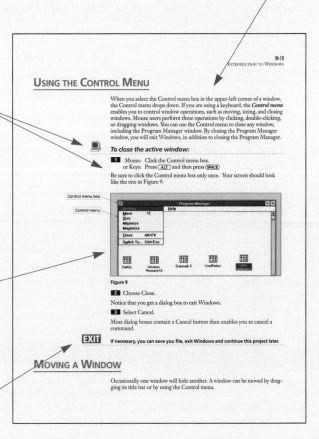

Each project begins with **Learning Objectives** that describe the skills and commands you will master.

Projects revolve around **Case Studies**, which provide real-world scenarios so you can learn an application in a broader context.

Each topic begins with a brief explanation of concepts you will learn and the operations you will perform.

Designing the Solution introduces you to important problem-solving techniques. You will see how to analyze the case study and design a solution before you sit down at the computer.

The **computer icon** provides a cue that you should begin working at the computer, and **Numbered steps** guide you step-by-step through each project, providing detailed instructions on how to perform operations.

Visual cues such as **screen shots** provide examples of what you will see on your own computer screen, reinforce key concepts, and help you check your work.

Exit points identify good places in each project to take a break.

Key Terms are boldfaced and italicized and appear throughout each project.

Margin figures show on-screen tools that are often convenient alternatives to menu commands presented in the numbered steps.

Tips, Reminders, Cautions, and **Quick Fixes** appear throughout each project to highlight important, helpful, or pertinent information about each application.

Study Questions (Multiple Choice, Short Answer, and For Discussion) may be used as self-tests or homework assignments.

Review Exercises present hands-on tasks to help you build on skills acquired in the projects.

Each project ends with **The Next Step** which discusses the concepts from the project and proposes other uses and applications for the skills you have learned, a **Summary,** and a list of **Key Terms and Operations**.

Assignments require critical thinking and encourage synthesis and integration of project skills.

WRD-12
WORD FOR WINDOWS

OPENING A NEW DOCUMENT

Word for Windows normally opens with a blank window and is ready to create a new document. If someone was using the computer before you, however, the window may already contain text. In that case, you will need to open a blank window for your new document. (If Word for Windows is not running already, start it by double-clicking the Word for Windows icon on the Windows desktop.)

To open a blank window for a new document:

1 Select New on the File menu or press `ALT` + `F7` and then type n

The New dialog box appears, as shown in Figure 1.1. This dialog box allows you to select from a variety of *templates* and *wizards*. **Templates** are preformatted skeleton documents ranging from memos to newsletters. **Wizards** ask a series of questions about a document format and then use that information to build a document for you to use. Right now, you need the default general-purpose template named Normal.

Figure 1.1

2 If Normal does not appear in the Template box, type Normal

3 Select OK.

Tip You can open a new document with a click of the mouse Use the New document button on the standard toolbar to open a Normal document with a single click.

The document area of the screen will be blank except for the blinking vertical *insertion point* (I), *the end-of-document mark* (_), and possibly a *paragraph mark* (¶). The **insertion point** marks the position where text will be inserted or deleted when you type at the keyboard. The **end-of-document mark** shows where the document ends; you cannot insert characters after the end-of-document mark. A **paragraph mark** indicates the end of a paragraph and forces the beginning of a new line. The paragraph mark may not show on your screen. If not, you will learn shortly how to make it visible.

Short Answer
1. What are the two main services offered by My Computer?
2. What objects are considered physical locations in My Computer?
3. Why is a directory structure sometimes called a tree?
4. How do you run a program from My Computer?
5. How do you create a new folder?
6. Will copying a file result in the original being changed in any way?
7. Why should you drag and drop objects using mouse button 2?
8. Will renaming a file cause a second copy of that file to be generated?

For Discussion
1. Why was the ability to create folders for file management on the PC so important?
2. My Computer will open a new window every time the user double-clicks on a drive or folder ol How could this create a problem?
3. Why should you expect there to be some sort of access restrictions on network drives?

Review Exercises

Examining the File System
Use My Computer to examine the root folders of your computer's local hard drive(s). If the computer part of a network, take a look at the network drives as well. Get some practice resizing, moving, and cl the many windows that will be created during this exercise. Draw a tree that shows how information is organized on your system and network—make note of the major folders in the root directories, and lo for other folders within these. You don't have to list the thousands of individual files!

Launching Programs from My Computer
Use My Computer to explore your student data diskette. Without using the Find command, look for program file AirMail and use My Computer to run the program. After closing AirMail, look on your hard drive(s) for a folder called Program Files. This is a standard directory on Windows 95 systems, though it may not be present, or may have a different name, on your system. Use My Computer to op the Program Files folder, and examine what's inside. There are probably more folders within Program Files; if an Accessories folder is present, open it and then use My Computer to launch MS Paint or W Pad.

Assignments

Drag-and-Drop Manipulation of Files and Folders
In this assignment, you will use My Computer to "juggle" files and folders. This will provide extensive practice with window management and using the mouse for drag-and-drop operations.

Open the Temp folder on your student data diskette. Create a folder within it called Reports. Open the Reports folder and create three new text documents called Rain Forest, Desert, and Coral Reef. Using drag-and-drop, *move* the Reports folder (which will include the files you just created) to the Text folder of the student data diskette. Select the two files Rain Forest and Coral Reef and, again using drag-and-drop, *copy* them to the Work subdirectory. Rename the file Desert to Tundra. Finally, delete the Reports folder (which will also delete the files it contains).

THE NEXT STEP

Access has many functions that are part of the You've already seen the Now() function in sev If you're interested in extending your knowled good place to start is the manual.
There are several other Report Wizards we reports have no Detail band. Tabular reports forms. The AutoReport Wizard will attempt that makes the most sense—at least, to the W Word Mail Merge, exports data in a format tha Merge feature can read. This is handy for proc
Experiment with fonts and print styles, an

SUMMARY AND EXERCISES

Summary
• Access includes ReportWizards for single-column, grouped, and tabular formats, as well as mailing labels. Wizards are also included that generate automatic reports and export data to Microsoft Word's Mail Merge format
• To build a report with fields from two or more tables, you can query by example to create a view first, and then create the report based on that view.
• Grouping lets you create reports with records collated according to the values in one or more fields.
• Grouping also lets you create subtotals for groups as well as a grand total for the report.
• You can display today's date with the Now() function.
• You can change the format in which the date is printed.
• The mailing label ReportWizard handles standard Avery label layouts.
• To insert text characters in a mailing label, you must use the text buttons provided by the ReportWizards.
• The UCase() function is helpful when you want to make sure report output is entirely upper case.

Key Terms and Operations

Key Terms	
group	report footer
group footer	report header
group header	UCase()
inner join	**Operations**
Now()	Create a new report
outer join	Page Preview
page footer	Report Design
page header	Sample Preview

FOLLOWING THE NUMBERED STEPS

To make the application modules easy to use in a lab setting, we have standardized the presentation of hands-on computer instructions as much as possible. The numbered step sections provide detailed, step-by-step instructions to guide you through the practical application of the conceptual material presented. Both keystroke and mouse instructions are used according to which one is more appropriate to complete a task. The instructions in the module assume that you know how to operate the keyboard, monitor, and printer.

Tip When you are using a mouse, unless indicated otherwise, you should assume that you are clicking the left button on the mouse. Several modules provide instructions for both mouse and keyboard users. When separate mouse and keyboard steps are given, be sure to follow one method or the other, but not both.

Each topic begins with a brief explanation of concepts. A computer icon or the ▶ symbol and a description of the task you will perform appear each time you are to begin working on the computer.

For Example:

To enter the address:

1 Type `123 Elm Street` and press (ENTER)

Notice that the keys you are to press and the text you are to type stand out. The text you will type appears in a special typeface to distinguish it from regular text. The key that you are to press mimics the labels of the keys on your keyboard.

When you are to press two keys or a key and a character simultaneously, the steps show the keys connected either with a plus sign or a bar.

For Example:
(SHFT) + (TAB)
(CTRL) + C

When you are to press keys sequentially, the keys are not connected and a space separates them.

For Example:
(CTRL) (PGDN)
(HOME) (HOME) (↑)

Be sure to press each key firmly, but quickly, one after the other. Keys begin repeating if you hold them down too long.

In some instances margin figures of single icons or buttons will appear next to the numbered steps. Margin figures provide visual cues to important tools that you can select as an alternative to the menu command in the numbered step.

For typographical conventions and other information unique to the application, please see *A Note to the Student* in the Overview of each module.

The *SELECT* Lab Series—A Connected Learning Resource

The *SELECT Lab Series* is a complete learning resource for success in the Information Age. Our application modules are designed to help you learn fast and effectively. Based around projects that reflect your world, each module helps you master key concepts and problem-solving techniques for using the software application you are learning. Through our web site you can access dynamic and current information resources that will help you get up to speed on the Information Highway and keep up with the ever changing world of technology.

Explore our web site **http://www.aw.com/bc/is** to discover:

- **B/C Link Online:** Our on-line newsletter which features the latest news and information on current computer technology and applications.
- **Student Opportunities and Activities:** Benjamin/Cummings' web site connects you to important job opportunities and internships.
- **What's New:** Access the latest news and information topics.
- **Links:** We provide relevant links to other interesting resources and educational sites.

The TechSuite

This module may be part of our new custom bundled system—the **Benjamin/Cummings TechSuite.** Your instructor can choose any combination of concepts texts, applications modules, and software to meet the exact needs of your course. The TechSuite meets your needs by offering you one convenient package at a discount price.

Supplements

Each module has a corresponding Instructor's Manual with a Test Bank and Transparency Masters. For each project in the student text, the Instructor's Manual includes Expanded Student Objectives, Answers to Study Questions, and Additional Assessment Techniques. The Test Bank contains two separate tests (with answers) consisting of multiple choice, true/false, and fill-in questions that are referenced to pages in the student's text. Transparency Masters illustrate 25 to 30 key concepts and screen captures from the text.

The Instructor's Data Disk contains student data files, answers to selected Review Exercises, answers to selected Assignments, and the test files from the Instructor's Manual in ASCII format.

ACKNOWLEDGMENTS

The Benjamin/Cummings Publishing Company would like to thank the following reviewers for their valuable contributions to the *SELECT Lab Series*.

Joseph Aieta
Babson College

Tom Ashby
Oklahoma CC

Bob Barber
Lane CC

Robert Caruso
Santa Rosa Junior College

Robert Chi
California State
Long Beach

Jill Davis
State University of New
York at Stony Brook

Fredia Dillard
Samford University

Peter Drexel
Plymouth State College

Ralph Duffy
North Seattle CC

David Egle
University of Texas,
Pan American

Jonathan Frank
Suffolk University

Patrick Gilbert
University of Hawaii

Maureen Greenbaum
Union County College

Sally Ann Hanson
Mercer County CC

Sunil Hazari
East Carolina University

Bruce Herniter
University of Hartford

Lisa Jackson
Henderson CC

Cynthia Kachik
Santa Fe CC

Bennett Kramer
Massasoit CC

Charles Lake
Faulkner State
Junior College

Ron Leake
Johnson County CC

Randy Marak
Hill College

Charles Mattox, Jr.
St. Mary's University

Jim McCullough
Porter and Chester
Institute

Gail Miles
Lenoir-Rhyne College

Steve Moore
University of
South Florida

Anthony Nowakowski
Buffalo State College

Gloria Oman
Portland State University

John Passafiume
Clemson University

Leonard Presby
William Paterson
College

Louis Pryor
Garland County CC

Michael Reilly
University of Denver

Dick Ricketts
Lane CC

Dennis Santomauro
Kean College of
New Jersey

Pamela Schmidt
Oakton CC

Gary Schubert
Alderson-Broaddus College

T. Michael Smith
Austin CC

Cynthia Thompson
Carl Sandburg College

Marion Tucker
Northern Oklahoma
College

JoAnn Weatherwax
Saddleback College

David Whitney
San Francisco State
University

James Wood
Tri-County
Technical College

Minnie Yen
University of Alaska,
Anchorage

Allen Zilbert
Long Island University

Contents

PROJECT 3: ENHANCING A DOCUMENT   78

ADDITIONAL ASSIGNMENTS   109

TERM PAPER PROJECT   111

PART II: SPREADSHEETS   115

PROJECT 1: CREATING A SPREADSHEET   117

PROJECT 2: REVISING AND ENHANCING A SPREADSHEET   138

Overview

Objectives

After completing this overview, you should be able to:

▶ Identify the components of integrated software

▶ Start Works 4 for Windows 95

▶ Access online Help

▶ Use the Help system's Introduction to Works

▶ Use menus to perform commands

▶ Work with dialog boxes

▶ Configure Works 4 for Windows 95

▶ Exit Works 4 for Windows 95

T o be productive with a computer, you often need a wide variety of software tools. A word processor is essential for creating documents such as letters and memos, a spreadsheet is necessary for developing accounting or financial applications, a database management system is the standard package for handling large amounts of data, a charting program is needed for creating visual representations of data, and a communications program is required for transferring data over phone lines. If you were to purchase all these products separately, you could easily spend more than $1000 and end up with a lot more power than you need. The best bet may be an integrated software package such as Microsoft Works 4 for Windows 95. To create Works, Microsoft gleaned the most popular features of various stand-alone programs and wrapped them into one reasonably priced package.

USING INTEGRATED SOFTWARE

Integrated software is an all-in-one product that typically consists of five components: a word processor, a spreadsheet program, a database management system, a charting package, and a communications program. Their similarity in terminology and operation—in other words, their high degree of integration—makes these products easy to use and enables the average computer user to become productive in a short time.

The first integrated software packages appeared on the market shortly after the first personal computers (PCs). Context MBA was released by Context Management Systems in 1983. In 1984, Lotus Development Corporation released Symphony, and Ashton-Tate introduced Framework. Compared to the slow-selling Context MBA, Symphony and Framework were fast and powerful, which led to their popularity in business environments. Microsoft introduced Works in 1987. The ease of use and attractive price of Works have made it a popular integrated software product in education, in the home, and in the workplace.

In the late 1980s, most integrated packages for PCs were character-based DOS applications. In the early 1990s, the advent of Windows 3.1 spawned a variety of graphical integrated applications including ClarisWorks for Windows, PFS:Window Works, and Microsoft Works for Windows. Adding to Microsoft Works' popularity is the fact that it is available in three versions: Works for DOS, Works for Windows 95, and Works for the Macintosh. In this module you will work with Works 4 for Windows 95.

USING MICROSOFT WORKS 4 FOR WINDOWS 95

Microsoft Works is a multipurpose program that consists of four tools for four types of tasks: word processing, spreadsheets, database management, and communications. In addition, analytical graphs can be produced using the charting capability available within the Spreadsheet tool; a drawing application can be used within any tool to create, edit, and modify drawings; pre-drawn clip-art images can be added to any document from the *ClipArt Gallery;* and *WordArt* can be used to create fancy headlines and interesting font effects. Designed to take advantage of the Windows *graphical user interface (GUI),* Microsoft Works 4 for Windows 95 provides users with a powerful applications program in which the various tools share a consistent "look and feel." This means the skills you develop within one tool can be used within the others, allowing you to be more creative and productive.

Using the Word Processing Tool

Word Processor

The *Word Processing tool* enables you to create a wide variety of text documents, from short letters and memos to lengthy term papers and multipage reports. Figure 0.1 shows a letter created with the Word Processing tool.

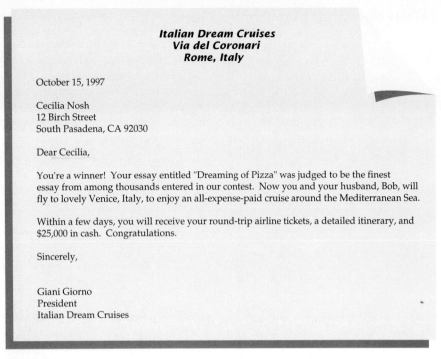

Italian Dream Cruises
Via del Coronari
Rome, Italy

October 15, 1997

Cecilia Nosh
12 Birch Street
South Pasadena, CA 92030

Dear Cecilia,

You're a winner! Your essay entitled "Dreaming of Pizza" was judged to be the finest essay from among thousands entered in our contest. Now you and your husband, Bob, will fly to lovely Venice, Italy, to enjoy an all-expense-paid cruise around the Mediterranean Sea.

Within a few days, you will receive your round-trip airline tickets, a detailed itinerary, and $25,000 in cash. Congratulations.

Sincerely,

Giani Giorno
President
Italian Dream Cruises

Figure 0.1

Using the Spreadsheet Tool

Spreadsheet

The *Spreadsheet tool* is ideal for performing mathematical calculations in a grid of rows and columns called a *spreadsheet* or *worksheet*. An electronic spreadsheet or worksheet allows you to enter text, numeric values, and formulas in the rows and columns that make a table. For example, you can create a checkbook-style register that automatically calculates the current balance after each transaction. A business can use a spreadsheet program to keep track of accounts receivable and accounts payable. A professor can enter students' test scores and use the Spreadsheet tool to calculate the average score. Figure 0.2 shows a checkbook register that was developed and then printed using the Spreadsheet tool.

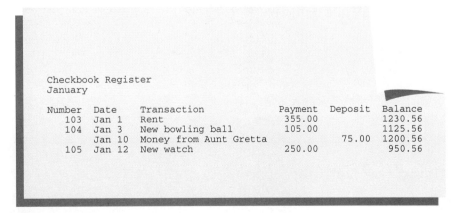

Checkbook Register
January

Number	Date	Transaction	Payment	Deposit	Balance
103	Jan 1	Rent	355.00		1230.56
104	Jan 3	New bowling ball	105.00		1125.56
	Jan 10	Money from Aunt Gretta		75.00	1200.56
105	Jan 12	New watch	250.00		950.56

Figure 0.2

Using the Charting Component

 In Works, the *charting* component is found within the Spreadsheet tool. Although charting is not considered a separate tool in Works, the package offers a sizable set of options that enable you to create a visual representation of spreadsheet data. You can create charts to forecast sales, to analyze the distribution of test data, or to track stock market trends. Figure 0.3 contains a bar chart and a pie chart that show the distribution of letter grades for Professor Brooks's class.

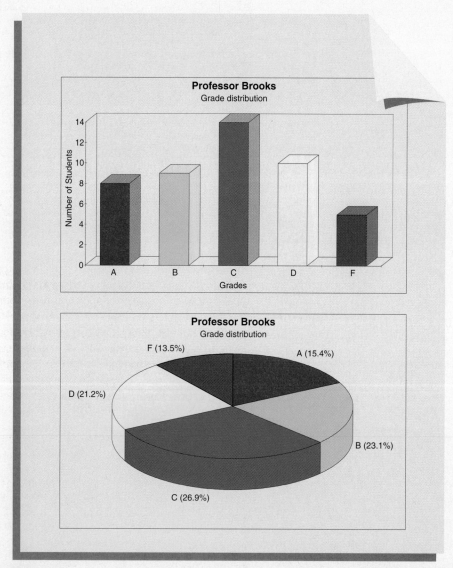

Figure 0.3

Using the Database Tool

 The *Database tool* enables you to manage large amounts of data. A *database,* which is a collection of highly structured data, can consist of a mailing list, a statement of warehouse inventory, or even data about a stamp collection.

For example, if you owned a video store, you could create a list of videos—this would be the database—and then quickly sort and print the entire list. You could find and edit information about specific video titles and add titles easily. Once you've created a database, you can create a *report,* which groups and summarizes data. Figure 0.4 presents a report in which video titles are sorted by category.

Video List

Title	Category	Rating	Price
Oh Yes, Oh Yes, Oh No	Comedy	PG-13	14.95
Aliens are Stealing My Socks	Comedy	R	15.75
Apache Helicopters and You	Documentary	G	11.95
My Life as a Banana Slug	Documentary	G	12.95
Raging Bees	Drama	PG	29.95
No Time to Scream	Horror	PG-13	15.95

Figure 0.4

Using the Communications Tool

Communications

The *Communications tool* allows the computer to communicate over telephone lines with another computer. You can look up current stock-market prices by calling a stock-market information service, and you can read about late-breaking news events by calling a news service and browsing through its news bulletins. You can even send, electronically, a letter to a friend in another part of the country. The following figure shows how Jim in Los Angeles uses telephone lines to communicate with Bob in New York City.

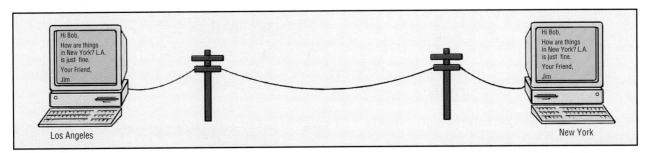

Figure 0.5

If you want to use the Communications tool, the computer must have a *modem.* A modem is a piece of hardware that translates computer signals into a form that can travel over phone lines.

Using the Tools Together

Although each tool in Works is not as robust as a stand-alone program, the combination of the tools provides you with a powerful, easy-to-learn product. For example, Works' word processing options are not as comprehensive as those of a full-featured word processor such as Microsoft Word for Windows. However, Works' simplified approach allows you to learn quickly how to create text documents. Once you understand how to use the word processor, you can readily learn the other tools, because they follow a consistent command structure.

Because all the Works tools are found in one package, using them together is a straightforward process. Figure 0.6 contains text that was created with the Word Processing tool and then combined with a spreadsheet and chart that were created with the Spreadsheet tool. Finally, a map was inserted from the ClipArt Gallery of images and a fancy title was created with WordArt.

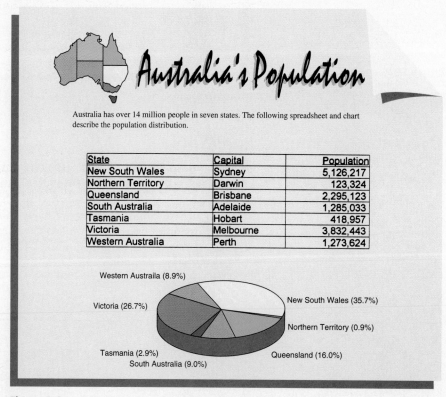

Australia's Population

Australia has over 14 million people in seven states. The following spreadsheet and chart describe the population distribution.

State	Capital	Population
New South Wales	Sydney	5,126,217
Northern Territory	Darwin	123,324
Queensland	Brisbane	2,295,123
South Australia	Adelaide	1,285,033
Tasmania	Hobart	418,957
Victoria	Melbourne	3,832,443
Western Australia	Perth	1,273,624

Western Austraila (8.9%)
Victoria (26.7%)
Tasmania (2.9%)
South Australia (9.0%)
New South Wales (35.7%)
Northern Territory (0.9%)
Queensland (16.0%)

Figure 0.6

USING THIS MODULE

This module is designed to make learning Microsoft Works easy. You will learn how to use all the Works tools by completing a variety of projects. Conceptual material is separated from numbered steps to make using the module in a lab setting straightforward. You will get your hands on the keyboard immediately and learn to use the Works online Help facility so you can get help when you need it.

The module is divided into an Overview and six parts. Each part consists of from one to four projects that describe how to use a particular tool or how to use the tools together. The material in the Overview and in each project is reinforced with a summary, a list of key terms and operations, and study questions; each project also has review exercises and additional assignments. Each part ends with one or more additional projects that draw on all the skills learned in that part. At the end of the module are an operations reference section; a glossary, which defines all the key terms; and an index.

STARTING WORKS

Microsoft Works can be started several ways. The following describes two methods for starting Works: using the menu system and using the desktop.

All programs can be started from the Windows 95 Start menu that typically appears in the bottom-left corner of the screen (some computers may have it on the top or side of the screen).

To start Works from the Start menu:

1 Turn on the computer. Windows 95 should start automatically.

2 Select the Start button in the bottom left of the screen.

3 Place the pointer on the Programs option. An additional menu should appear.

4 Place the pointer on the Microsoft Works 4 option. In the small menu that appears, place the pointer on Microsoft Works 4.
The screen should look similar to Figure 0.7.

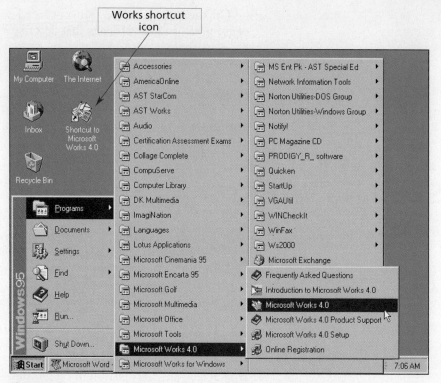

Figure 0.7

5 Select Microsoft Works 4 to start Works.

Many computers are set up with shortcuts for starting programs. The desktop may have an icon called "Shortcut to Microsoft Works 4" as shown in Figure 0.7.

To start Works with the shortcut icon:

1 Double-click the Shortcut to Microsoft Works icon on the desktop.

2 If you get a dialog box that asks whether you want to run a short demo of Works, select Cancel.

Working with the Opening Screen

The first thing to appear in Works is the Works *Task Launcher,* a starting point for creating documents, as shown in Figure 0.8. This dialog box includes three tabs: TaskWizards, Existing Documents, and Works Tools. Each tab provides a different approach for working on a document. When you select a tab, that tab moves in front of the other tabs so you can access its features.

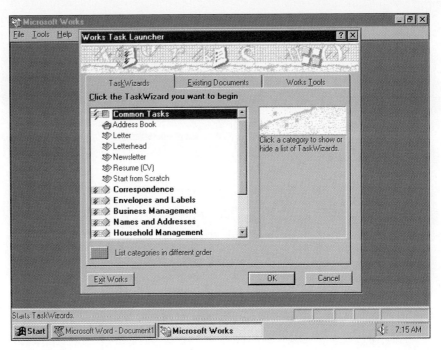

Figure 0.8

Quick Fix If you accidentally close the Works Task Launcher dialog box or if it is not visible, choose New from the File menu.

The ***TaskWizards*** tab shown in Figure 0.8 provides step-by-step instructions for performing common tasks, such as writing a business letter, laying out a résumé, or designing an address book. If you need to write a résumé, you can choose Résumé and answer a few questions about what style of résumé you desire. Then the TaskWizard will lay out the résumé according to your specifications. All you have to do is enter pertinent information such as your name, work history, and education.

The Existing Documents tab lets you open any document that you have already created. If you create a résumé and then several days later you decide to revise it, you can access the résumé again by selecting it from among the existing documents, as shown in Figure 0.9. In several projects, you will open existing files to continue developing them.

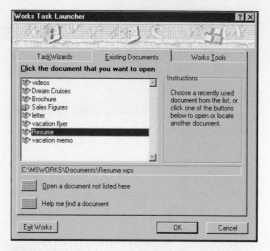

Figure 0.9

You can go directly to one of Works' four main tools by selecting the Works Tools tab. Four tools will be listed, as shown in Figure 0.10. To start the Word Processing tool, you would select the *button* that appears to the left of the tool name. You will be using these tools in later projects as this module guides you through the process of creating new files, such as word processing or spreadsheet files.

Figure 0.10

GETTING ONLINE HELP

Before you begin creating documents with Works, it is important to know how to get help from within the program. Works has a comprehensive Help system that provides information on commands, functions, messages, and procedures. The Help system is similar in format to the Windows Help system described in the Windows 95 module.

To view the Help menu:

1 If you see the Works Task Launcher dialog box, select the Cancel button to close the box.

Three menu names should appear across the top of the screen. You may also see a Help window on the right.

2 Choose the Help menu.

The screen should now look like Figure 0.11. Figure 0.11 has a Display Help Window button on the right side of the screen; your screen may not.

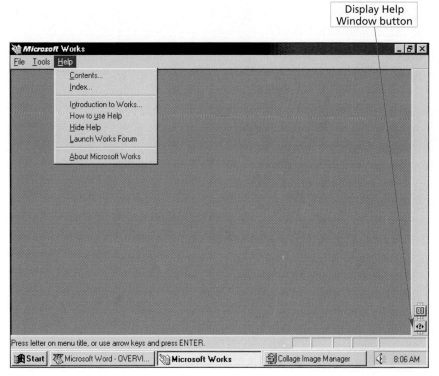

Figure 0.11

Working with the Help Window

Depending on how the computer is set up, you may see a Help window or a Display Help button on the right of the screen. In the Help window, Works continuously displays help related to your current task. If you do not like the Help window, there are two ways to remove it. You can hide it or you can temporarily shrink it.

 To hide and redisplay the Help window:

1 Choose Hide Help from the Help menu.

The Help window should be hidden. If you cannot find the Hide Help command in the Help menu, that's okay. It means the Help window is already hidden.

2 To redisplay the Help window, choose Show Help from the Help menu.

You should see a Help window as shown in Figure 0.12.

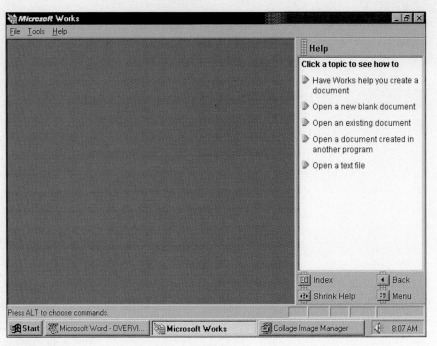

Figure 0.12

Notice in Figure 0.12 that there are four buttons at the bottom of the Help window. The Index button displays the Help Index, the Shrink Help button shrinks the Help window, the Back button takes you back to previous Help windows, and the Menu button displays the main Help menu within the Help window.

The Shrink Help button lets you temporarily shrink the Help window and also provides you with a button to redisplay the window at any time.

To shrink the Help window:

1 Select the Shrink Help button.
The screen should look like Figure 0.11. The Display Help button appears on the right of the screen.

The projects in this module assume that the Help window has been shrunk. You can display the Help window at any time by selecting the Display Help button.
Let's take a look at other components of the Works Help system.

Using the Help System's Introduction to Works

The Help System's Introduction to Works provides a quick overview of many tasks that can be performed in Works. Introduction to Works is an option in the Help menu.

To view the Introduction to Works:

1 Choose the Help menu.

2 Choose Introduction to Works.
The screen should look like Figure 0.13. The introduction takes about ten minutes.

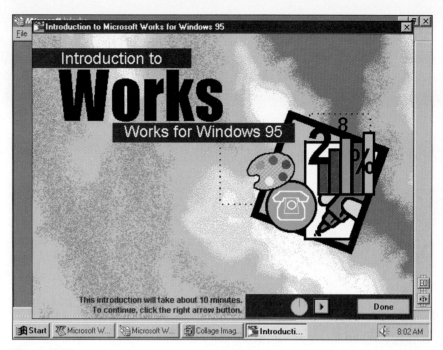

Figure 0.13

3 Move from one screen to the next by selecting the right-arrow button at the bottom of the screen.

4 Select Done when you are finished.

Accessing the Help Contents

The Help Contents is a good place to start when you aren't sure how to do something in one of the four main tools. The Help Contents lists major topics related to each of the tools and then provides step-by-step help for each topic. Suppose you need help aligning paragraphs.

To get help on aligning paragraphs:

1 If you see the Works Task Launcher, select Cancel; otherwise, go on to the next step.

2 Choose Contents from the Help menu.

3 Select the Word Processor button at the bottom of the Help Topics: Microsoft Works dialog box.
Your screen should look like Figure 0.14. By selecting the Word Processor button you indicate to Works that you want to list the Help topics related to the Word Processing tool. You would select the Spreadsheet, Database, or Communications buttons for more related topics.

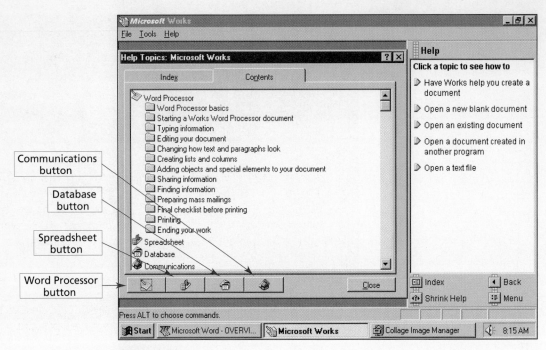

Figure 0.14

4 Select Changing how text and paragraphs look.

5 Select Alignment and spacing.

6 Select To change paragraph alignment.
As shown in Figure 0.15, on the right side of the screen there are step-by-step instructions labeled To change paragraph alignment. You can scroll down to read the entire description.

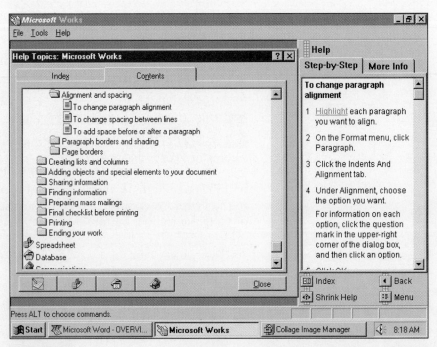

Figure 0.15

7 Select the Close button when you are finished reading about aligning paragraphs.

8 Select the Shrink Help button to shrink the Help window on the right side of the screen.

By navigating through the Help Contents system, you can receive help on almost any command or procedure related to any tool.

Using the Index to Search for Help

The Works Help system allows you to search for help on almost any topic by using the *Help Index.* To use the index search feature, you can choose Index from the Help menu and then type a word or phrase describing a search topic. Assume that you want help on creating text using WordArt, a small program that creates fancy headlines and titles.

To search for help on WordArt:

1 Choose Index from the Help menu.
A dialog box with a list of index entries appears, as shown in Figure 0.16. The dialog box is waiting for you to specify an index topic.

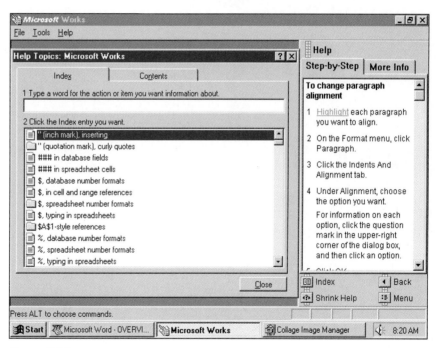

Figure 0.16

2 Delete any text in the text box.

3 Type **wordart**
A list of available WordArt topics appears. Notice that the index is not *case sensitive,* which means uppercase characters are not distinguished from lowercase characters. You can type WordArt or wordart.

4 Select WordArt: creating.

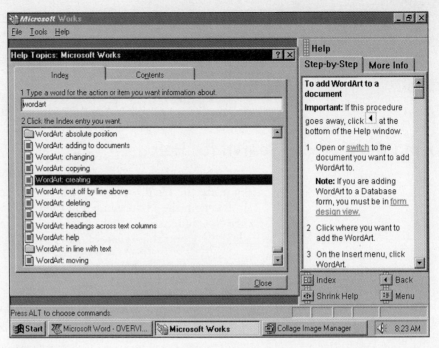

Figure 0.17

As shown in Figure 0.17, on the right side of the screen is a Help window with step-by-step instructions for adding WordArt to a document.

5 Select Close to close the Help Index window.

6 Shrink the Help window.

When searching for help from the Help menu, you can use Contents when you want to browse through Help Topics related to one of the four main tools. You can use Index when you want to search for help on any specific topic, including help on any of the tools or any of the add-on programs such as ClipArt or WordArt.

Finding Context-Sensitive Help

The Works Help system is *context sensitive,* which means you can get help related to your current task. If you are in the process of performing a command, you can press F1 to get information on that particular command.

Assume that you are in the Word Processing tool. If you press F1 while the Font and Style dialog box is active, the Help message shown in Figure 0.18 will appear.

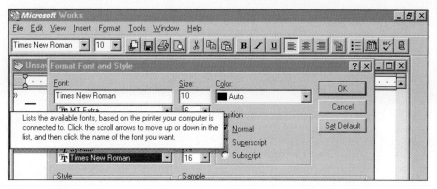

Figure 0.18

Help is also context sensitive with many Works messages. If you get an error message, you can press (F1) for an explanation of the message.

USING THE WORKS SCREEN

Works has a consistent "look" to all its tools. The word processing screen is a good example. To access the Word Processor, you must first tell Works what tool you want to use.

To start the Word Processor tool:

1 Choose New from the File menu.
The Works Task Launcher dialog box should appear.

2 Select the Works Tools tab. (It probably is selected already.)

3 Select the Word Processor button.

4 Choose the File menu.
The screen shown in Figure 0.19 appears. The parts of the screen that are labeled are common to all Works tools.

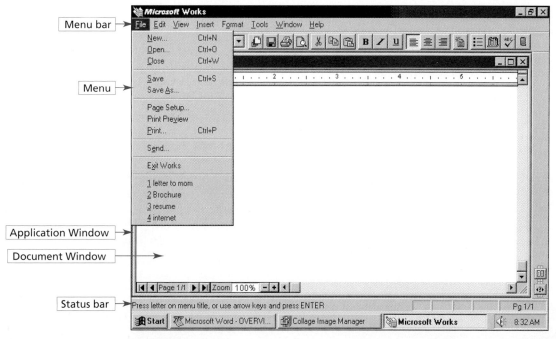

Figure 0.19

5 Click the word *File* on the menu bar to remove the File menu. The screen should look like Figure 0.20.

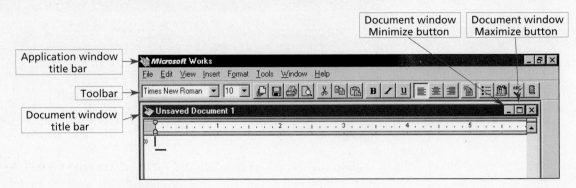

Figure 0.20

Each tool displays the names of its menus in the ***menu bar.*** In Works, menus list groups of related commands. For example, in Figure 0.19, the File menu lists commands related to file operations. You can also choose commands from a menu by pressing (ALT) and an underlined letter from the menu bar. If you press (ALT) + **F,** for example, the File menu will appear. You can then use the arrow keys to highlight a command and then press (ENTER) to choose the command.

The ***Toolbar*** shows ***icons*** or buttons that provide a quick way to accomplish common operations. For example, the scissors icon, or Cut button, lets you quickly cut selected text from the current document so you can later paste that text somewhere else. You will use buttons from the Toolbar in each of the projects.

The ***status bar*** at the bottom of the screen provides several pieces of useful information, such as your current location in a file, the settings of certain keys on the keyboard, and short explanations of commands or brief reminders about the action to take. In Figure 0.19, the status bar indicates that you can choose a command by pressing a letter or using arrow keys.

Windows 95 places programs and documents into rectangular areas on the screen called ***windows.*** The main Works program is placed into an ***application window,*** and the file you are developing is placed into a ***document window.*** Document windows are always located within application windows. Notice that both windows also have titles across the top in the ***title bar,*** as shown in Figure 0.20. The Works window title bar contains the name of the current application, "Microsoft Works." The document window title bar contains the title "Unsaved Document 1." Works uses this standard title until you save a document and give it a ***file name,*** which is a descriptive name for your work.

The ***Maximize button,*** shown in Figure 0.20, is used to increase a window to its largest size. You may want to maximize the document window to give yourself the maximum amount of workspace. You can shrink the document window into an icon by using the ***Minimize button.*** A minimized document remains active, and you can click the document icon to restore the document to its original size.

To maximize the document window:

1 Click the document window Maximize button.
The screen should look like Figure 0.21. The document window title bar is gone and the document title now appears at the top of the screen. (For more information on maximizing windows, see the Windows 95 module.)

Document window
Restore button

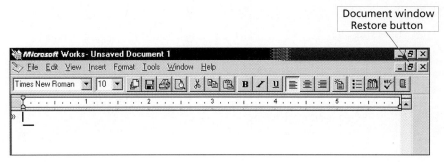

Figure 0.21

2 Click the document window *Restore button* to restore the window to its previous size.

The projects in this module will not have maximized document windows.

RESPONDING TO DIALOG BOXES

When you choose a command followed by three dots (. . .), such as the New, Open, or Save As commands in Figure 0.19, a *dialog box* will appear. A dialog box is a rectangular box that asks you to provide data to complete a command. For example, the Save As command will prompt you to enter a new file name for your file.

 To save a file with a new file name:

1 Choose Save As from the File menu.
The screen should look like Figure 0.22. The dialog box is waiting for you to enter a file name.

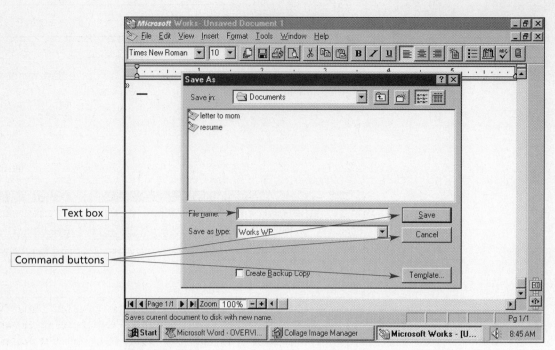

Figure 0.22

2 Select the Cancel button to close the dialog box without completing the command.
Normally you select the Save button to close this dialog box, but because you don't have anything yet to save, you select Cancel here instead.

   Dialog boxes provide different ways for completing a command. Typically you would select a *command button* such as OK (Figure 0.22 has a Save button instead of OK) or Cancel. Another way to cancel a dialog box is by pressing ESC. Command buttons are different from other elements of a dialog box, because command buttons perform actions as soon as they are selected. Other elements of a dialog box can be set and reset without any action taking place until you select OK. Figures 0.22 and 0.23 show some of the different types of options you may encounter.

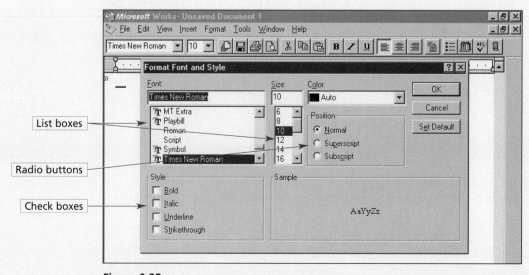

Figure 0.23

In a ***text box,*** you would type data. For example, in Figure 0.22, File Name labels a text box into which you would enter a file name.

A ***list box*** displays a list of choices from which you can choose only one. Figure 0.23 shows the Format Font and Style dialog box, which contains several list boxes. To move within a list box you can click the scroll bar, the vertical bar along the right edge of the box. You can scroll in a particular direction by clicking the appropriate arrow at the top or bottom of the scroll bar or by dragging the scroll box. See the Windows 95 module for more information on scrolling.

The box labeled *Position* in Figure 0.23 contains three ***radio buttons,*** which allow only one option to be selected. ***Check boxes,*** like the ones under Style, act as ***toggles*** (something that can be switched on or off). A check box is selected or deselected by marking or unmarking the box. Unlike radio buttons, check boxes allow for multiple selections. Figure 0.23 does not have any checked boxes.

A Note to the Student

Word processing examples in this module use 10-point Times New Roman as the default font. For the screen to match the figures in the word processing module, your default font should be the same. The default font can be set from within the Word Processing tool. If the screen does not match the figures shown in the projects, you can change the default font.

To change the default font to 10-point Times New Roman:

1 From within the Word Processing tool, choose the Format menu and then choose Font and Style.
Compare the screen with Figure 0.23.

2 If the font is not Times New Roman, scroll through the font list box and select Times New Roman.

3 If the size is not 10, select 10 from the list box.
The screen should now look like Figure 0.23.

4 Select the Set Default button.

5 When asked whether you want to change the default, select Yes.

The default font in the Spreadsheet and Database tools is 10-point Arial. You can set the font by using the Font and Style command within each tool.

Tip Now that you have seen how to access menu commands and screen buttons using either the mouse or the keyboard, you can use the method or combination of methods you prefer. From now on, the instructions will be stated in more general terms, and will look like this:

Choose Contents *or* Select Search

The word *choose* refers to menu commands, and the word *select* refers to options (such as the Help buttons).

CONFIGURING WORKS

There may be times when you need to change the configuration of Works. For example, you may want to change the units of measure, the dictionary that the Spelling Checker will use, the display of numbers in the Spreadsheet and Database tools, or modem settings in the Communications tool. These settings can be changed from within the Options dialog box. The following numbered steps show you how to access the Options dialog box, but do not make any changes until you are more familiar with Works.

To change Works options:

1 Choose Options from the Tools menu.
The dialog box shown in Figure 0.24 appears.

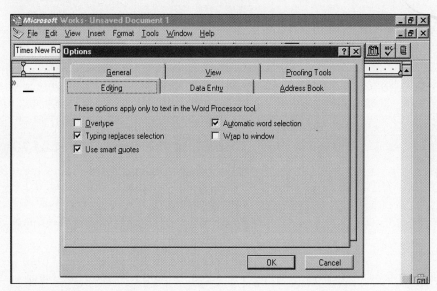

Figure 0.24

2 Select the different tabs to see what options are available.

3 Select Cancel to close the dialog box without making changes. Remember, don't make any configuration changes unless you are really familiar with Works.

EXITING WORKS

Before exiting Works, you must be sure to save any documents you have developed. After you choose the Exit command, the program will prompt you to save your work if you haven't done so already. Because you have not created any documents in this Overview, you will not be saving any work.

To exit Works:

1 Choose Exit Works from the File menu.

2 When asked whether to save your work, select No.

In general, when asked whether to save your work, you will select Yes. If you don't want to save any changes made to the document, you will select No. In this case, you selected No because you have not created anything yet.

In the projects that follow, you will use all the Works tools to create individual and integrated documents.

This concludes the Overview. You can either exit Works or go on to work the Study Questions.

SUMMARY AND EXERCISES

Summary

- Most integrated software packages consist of five components: word processing, spreadsheet, database management, charting, and communications.
- Microsoft Works for Windows is a popular, easy-to-use, integrated software package.
- Works' opening screen provides several startup options, such as creating a new file, opening an existing file, and TaskWizards.
- Help is available by choosing the Help menu or by pressing F1.
- You can get context-sensitive help by pressing F1 while using a menu or a dialog box.
- To perform a command, you would first open the appropriate menu and then choose the command.
- Choosing some commands causes a dialog box to appear. The dialog box prompts you to provide specific data that will allow Works to complete the command.

Key Terms and Operations

Key Terms
application window
button
case sensitive
charting
check box
ClipArt Gallery
Command button
Communications tool
context sensitive
database
Database tool
dialog box
document window
file name
Help Index
graphical user interface
    (GUI)

icon
integrated
    software
list box
Maximize button
menu bar
Minimize button
modem
Option button
report
Restore button
spreadsheet
Spreadsheet tool
status bar
Task Launcher
TaskWizards
text box
title bar

toggle
Toolbar
window
Word Processing
    tool
WordArt
worksheet

Operations
Change defaults
Configure Works
Exit Works
Get online Help
Maximize and
    minimize
    windows
Start Works
Use menus

Study Questions

Multiple Choice

1. Microsoft Works is what kind of application?
   a. word processing
   b. integrated
   c. database
   d. spreadsheet

2. Which tool requires a modem?
   a. Word Processing
   b. Spreadsheet
   c. Database
   d. Communications

3. Which version of Works are you using?
   a. Works for DOS
   b. Works for the Macintosh
   c. Works for Windows 95
   d. Works for Windows 3.1

4. Which of the following is an integrated software package?
   a. ClarisWorks
   b. Lotus Symphony
   c. Microsoft Works
   d. All of the above

5. Which tool provides the charting component of Works?
   a. Word Processing
   b. Spreadsheet
   c. Database
   d. Communications

Short Answer

1. All menu names are displayed in the _____.

2. Within a dialog box, a(n) _____ displays a list of settings from which you can choose only one.

3. To _____ a command in a dialog box is to turn it on and off by placing a mark in front of its name.

4. The _____ is the name of the opening dialog box that appears when you start Works and provides a starting point for creating documents.

5. If you press _____ while executing a command, you will get help.

For Discussion

1. In what situations do dialog boxes appear?

2. On the system you are using, how do you start Works?

3. What is an integrated software package?

4. How do you search for help on a particular item in Works?

5. How do you perform the Save command in the File menu?

PART I

Word Processing

Over the past few thousand years, people have gone to great lengths to express themselves in writing. Words have been carved into stone, scratched into wood, pressed into clay, and drawn on papyrus. The pen and paper greatly simplified the processing of words, as did the typewriter. Today, the electronic computer combined with a tool called a word processor has enabled us to take a giant leap forward in the creation and manipulation of the written word. A word processor such as the one found in Works enables you to create, edit, format, store, and print text.

Objectives

After completing this project, you should be able to:

▶ Create a document in the Word Processing tool

▶ Display all special characters

▶ Save and open a document

▶ Move the insertion point within a document

▶ Insert and delete text

▶ Select text

▶ Use the Undo command

▶ Preview and print a document

CASE STUDY: WRITING A CUSTOMER LETTER

Assume you are the president of Excellent Vacations, Inc., a company that specializes in organizing vacations to Europe. You need to create a letter that will be used to respond to potential customers. You know a word processor can be used to automate this task. Creating a letter with a word processor usually involves at least five steps. First, the Word Processing tool in Works would be selected. Second, text would be entered to create the letter. Third, the new document would be saved to disk so it can be worked on in the future. Fourth, the document would be reexamined and text would be edited so the letter reads as you want it to. Fifth, the letter would be previewed and printed.

Designing the Solution

When creating a letter you should always keep the overall design in mind. Writing a letter with a word processor is similar to using a typewriter or pen and paper: characters are entered from left to right and from top to bottom on the page. A letter usually begins with the sender's address. This address, which is not included in Figure 1.1, is often in the form of a preprinted letterhead. The letter should also include the date and the recipient's address. These are followed by a salutation, the body of the letter, and a closing. Plan to design a letter that can be easily read by the recipient. In this project, you will create the letter shown in Figure 1.1.

```
November 5, 1996

Ms. Danielle Fobrant
57 South Mercado Drive
San Jacinto, CA 92556

Dear Danielle:

Thank you for your interest in our exciting vacation
programs to Spain. All of our travel plans are designed to
enable you to experience the warm embrace of Spain's
continuous celebration of life.

Since Roman times, people have flocked to Spain to visit a
people and culture shaped by two diverse land masses, Europe
and Africa, and two distinct bodies of water, the
Mediterranean Sea and the Atlantic Ocean. Today, interest in
Spain is especially keen due to the 1992 Summer Olympic
Games, which were held in Barcelona, and Expo '92, which
took place in Seville.

Enclosed you will find a one-page brochure describing our
available travel packages.  Please let us know how we can
assist you in making this the most memorable vacation of
your life.

Sincerely,

Bob R. Mayton
President
Excellent Vacations
```

Figure 1.1

CREATING THE LETTER

The first step in creating a letter is telling Works what tool you want to use. Usually, this is a straightforward procedure. To create the letter, you will tell Works to open the Word Processing tool.

To create a new word processing document:

1 Start Windows 95.

2 Start Works for Windows 95.
If you do not know how to start Works for Windows 95, see the section titled "Starting Works" in the Overview. After starting Works, you should see the Works Task Launcher, as shown in Figure 1.2.

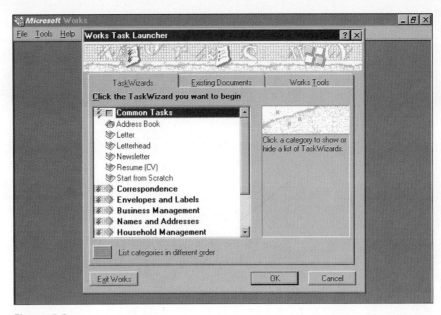

Figure 1.2

3 Select the Works Tools tab.

4 Select the Word Processor button.

5 Choose Normal from the View menu.
In this project you will use Works' Normal view.
The screen now should look like Figure 1.3.

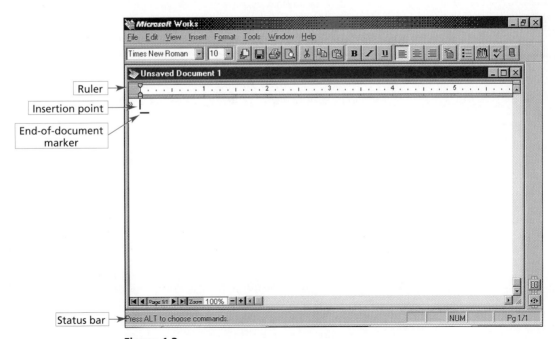

Figure 1.3

EXPLORING THE WORD PROCESSING SCREEN

The screens from the various tools of Works have a consistent user interface, which means that once you become familiar with the Word Processing tool, the spreadsheet, database, and communications screens will appear similar.

> **Tip**   The projects in this module assume that you do not have the Help window open. To shrink the Help window, select the Shrink Help button. See "Working with the Help Window" in the Overview for more information.

The menu bar appears at the top of the screen. Program commands are selected here by using the menus.

Below the menu bar is the Toolbar, which allows you to perform frequently required tasks more easily than by using the menus. Each button is an icon representing the tool's functions. If you move the pointer directly over a button and pause for a moment you can see a label indicating that button's function. The Toolbar also shows the current font style and size.

Works gives the first document you create in the word processor the generic name Unsaved Document 1, as you can see in the title bar of Figure 1.3. The name Unsaved Document 1 is changed when you save the document.

The *ruler* contains a series of numbers that represent inches. The *default,* or standard setting, allows you to type from 0 to 6 inches across the page.

The *insertion point,* which is the small, blinking vertical line, is the position where text is inserted into the document. After you have typed some text, you can move the insertion point within the typed area by using the arrow keys or the mouse.

The double arrows (>>) represent the top of the page. The horizontal line after the insertion point is the *end-of-document marker.* The insertion point cannot move before the double arrows on the first page or beyond the end-of-document marker. The document window also contains horizontal and vertical scroll bars that are used to navigate through a document.

In the status bar, *Pg 1/1* indicates the current page number and the total number of pages in the file. Currently the insertion point is on page 1 out of a total of 1 page. If the status bar displayed 3/7, the insertion point would be on page 3 of 7 pages. The status bar also shows the current settings of the Num Lock, Cap Lock, and Scroll Lock keys. In Figure 1.3, *NUM* indicates that the Num Lock key is on.

> **Caution**   If the characters OVR appear in the box immediately to the left of the page-number and total-pages indicators, (INS) has been pressed and Works is in *Typeover mode.* This means that any text you type will replace existing text. Press (INS) to toggle between Typeover and *Insert modes.* This project does not use Typeover mode.

ENTERING TEXT

As soon as you select the Word Processing tool, you can begin to enter text. In this case, you will begin by typing the date.

To enter the date:

1 Make sure the insertion point is in the upper-left corner of the document window.

If you see an H and F (*Header* and *Footer*) on the screen, do not place the insertion point in these rows. These concepts are discussed in a subsequent project.

2 Type **November 1, 1996** and then press (ENTER)

3 Press (ENTER) again to insert a blank line.

Pressing (ENTER) places a ***hard return*** into a document, which forces the insertion point to move to the next line. You can press (ENTER) to end a line of text or to insert a blank line.

To enter the address:

1 Type **Ms. Danielle Fobrant** and then press (ENTER)

2 Type **57 Mercado Drive** and then press (ENTER)

3 Type **San Jacinto, CA 92556** and then press (ENTER)

4 Press (ENTER) to insert a blank line.

To enter the salutation:

1 Type **Dear Danielle:** and then press (ENTER)

2 Press (ENTER) once to insert a blank line.

Your letter is starting to take shape. Compare what you have so far with the letter in Figure 1.4.

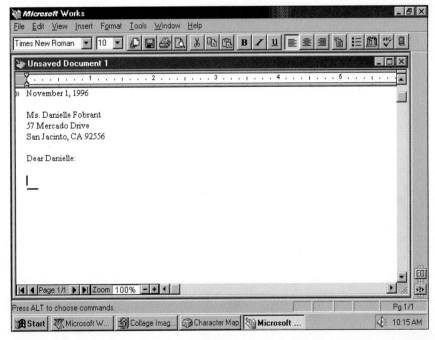

Figure 1.4

Typing a paragraph is a little different from typing a simple line of text. When you are typing a paragraph, you will not press (ENTER) at the end of each line. Instead, you will press (ENTER) only at the end of each paragraph. When you reach the end of a line, you will continue typing and Works will insert a *soft return,* which automatically moves the insertion point to the next line. If you are typing a word when you reach the end of a line, a Works feature called *word wrap* places the entire word on the following line so the text never goes past the right margin.

To create a paragraph:

1 Type the following paragraph. Be sure to press (SPACE) once at the end of each sentence. Do not press (ENTER) until step 2.

`Thank you for your interest in our vacation programs to Spain. All of our travel plans are designed to enable you to experience the warm embrace of Spain's continuous celebration of life.`

2 Press (ENTER) twice at the end of the paragraph. Your document should now look like the one shown in Figure 1.5.

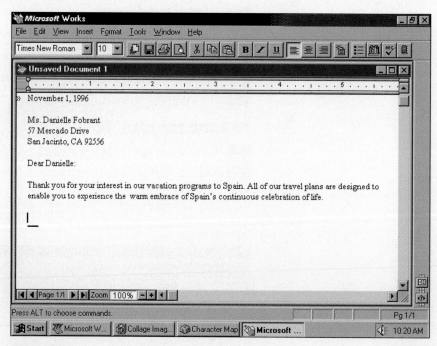

Figure 1.5

DISPLAYING ALL CHARACTERS

Figure 1.5 shows all the characters that you have typed so far, except the spaces and hard returns. You can see special characters, such as spaces and hard returns, by choosing the All Characters command from the View menu.

To show all special characters:

1 Choose the View menu from the menu bar.
The menu shown in Figure 1.6 appears.

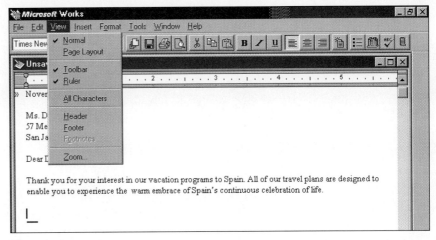

Figure 1.6

Notice that the Normal, Toolbar, and Ruler options have a checkmark preceding them. This indicates that these options are currently active.

2 Choose All Characters to make this option active. Your screen should look like Figure 1.7.

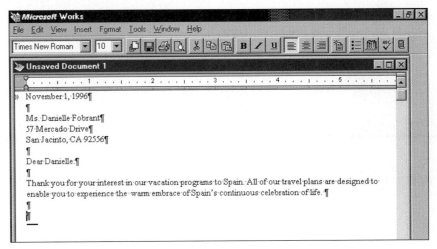

Figure 1.7

A little dot (•) on the screen marks a spot where you have pressed (SPACE). The paragraph mark (¶) indicates where you have pressed (ENTER).

Many people like having a continuous display of special characters on the screen, because it gives them a precise indication of all the keystrokes they have made. Others do not like seeing special characters, because these characters tend to make the screen look cluttered. This project assumes that you will not be displaying special characters, but if you want to keep them on the screen, that's okay. Removing the display of special characters is done in the same manner they were displayed.

To remove special characters from the screen:

1 Choose the View menu. Notice that a checkmark appears before All Characters.

2 Choose All Characters to toggle this option off.
All special characters should disappear from the screen.

SAVING A NEW DOCUMENT

Although you have not finished the letter yet, this is a good opportunity to learn how to close and then reopen a file. Often when you are creating a document, you will have to stop and resume your work at a later time. It is important to know how to save your work and exit Works properly.

The first time you save a file with either the Save or the Save As command, the Save As dialog box will appear and prompt you for a file name. Afterward, the Save and Save As commands work differently. The Save command immediately saves your work with the current file name. The Save As command lets you save your work with a different file name by redisplaying the Save As dialog box.

Any document saved in Works requires a file name. Works will add one of four small icons to the file depending on what tool you are using. Table 1.1 shows these four icons.

Table 1.1

Icon	File Type
	Word processing
	Spreadsheet
	Database
	Communications

Do not place an asterisk (*) or a question mark (?) in a file name. Letters of the alphabet, digits from 0 to 9, and spaces are acceptable. For example, *Letter*, *Spain*, and *Letter to Danielle* are all acceptable file names.

To save a document:

1 Choose Save from the File menu.
Because this is the first time you are saving this document, the Save As dialog box shown in Figure 1.8 appears.

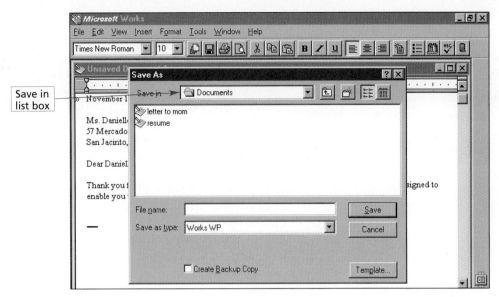

Figure 1.8

2 Click the downward-pointing arrow next to Save In to see a list of places where you can save your work.

3 Select 3½ Floppy (A:).
If you wish to save your work on a disk drive other than drive A:, select the appropriate drive. For example, you might select drive B: or drive C:.

4 Click in the text block next to File Name.

5 Type **Letter to Danielle**
Letter to Danielle is a good file name because it describes the file and follows the rules for naming a file. *Spain*, *Letter to Customer*, and *Vacation* are typical file names for this document. You can type up to 255 characters including spaces. Figure 1.9 shows that drive A: is selected and that the file name is *Letter to Danielle*.

6 Select Save to complete the command and save the file.

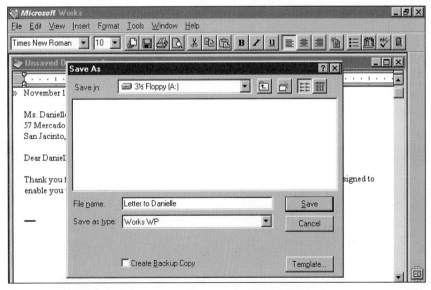

Figure 1.9

Caution Once a document has been saved, choosing the Save command will automatically overwrite the existing version of the file. To save a copy of the file, you can use Save As to save the file with a different name and maintain the original version as it was.

After you specify a file name, Works will place the new file name in the title bar of the document window. You can then safely exit Works without losing your work by choosing the Exit Works command from the File menu. Because you have not really finished the current document, you will close the window to simulate that you are done with your work and are exiting Works. This action will take you back to the opening screen of Works.

To close a window:

1 Choose the File menu.

2 Choose Close to close the file without saving.
You should have a display of the opening screen, the one you see when none of Works' tools are open. The Works Task Launcher dialog box should be on the screen.

If necessary, you can save your file as *Letter to Danielle,* exit Works now, and continue this project later.

Assume you have just started Works and want to continue editing an existing file. The Works Task Launcher should be on the screen, just as it is when you first start Works.

To open an existing file:

1 Select the Existing Documents tab.
You should see a dialog box similar to the one in Figure 1.10.

2 If you do not see the file you want in the file list, select Open a Document Not Listed Here, and then select 3½ Floppy (A:) or the drive location you are using to save your files.

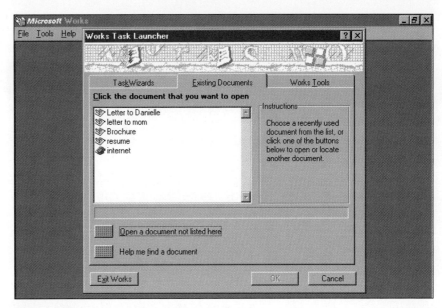

Figure 1.10

3 Select the file name *Letter to Danielle* and then select OK to open the file.

The selected file—in this case, *Letter to Danielle*—appears on the screen.

MOVING AROUND IN A DOCUMENT

While developing a document, you often will need to move through the document to review your work or to insert or delete text. To use the mouse to move the insertion point, you would first place the pointer at the desired location and then you would click.

The scroll bars can be used to move to a document location that is not currently visible on the screen. When you move through a document using the scroll bars, the insertion point will remain at its previous location until you click at a new location.

The insertion point also can be moved to any point within the document by using the keys shown in Table 1.2. You may prefer using the keyboard to move the insertion point because often it is faster to keep your hands on the keyboard than to reach for the mouse.

Table 1.2

Key(s)	Direction of Movement
←, →	One character left, one character right
↑, ↓	One line up, one line down
HOME, END	To beginning of line, to end of line
CTRL + →	One word right
CTRL + ←	One word left
CTRL + ↑	To beginning of the previous paragraph
CTRL + ↓	To beginning of the following paragraph
PGUP	One screen up
PGDN	One screen down
CTRL + HOME	To beginning of file
CTRL + END	To end of file

To move through a document using the arrow keys:

1 Press ↓ until you reach the end of the document.

2 Press ↑ until you reach the beginning of the document.

3 Use the arrow keys to place the insertion point before the letter *M* in *Mercado*.

To quickly move through a document using the keyboard:

1 Press CTRL + HOME to move to the beginning of the document.

2 Press CTRL + END to move to the end of the document.

3 Press CTRL + ← several times to jump quickly from one word to the previous word.

4 Press CTRL + → until you reach the end of the document.

INSERTING AND DELETING TEXT

The document *Letter to Danielle* needs several changes; to make them, you will have to insert and delete text. A word processor's tremendous capability to modify, or *edit,* text distinguishes it from a typewriter. Changes to a typewritten document can look rather messy; in some cases, you have to retype the entire document. With a word processor, you make the changes only. The document never has to be retyped, and corrected printouts always look neat.

The street address in the letter needs to be changed to 57 South Mercado Drive. You will insert the word *South* right before the word *Mercado*.

To insert the word South:

1 Make sure OVR is toggled off in the status bar (press INS if necessary).

2 Place the insertion point just before the letter *M* in *Mercado*.

3 Type **South** and press SPACE

The new text is inserted and the existing text is pushed to the right.

When you insert text into an existing paragraph, Works will automatically rearrange the entire paragraph.

To insert the word exciting:

1 In the first sentence of the paragraph, place the insertion point before the letter *v* in the word *vacation*.

2 Type **exciting** and then press (SPACE)
Notice how all the text in the paragraph is rearranged to accommodate the word *exciting*.

To delete a character, you can press (DEL) or (BKSP). Pressing (DEL) will delete the character to the right of the insertion point; pressing (BKSP) will delete the character to the left of the insertion point. In Figure 1.11, pressing (DEL) would delete the comma; pressing (BKSP) would delete the letter *o*.

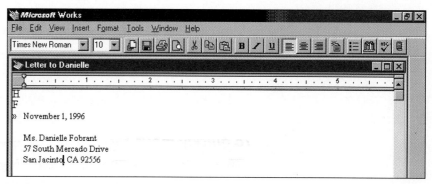

Figure 1.11

To change the word Jacinto *to* Diego:

1 Place the insertion point immediately to the left of the comma that appears after the word *Jacinto*, as shown in Figure 1.11.

2 Press (BKSP) until *Jacinto* is deleted.

3 Type **Diego**
Within the letter, the word *Spain* is mentioned two times. In the following numbered steps you will change the country from Spain to England.

To change Spain *to* England:

1 Place the insertion point on the first occurrence of the word *Spain*.

2 Press (DEL) or (BKSP) to delete the word *Spain*.

3 Type **England**

4 Place the insertion point on the second occurrence of the word *Spain*.

5 Delete *Spain* and type **England**

Reminder Pressing (DEL) will delete the character to the right of the insertion point; pressing (BKSP) will delete the character to the left.

Now you realize that you've made a mistake and the country really should be Spain, not England.

To change England *back to* Spain:

1 Place the insertion point on the first occurrence of the word *England*, delete *England*, and then type **Spain**

2 Place the insertion point on the second occurrence of the word *England*, delete *England*, and then type **Spain**

Tip You can replace multiple occurrences of a word by using the Replace command. You would choose Replace from the Edit menu and then type the word or words you want to find as well as the words to replace them with.

To enter additional text:

1 Press (CTRL) + (END) to move the insertion point to the end of the document.

2 Type the remainder of the letter. Use (ENTER) to place one blank line after each paragraph and two after the word *Sincerely*.

```
Since Roman times, people have flocked to Spain to visit a people
and culture shaped by two diverse land masses, Europe and Africa,
and two distinct bodies of water, the Mediterranean Sea and the
Atlantic Ocean. Today, interest in Spain is especially keen due to
the 1992 Summer Olympic Games, which were held in Barcelona, and
Expo '92, which took place in Seville.

Enclosed you will find a short flyer describing our available travel
packages. Please let us know how we can assist you in making this
the most memorable vacation of your life.

Sincerely,



Bob R. Mayton
President
Excellent Vacations
```

SELECTING TEXT

To delete a character or a small word, (DEL) and (BKSP) work well. To delete larger amounts of text, it is more efficient to first select the text and then press (DEL).

Selecting text is the process of highlighting a word, sentence, paragraph, or entire document. Then the selected text can be moved, copied, or deleted. Table 1.3 describes how to select text using the keyboard or the mouse.

Table 1.3

Text Selected	Using the Keyboard	Using the Mouse
Word	Press (F8) twice	Double-click the word
Sentence	Press (F8) three times	Click while holding down (CTRL)
Paragraph	Press (F8) four times	Double-click in the left margin of the document window beside the paragraph
Entire document	Press (F8) five times	Hold down (CTRL) and click in the left margin of the document window

You can use the keyboard to select a block of text that does not appear in Table 1.3 by pressing (F8) once and then using the arrow keys to highlight the text. You can also select text by pressing the arrow keys while holding down (SHFT). You can deselect text by pressing an arrow key.

You can use the mouse to select a block of text that does not appear in Table 1.3 by holding down the left mouse button while dragging the pointer over the desired text. You can deselect text by clicking at a new location.

To change the date:

1 Place the pointer in the left margin beside *November 1, 1996*. The pointer should be an arrow that points to the right.

2 Click to select the date.
The screen should look like Figure 1.12.

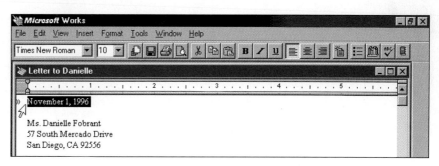

Figure 1.12

3 Press (DEL) to delete the selected text.

4 Type the current date and then press (ENTER)

To delete **Bob R. Mayton** *and insert your name:*

1 Place the pointer in the left margin beside the name *Bob R. Mayton*.

2 Click to select the name.

3 Press (DEL) to delete the selected text.

4 Type your name and then press (ENTER)

To delete short flyer _and insert_ one-page brochure:

1 Place the pointer on the letter *s* in *short flyer*.

2 Press and hold down the mouse button and drag the pointer over *short flyer* until the phrase is selected.

3 Release the mouse button.
Your letter should look like Figure 1.13.

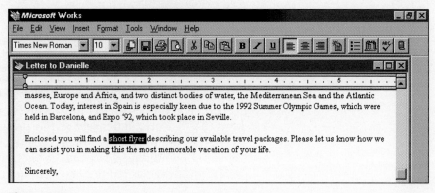

Figure 1.13

4 Press (DEL) to delete the selected text.

5 Type **one-page brochure** and then press (SPACE)
Your letter should look like Figure 1.14. (Of course, you should see your name instead of that of Bob R. Mayton.)

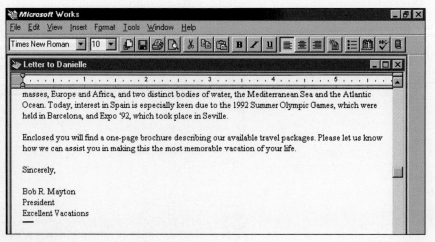

Figure 1.14

USING THE UNDO COMMAND

The Undo command in the Edit menu "undoes" the most recent editing or formatting operation. Many people use Undo to "undelete" text that has been deleted accidentally. To undelete text, you must use the Undo command immediately after deleting the text.

 ### To delete and undelete the word Olympic:

1 Place the insertion point anywhere in the word *Olympic*.

2 Double-click to select the word.

3 Press ⬚ DEL ⬚ to delete the selected text.

4 Choose Undo Editing from the Edit menu to restore the deleted text. The word *Olympic* should reappear.

Tip You can undelete words, paragraphs, and even entire pages—provided that you choose Undo immediately after the deletion.

SAVING AN EXISTING DOCUMENT

After creating a document, you will usually save your work to a disk so you can use the document again in the future. For example, if you were the president of Excellent Vacations, you would save the file *Letter to Danielle* so you could perhaps use it again with a different customer. Of course, you would have to change the customer name and address each time.

When you create or edit a document, your work is kept in a temporary storage area called ***random-access memory (RAM)***. The contents of RAM disappear when you turn off the computer or when there is a power failure, so it is a good practice to save your work about every 15 minutes. If there is a power failure, the document will disappear from RAM, but you will have a copy that was saved to disk within the past 15 minutes.

Saving an existing document involves choosing Save from the File menu. Because you already named this document when you saved it the first time, you will not be prompted for a file name this time.

 ### To save your work:

1 Choose Save from the File menu.

PREVIEWING AND PRINTING A DOCUMENT

When you have finished creating and saving a document, the next step is to print it. After examining the printout, you may find mistakes that need to be corrected. Works enables you to preview a document before printing it so you can see on the screen how the document will look on paper. The preview gives you a chance to find mistakes before you've committed the document to paper, especially mistakes related to the format of the document.

 ### To preview a document on-screen:

 1 Choose Print Preview from the File menu. The screen should look like Figure 1.15.

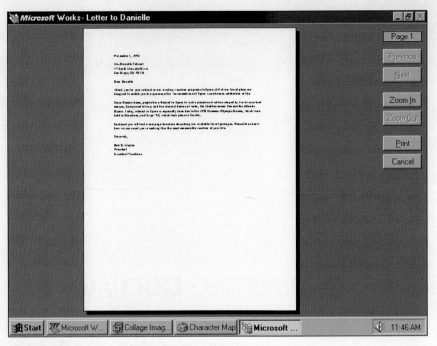

Figure 1.15

Notice that the characters are small and difficult to read and that the document cannot be edited while in Preview mode. The preview works well, however, in presenting the overall format of the document.

2 Select the Cancel button to cancel the preview.

> *Tip* As you move the pointer into a document in Preview mode, the pointer becomes a magnifying-glass icon. You can zoom (enlarge) the preview by moving the pointer to any portion of the document and clicking. If you click twice, you zoom in even more. Three clicks takes you back to the full page.

Once you are satisfied with the document, it is ready to be printed. If the computer is attached to a printer, you should first make sure the printer is on.

If a printer is not attached to the computer, you can exit Works and open the file on a computer that has a printer.

> *Caution* Be sure to save your latest changes before exiting Works.

To print a document:

1 Choose Print from the File menu.
If you are asked for First-time Help, select OK to bypass the Help.
A dialog box appears, similar to the one shown in Figure 1.16.

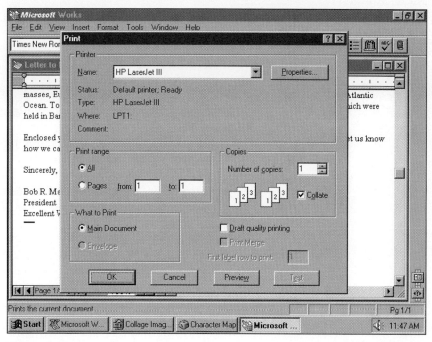

Figure 1.16

2 Make sure the number of copies is set to 1 and the print range is set to All.

3 Select OK to print the document.
The Windows Print Manager processes the print job.

THE NEXT STEP

In this project you have created your first word processing document and learned some basic skills. Creating, saving, editing, and printing a document are essential components of a document cycle: the steps you follow to successfully use a computer to automate common word processing tasks.

In Works, multiple documents can be open at the same time. When you need to copy text from one document to another, both documents can be opened using the File menu. The text can be selected in the first document, copied, and pasted into the second document. Think of other ways the word processing skills you learned in this project can be used to simplify the process of creating other types of documents, such as a research paper.

This concludes Project 1. You can either exit Works or go on to work the Study Questions, Review Exercises, and Assignments.

SUMMARY AND EXERCISES

Summary

- To create a text document, you would choose the Word Processing tool.
- The insertion point, the vertical line that marks the location where text is inserted, can be moved to any point within a document by using the arrow keys or the mouse.
- The status bar indicates the current page number; the total number of pages in the file; and the status of the Num Lock, Caps Lock, and Scroll Lock keys.
- You should press (ENTER)—that is, enter a hard return—to end a line of text, to end a paragraph, or to insert a blank line.
- When you reach the end of an on-screen line while typing a paragraph, you can continue typing. Works will cause the insertion point to move automatically to the next line. If you are in the process of typing a word at the end of an on-screen line, Works will place the entire word on the following line by using a capability called word wrap.
- To insert text, you can type the new text at the desired location. Works will rearrange the existing text to accommodate the new text.
- To delete small amounts of text, you can press (BKSP), which deletes characters to the left of the insertion point, or you can press (DEL), which deletes text to the right of the insertion point. To delete large amounts of text, such as words, sentences, or paragraphs, you can first select the text and then press (DEL).
- To undelete text, you can choose Undo from the Edit menu. The Undo command undoes the last operation.
- You should periodically save the document you are working on. This practice will help you avoid losing too much data in case of power loss or other accident.
- It is a good idea to preview a document on the screen before printing it.

Key Terms and Operations

Key Terms	Operations
default	Close a file
edit	Create a new file
end-of-document marker	Edit a file
hard return	Open an existing file
Insert mode	Preview a document
insertion point	Print a document
random-access memory (RAM)	Save a new file
ruler	Save an existing file
soft return	Select text
Typeover mode	Undo a deletion
word wrap	

Study Questions

Multiple Choice

1. Which command is used to access a document previously saved to disk?
   - a. Open
   - b. Create
   - c. Preview
   - d. Save

2. In the Word Processing tool, menus are opened from which of the following?
   - a. Toolbar
   - b. status bar
   - c. document window
   - d. menu bar

3. Which screen element contains icons that are used to quickly perform common procedures?
   - a. Toolbar
   - b. status bar
   - c. document window
   - d. menu bar

4. After you choose the All Characters command in the View menu, the _____ symbol marks the ends of paragraphs.
   - a. ¶
   - b. &
   - c. @
   - d. %

5. Which command is used to examine a document before a hard-copy printout is generated?
   - a. Print
   - b. Insert
   - c. Undo
   - d. Print Preview

6. File names should not contain:
   - a. asterisks (*) or question marks (?).
   - b. spaces.
   - c. numbers.
   - d. All of the above.

7. To create a new file you can choose _____ from the File menu.
   - a. Open
   - b. Create
   - c. New
   - d. Edit

8. Which option allows the last editing step to be reversed?
   - a. search and replace
   - b. Delete
   - c. Undo
   - d. Copy

9. What command lets you see special characters such as spaces and hard returns?
   - a. Show All from the File menu
   - b. All Characters from the View menu
   - c. Special Characters from the Edit menu
   - d. Show All from the View menu

10. The default name given to new documents is:
    - a. Unsaved Document 1.
    - b. Word Processing Document 1.
    - c. WORD1.
    - d. Save Me Now Please.

Short Answer

1. To insert a hard return, press _____.

2. To delete a character to the left of the insertion point, press _____.

3. An alternate way of selecting text is to hold down _____ while using the arrow keys to highlight the appropriate text.

4. To move quickly to the beginning of a document, press _____.

5. To move quickly to the end of a document, press _____.

6. The _____ command enables you to undelete text.

7. Your work is temporarily contained in _____ until you save it to a disk.

8. The _____ displays how many total pages are in a document.

9. A word processing document cannot be edited while Works is in _____ mode.

10. The _____ is marked off in inches and displays the left and right margins of a document.

For Discussion

1. Why is it a good idea to preview a document before printing it?

2. What is the difference between the Save and Save As commands?

3. In this project you created a letter. What other types of documents can be created in the Word Processing tool?

4. How is a word processor different from a typewriter?

5. Describe word wrap.

Review Exercises

Creating a Business Letter

1. You are the president of a company that markets three products. Invent a name for your company and think about three products you would like to sell.

2. Write a letter to Danielle Fobrant that describes your three products. Explain why she should purchase them. Your letter should include the current date, Danielle's name and address, your title, and the name of your company.

3. Delete the name *Danielle Fobrant* and insert a new name. You do not need to change the address. Also, be sure to change the name *Danielle* after the word *Dear*.

4. Select the second paragraph of the document and then delete it.

5. Undelete the second paragraph.

6. Save the document and assign it the file name *Products*.

7. Preview the document.

8. Print the document.

9. Exit Works.

Editing a Business Letter and Changing the File Name

1. Your marketing company has just approved two new products for distribution. The letter you created in the previous exercise needs to be modified and the updates saved to a new file.

2. Retrieve the file *Products.* Add a paragraph describing two additional products.

3. Save the file as *More Products.* Remember to use the Save As command from the File menu and not the Save command.

4. Preview the document.

5. Print the document.

Assignments

Writing a Personal Letter

You are planning to take a vacation and you want to discontinue newspaper service. Using the Works Word Processing tool, create the short letter shown in Figure 1.17. Add a second paragraph explaining how the delivery service has been for the past month. Save the letter to a data disk with the file name *Cancel Paper.* Preview and print the letter.

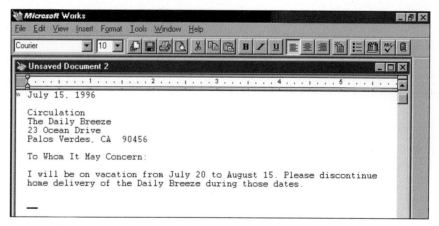

Figure 1.17

Requesting a Course Schedule

As a returning student for spring semester, you have not received confirmation of your course schedule. Using the Works Word Processing tool, create the memo shown in Figure 1.18. The line across the center of the memo can be created by pressing the minus sign, ⊖, multiple times. Use 12-point Times New Roman. Save the memo as *Course Schedule.* Print a copy of the memo.

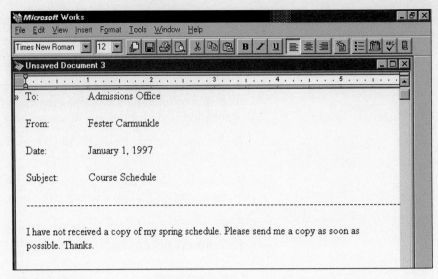

Figure 1.18

Creating a Memo

As president of First Savings and Loan, you want to inform all bank tellers that a number of bad checks have been cashed in the past few weeks. Use Figure 1.18 as a guide for creating the memo. Include your name as sender and all tellers as the recipients of the memo. The first paragraph should explain that extra precautions should be taken, such as checking signatures and requesting photo ID. In a second paragraph, announce a meeting for all employees the next week. Save the memo to a data disk as *Bad Checks*. Print the memo.

PROJECT 2:   FORMATTING A DOCUMENT

Objectives

After completing this project, you should be able to:

▶ Set left and right margins

▶ Center text

▶ Apply bold, underline, and italic character styles

▶ Indent paragraphs

▶ Justify paragraphs

▶ Check the spelling in a document

CASE STUDY: DESIGNING A BROCHURE

In Project 1 you learned how to create, save, edit, and print a business letter. Although these are common word processing tasks, it is also important to know how to format a document. *Formatting* allows you to modify a document's appearance to enhance readability.

As president of Excellent Vacations, you need to create a one-page brochure that describes various vacation packages to Spain. Because this document is a marketing tool, you will need to format the brochure so it appeals to readers. This can be accomplished in a variety of ways such as applying character styles, changing the margin settings, and indenting text.

Designing the Solution

In this project you will use a variety of character styles and paragraph formats to modify the appearance of a brochure. Character styles such as bold, italic, and underline can be used to make characters stand out from surrounding text. Paragraph formats affect the appearance of paragraphs and include indentation, text alignment, and tabs. When all the desired formats have been applied, you will use the Works Spelling Checker to check for any misspelled words. You will create the word processing document shown in Figure 2.1.

```
                        Excellent Vacations
                        3441 Drummond Street
                      Moreno Valley, CA  92553


                      Vacation Packages to Spain

      Excellent Vacations is delighted to announce our exciting new
      vacation packages to the regions of Andalusia, Castile, and
      Catalonia.

      Andalusia

            The sunny southern region of Spain, Andalusia is
            known for its sandy beaches, vast olive groves,
            and lush vineyards.  Seville, an ancient city in
            the center of Andalusia, played host to Expo '92.


      Castile

            Castile lies on a vast plateau that is dotted with
            ancient structures erected by the Romans and
            Moors.  Madrid, a bustling city in the heart of
            Spain, is a leading European cultural center.


      Catalonia

            The Mediterranean Sea brushes up against
            Catalonia's beautiful east coast.  Barcelona,
            Spain's second largest city, was the site of
            the 1992 Summer Olympic Games.


      Our vacation packages to Spain have received glowing reviews from
      many leading travel magazines, including Travel Today. Excellent
      Vacations offers the best vacation value for your dollar.
```

Figure 2.1

CREATING THE DOCUMENT

A brochure is an example of a word processing document. From the Works Task Launcher you need to open the Word Processing tool.

 To create a new word processing document:

1 Start Windows 95.

2 Start Works.
The Works Task Launcher dialog box appears.

3 Select the Works Tools tab.

4 Select the Word Processor button.

5 Choose Normal from the View menu.
You are now ready to begin your brochure.

SETTING MARGINS

Before you begin writing the brochure, you need to set the margins. On a printed page, *margins* are the white space surrounding the text. As you enter text, you probably are not too aware of the margins because Works does not show blank space around the text on-screen. On a printed document, however, margins are clearly visible and desirable, as you can see by looking at the mockup shown in Figure 2.2.

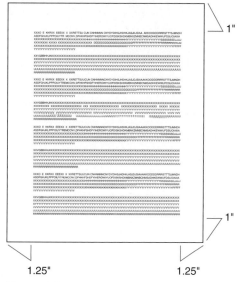

Figure 2.2

You can control the amount of white space around the edges of a document by choosing the Page Setup command from the File menu and then selecting the tab for margins. By default, the left and right margins are 1.25 inches, and the top and bottom margins are each 1 inch. On standard 8.5- by 11-inch paper, the left and right margins add up to 2.5 inches, which means that each typed line can be up to 6 inches (2.5 + 6 = 8.5). From top to bottom, you have a 1-inch margin, 9 inches of text, and another 1-inch margin (1 + 9 + 1 = 11).

Your one-page brochure will look better if you have 6.5 inches of text across the page. To get 6.5 inches, you need to set the left and right margins to 1 inch each, which will cause the right-margin mark (triangle) on the ruler to move halfway between 6 and 7.

To set the left and right margins to 1 inch:

1 Choose Page Setup from the File menu.
The dialog box shown in Figure 2.3 appears.

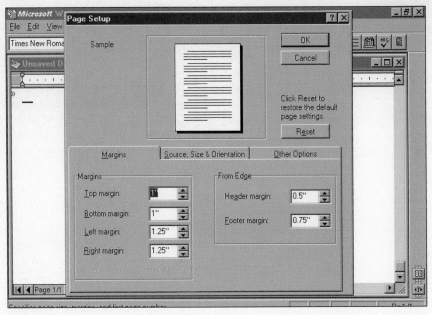

Figure 2.3

2 Press ⌗TAB⌗ until the insertion point is in the box labeled Left Margin.

3 Type **1** to set the left margin to 1 inch, and then press ⌗TAB⌗

4 In the box labeled Right Margin, type **1** to set the right margin to
1 inch.

5 Select OK or press ⌗ENTER⌗ to accept the new settings.
The left-margin symbol appears as two triangles at position 0. You will not
see the right-margin marker.

6 Click the right arrow on the horizontal scroll bar a few times to move
to the right.
When the view shifts to the right, you can see that the right-margin marker
on the ruler is now halfway between 6 and 7, as shown in Figure 2.4.

7 Click the left arrow on the horizontal scroll bar to move back to the
left.

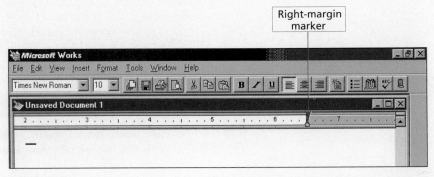

Figure 2.4

CENTERING TEXT

If you are using a letterhead or title in a document, it usually looks best to center the title between the left and right margins. On the brochure, you will start by typing the address of Excellent Vacations. Then you will center the address.

To enter the address:

1 Type **Excellent Vacations** and press (ENTER)

2 Type **3441 Drummond Street** and press (ENTER)

3 Type **Moreno Valley, CA 92553** and press (ENTER)

4 Press (ENTER) to insert a blank line.

To center the address:

1 Place the pointer in the left margin beside the *E* in *Excellent.*
The pointer should point to the right like the one shown in Figure 2.5.

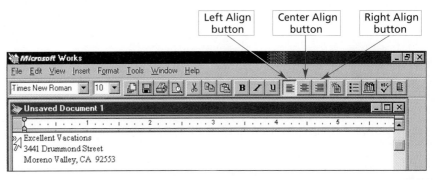

Figure 2.5

2 Hold down the left mouse button and then drag the pointer downward to select the first three lines of the document.

3 Select the Center Align button on the Toolbar.
The address should be centered, as shown in Figure 2.6.

Figure 2.6

There are times when you want text to be automatically centered as it is entered. Just below the address, you will type and center the title *Vacation Packages to Spain* by first selecting the Center Align button on the Toolbar and then typing the text. As you type, the text will be centered automatically between the left and right margins.

To center text as it is entered:

1 Press (CTRL) + (END) to move to the end of the document.

2 Select the Center Align button on the Toolbar.

3 Type **Vacation Packages to Spain** and press (ENTER)

4 Select the Left Align button on the Toolbar.
Text returns to normal (left-aligned) formatting.

5 Press (ENTER) to insert a blank line.
Your brochure should look like Figure 2.7.

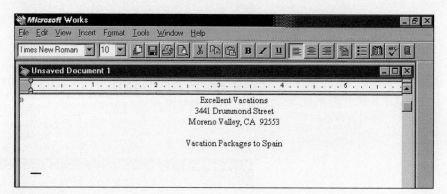

Figure 2.7

Rather than having Works center text as you type, you may find it easier to type the text first and then format it, as you did with the company address. Remember, to center existing text, you would first select the text and then select the Center Align button. To center new text, you would select the Center Align button on the Toolbar, type the new text, and then select the Left Align button on the Toolbar.

APPLYING CHARACTER STYLES

To emphasize words and phrases in a document, you can change the *style,* or appearance, of the text. Several character styles are available, including bold, italic, and underlining. **Bold** text is thicker, heavier type than normal text. *Italic* characters slant to the right. **Underlined** characters have a line beneath them.

In Works, you can change text styles by using either the pull-down menus or the appropriate buttons on the Toolbar. You can set text enhancements by choosing Font and Style in the Format menu. Figure 2.8 shows the dialog box that appears when Font and Style is chosen.

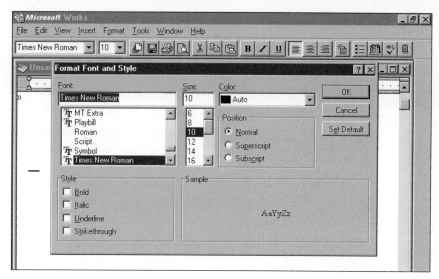

Figure 2.8

Now look at the Toolbar at the top of the Works screen. Notice that the buttons for bold, italic, and underline look like the style they accomplish. Figure 2.9 shows plain text followed by several styles that were created using these style buttons. The appearance of text in the document will be identical whether the Toolbar buttons or the Font and Style dialog box is used to apply character styles.

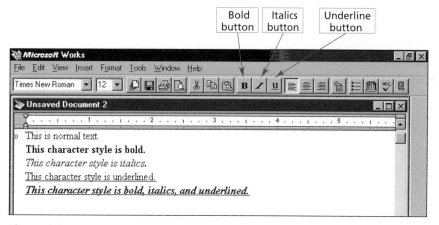

Figure 2.9

You can change a character style back to plain text by selecting the text and then selecting the Bold, Underline, or Italic buttons on the Toolbar.

Tip When text is selected and a character style is applied, the appropriate style button will change to reverse color, indicating that the character style applies to the currently selected text.

Different character styles create different effects. For example, a bold style can be used for emphasis. In the following numbered steps, you will type a paragraph that mentions vacation packages to three areas in Spain:

Andalusia, Castile, and Catalonia. You will use the Bold button on the Toolbar to emphasize these names.

To enter additional text:

1 If you are not at the end of the document, press (CTRL) + (END)

2 Type the following paragraph:

Excellent Vacations is delighted to announce our exciting new vacation packages to the regions of Andalusia, Castile, and Catalonia.

3 Press (ENTER) to complete the paragraph.

4 Press (ENTER) to insert a blank line.

You can apply a bold style to existing text by selecting the text and then selecting the Bold button on the Toolbar.

To apply a bold style to the word Andalusia:

1 Place the insertion point anywhere in the word *Andalusia*.

2 Double-click to select the word.

3 Select the Bold button on the Toolbar.

4 Click outside the word to deselect the text.

Bold text appears on the screen as dark, thick type. What you see on the screen is basically what you will see in the printed document. This feature is known as *WYSIWYG* (what you see is what you get). To get true WYSIWYG you should choose Page Layout from the View menu. In these projects you will not use the Page Layout mode.

Tip Once text is selected, you can press (CTRL) + **B** to change the character style of that text to bold.

To apply a bold style to the words Castile and Catalonia:

1 Place the insertion point anywhere in the word *Castile*.

2 Double-click to select the word.

3 Apply a bold style to *Castile*.

4 Select the word *Catalonia*.

5 Apply a bold style to *Catalonia*.

6 Click anywhere to deselect *Catalonia*.

The screen should look like Figure 2.10.

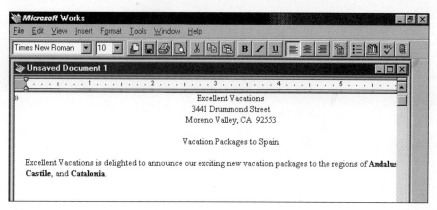

Figure 2.10

You can also apply a bold style to new text by first selecting the Bold button on the Toolbar, typing the new text, and then again selecting the Bold button to reset the text style to normal. The method you use to apply a bold style is usually a matter of personal preference.

INDENTING PARAGRAPHS

The Indents and Alignment tab in the Format Paragraph dialog box enables you to indent a paragraph. *Indentations* are somewhat different from margins. Margins affect the amount of white space surrounding the entire document, whereas indentations set the amount of white space on the sides of a paragraph.

So far, the brochure describes three vacation packages. Next you will describe each package in more detail and, in the process, indent several paragraphs.

To add the heading Andalusia *and enter a short paragraph:*

1 Press (CTRL) + (END) to make sure the insertion point is at the end of the document.

2 Type **Andalusia** and press (ENTER)

3 Press (ENTER) to insert a blank line.

4 Type the following paragraph:
The sunny southern region of Spain, Andalusia is known for its sandy beaches, vast olive groves, and lush vineyards. Seville, an ancient city in the center of Andalusia, played host to Expo '92.

5 Press (ENTER) twice at the end of the paragraph.

You can indent an existing paragraph by placing the insertion point in the paragraph and then specifying the size of the indentation in inches. The paragraph describing Andalusia will look better if it is indented a little on each side.

To indent an existing paragraph:

1 Place the insertion point anywhere in the Andalusia paragraph.

2 Choose Paragraph from the Format menu.

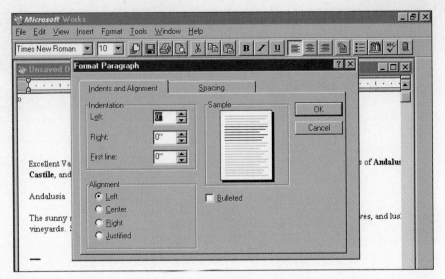

Figure 2.11

The Format Paragraph dialog box appears.

3 Select the Indents and Alignment tab.
The screen should look like Figure 2.11.

4 In the Left text box in the Indentation area, type **.75** and then press (TAB)
You have specified a left indent of .75 inch.

5 In the Right text box in the Indentation area, type **.75** and then press (ENTER)
The paragraph now is indented .75 inch from the left and right margins.
The brochure should look like Figure 2.12.

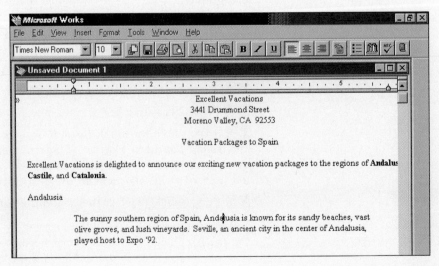

Figure 2.12

Notice that the triangles on the left and right of the ruler now reflect the paragraph indentation, not the original margins. When you move the insertion point out of the indented paragraph, the triangles in the ruler will indicate the document margins.

You can automatically indent a new paragraph by first setting the indentation and then typing the paragraph. You will do this for the description of Castile.

To add the heading Castile:

1 Press (CTRL)+(END) to move the insertion point to the end of the document.

2 Type **Castile** and press (ENTER)

3 Press (ENTER) to insert a blank line.

To indent a new paragraph:

1 Choose Paragraph from the Format menu.
The dialog box appears.

2 Select the Indents and Alignment tab.

3 In the text box for the left indentation, type **.75** and then press (TAB)

4 In the text box for the right indentation, type **.75** and then press (ENTER)

5 Type the following paragraph:
Castile lies on a great plateau that is dotted with ancient structures erected by the Romans and Moors. Madrid, a bustling city in the heart of Spain, is a leading European cultural center.
The screen should look like Figure 2.13.

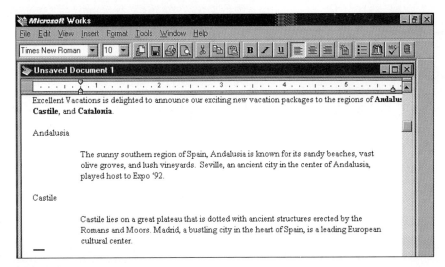

Figure 2.13

6 Press (ENTER) to go to a new line.

7 Choose Paragraph from the Format menu, and then select the Indents and Alignment tab.

8 Type **0** for the left indentation and press (TAB)

9 Type **0** for the right indentation and then press (ENTER)
If you do not reset the indentations to 0, Works will indent all subsequent text in this document.

10 Press (ENTER) to insert a blank line.

EXIT If necessary, you can save your file as *Brochure,* exit Works now, and continue this project later.

UNDERLINING TEXT

Underlined characters can be used for emphasis. The headings *Andalusia* and *Castile* need to be emphasized. To underline text that already appears on-screen, you will select the text and then select the Underline button on the Toolbar.

To underline the heading Andalusia:

1 Place the insertion point anywhere in the word *Andalusia*.

2 Double-click to select the entire word.

3 Select the Underline button on the Toolbar.
The screen should look like Figure 2.14.

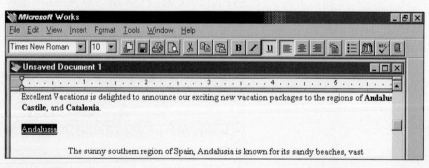

Figure 2.14

4 Click anywhere to deselect the word.

> *Tip*   Once text is selected, you can press (CTRL) + **U** to change the character style of that text to underline.

To underline the heading Castile:

1 Place the insertion point in the heading *Castile*.

2 Select the entire word.

3 Apply the underline style.

You can underline text as it is typed by first selecting the Underline button on the Toolbar, typing the new text, and then again selecting the Underline button to reset the text style to normal.

To type and underline the heading Catalonia:

1 Press (CTRL)+(END) to move to the end of the document.

2 Select the Underline button on the Toolbar.

3 Type **Catalonia**
Notice that *Catalonia* is underlined as you type it.

4 Again select the Underline button on the Toolbar.
Underlining is now deactivated.

5 Press (ENTER) twice.

To type and indent a paragraph:

1 Indent and type the following paragraph. You can either type the paragraph first and then indent it or define the indentation before typing.
The Mediterranean Sea brushes up against Catalonia's beautiful east coast. Barcelona, Spain's second largest city, was the site of the 1992 Summer Olympic Games.

2 Press (ENTER) at the end of the paragraph.

3 Select and indent the paragraph if needed.

4 If you indented before typing, choose Paragraph from the Format menu and then select the Indents and Alignment tab.

5 Make sure the left and right indentations are set to 0; then select OK to complete the command.

6 Press (CTRL)+(END) to go to the end of the document.

7 Press (ENTER) to insert a blank line at the end of the document.
The screen should look like Figure 2.15.

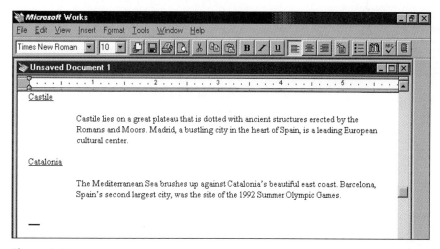

Figure 2.15

JUSTIFYING PARAGRAPHS

Usually, paragraphs such as the ones in Figure 2.15 are aligned along the left edge but have a "jagged" edge along the right. Paragraphs with left alignment are suitable in many documents, including letters and memos. Paragraphs in magazines, newspapers, and brochures tend to be *justified,* or aligned on both the left and right edges. A justified paragraph has extra spaces inserted between words so that lines of text are pushed to the right to create a smooth alignment along the right edge of the paragraph. For example, if you justify the paragraph about Castile from Figure 2.15, it will look like Figure 2.16.

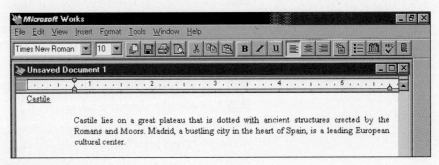

Figure 2.16

To justify the paragraph that describes Castile:

1 Place the pointer anywhere in the left margin of the paragraph that describes Castile.
The pointer must be close to the left edge of the screen and should point to the right.

2 Double-click to select the paragraph.

3 Choose Paragraph from the Format menu.

4 Select the Justified option.

5 Select OK to complete the command.

6 Click anywhere in the document to deselect the text.
The screen should look like Figure 2.16.

> **Tip** If the Justified option is not visible in the Format Paragraph dialog box, you can select the Indents and Alignment tab.

To justify the first paragraph in the brochure:

1 Place the pointer in the left margin of the first paragraph, which begins with *Excellent Vacations is delighted. . .*
The pointer should point to the right.

2 Double-click to select the paragraph.

3 Justify the paragraph.

To justify the remaining paragraphs in the brochure:

1 Select the paragraph describing Andalusia.

2 Justify the selection.

3 Select the paragraph describing Catalonia.

4 Justify the selection.

All the paragraphs should now be justified.

If you want to justify a paragraph as you type it, you should first select the Justified option and then type the text. Each subsequent paragraph will be justified until you reset the alignment to the left.

 To type a justified paragraph:

1 Press CTRL + END to move the insertion point to the end of the document.

2 Choose Paragraph from the Format menu.

3 Select Justified.

4 Select OK to apply the justified format.

5 Type the following paragraph:

Our vacation packages to Spain have received glowing reviews from many leading travel magazines, including Travel Today. Excellent Vacations offers the best vacation value for your dollar.

6 Press ENTER to complete the paragraph.

7 Deselect the Justified option by selecting the Left Align button on the Toolbar.

8 Press ENTER to insert a blank line.

The screen should look like Figure 2.17.

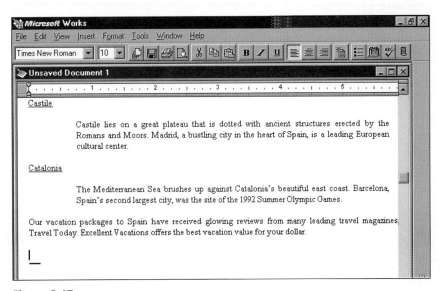

Figure 2.17

USING ITALICS

The names of newspapers, magazines, and similar periodicals are usually italicized. Foreign words, except foreign proper nouns, also are usually italicized. In addition, italics can be used to emphasize or define a word. The last paragraph of the document has a magazine name that needs to be italicized.

To italicize Travel Today:

1 Select the text *Travel Today*.

2 Select the Italic button on the toolbar.

3 Click to deselect the text.

> **Tip** Once text is selected, you can press (CTRL) + **I** to change the character style of the selected text to italic.

On the screen, italicized text will look like the italicized text in Figure 2.18.

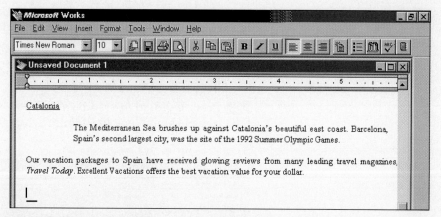

Figure 2.18

CHECKING SPELLING

The Works **Spelling Checker** enables you to check a document for spelling mistakes. Works compares words from the document to an internal list of words. Whenever the program cannot find a word in its list, Works notifies you that the word is misspelled and offers alternative spellings.

Because this document is probably error-free, you need to purposely misspell something to see how the Spelling Checker works. In the following numbered steps you will insert an extra *e* in the word *Excellent* and then correct the word by choosing Spelling from the Tools menu.

To check the spelling of a word:

1 Move the insertion point to the top of the document.

2 Place the insertion point immediately to the left of the letter *c* in *Excellent*.

3 Type **e** to misspell the word.

4 Double-click to select *Execellent*.

5 Choose Spelling from the Tools menu.
Works should identify *Execellent* as being misspelled and provide a dialog box like the one in Figure 2.19. Notice that the word *Excellent* is in the box labeled Change To. The box labeled Suggestions usually contains a list of possible alternate spellings.

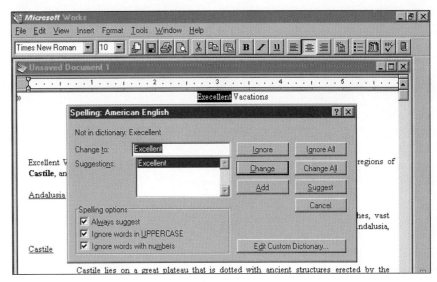

Figure 2.19

6 Select the Change button to replace the misspelled word with the suggested one.

7 When a small dialog box appears indicating that Works is finished, select OK. Works returns you to the document, and the word is now spelled correctly.

8 Click anywhere in the document to deselect the text.

In the previous numbered steps you checked the spelling of the word that was selected. You also can check the spelling of an entire document.

To check the spelling of an entire document:

1 Press (CTRL) + (HOME) to go to the top of the document.

2 Choose Spelling from the Tools menu.
The screen should look like Figure 2.20. Notice that all the check boxes are checked. Yours should be checked, too.

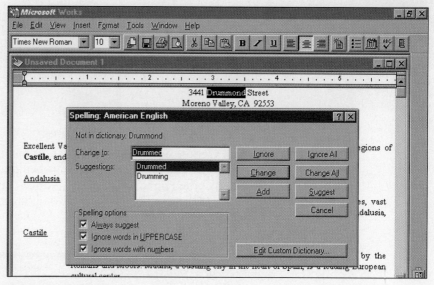

Figure 2.20

The Spelling Checker has identified the word *Drummond* as being misspelled. Although *Drummond* is spelled correctly, Works could not find the word when it compared the word to its internal dictionary of correctly spelled words. Tell Works to ignore this word and continue.

3 Select the Ignore button to skip this word.
The Spelling Checker should continue and then stop on *Moreno*.

4 Select Ignore All to skip all occurrences of this word.

5 Continue checking the rest of the document. Use Ignore or Ignore All to bypass proper nouns.

> **Tip** You can select Ignore during spell-checking to tell Works to ignore the current occurrence of a misspelled word. You can select Ignore All to tell Works to ignore all occurrences of a specific word.

If Works doesn't suggest an alternate spelling, you can type the correct spelling in the Change To text box and then select the Change button. You also can select the Add button to add the word to the dictionary so Works will suggest this spelling in the future.

USING THE THESAURUS

Works contains a ***thesaurus*** with close to 200,000 words. A thesaurus provides synonyms and antonyms to help you select a more appropriate word. Using the Works Thesaurus is similar to using the Spelling Checker. You will select a word and then activate the thesaurus.

To have Works suggest a synonym for a selected word:

1 Select the word *great* in the third paragraph.

2 Choose Thesaurus from the Tools menu.
The Thesaurus dialog box appears.

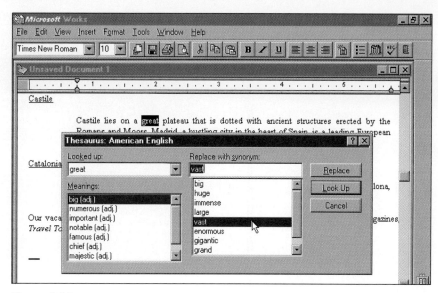

Figure 2.21

3 Select *vast* as a replacement word, as shown in Figure 2.21.

4 Select the Replace button to change *great* to *vast*.

CHANGING LINE SPACING

The brochure is almost ready to print! As you look at the title, however, you decide that the ***line spacing*** should be increased to make the title stand out from the rest of the text. Works will allow you to change the line spacing for individual paragraphs or for the entire document.

To change the title's line spacing:

1 Select the three lines at the top of the brochure that provide the company's name and address.

2 Choose Paragraph from the Format menu.

3 Select the Spacing tab.
Make sure the cursor is in the Line Spacing text box.

4 Type **1.5** to specify line-and-a-half-spacing.
The Line Spacing text box should contain 1.5, as shown in Figure 2.22.

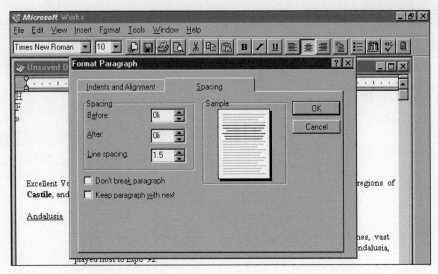

Figure 2.22

5 Select OK to apply the line spacing.

6 Click in the document to deselect the text.
The line spacing for the title changes to 1½-line spacing.

SAVING AND PRINTING THE DOCUMENT

You should always save a document before printing it, just in case some unforeseen error occurs while printing.

To save the document:

1 Choose Save from the File menu.

2 Select 3½ Floppy (A:) in the Save In box.
To save your work to a disk other than drive A:, choose the appropriate location.

3 In the File Name text box, type **Brochure**
Brochure is a good file name because it describes the document and follows the rules for naming a file.

4 Select Save to complete the command.

The preview feature in Works shows the overall format of a document. Because the current document has several paragraph formats, you would be wise to use the preview feature to check how the document will print. If you are satisfied that the document is ready to be printed, you can print right from the Print Preview screen.

To preview the document on-screen:

1 Choose Print Preview from the File menu.
The document should look like Figure 2.23. Notice that if you like the preview, you can print right from this screen.

2 Select Print to print the document.

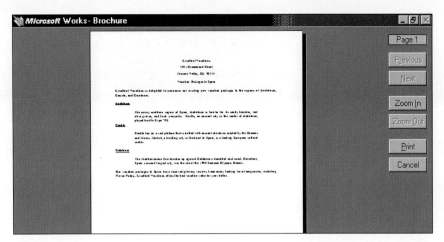

Figure 2.23

THE NEXT STEP

Document formatting and character styles can both enhance the look of a document and improve readability. In some situations you may be required to follow a specific format and style. For example, a résumé usually has some words and phrases that use bold, underline, and italic styles. The title is often centered, and the justification of certain sections will vary. Or consider a research paper. Most papers are double-spaced with 1-inch left and right margins. Of course, the Spelling Checker is a valuable proofreading tool.

This concludes Project 2. You can either exit Works or go on to work the Study Questions, Review Exercises, and Assignments.

SUMMARY AND EXERCISES

Summary

- Margins consist of white space that surrounds text on a printed page.
- Text can be centered horizontally with the Center Align button on the Toolbar.
- Bold text, which is heavier and thicker than regular text, can be used for emphasis.
- Underlined text can be used for emphasis.
- The default alignment for paragraphs is left alignment. Justified paragraphs are aligned along both the left and right edges.
- Italic characters, which slant to the right and are slightly rounded, usually are used for the titles of periodicals and for foreign words. Italics also can be used for emphasis.

- You can use the Spelling command in the Tools menu to check the spelling of one word or an entire document. You can use the Thesaurus to select synonyms.
- You can choose Print Preview from the File menu to check paragraph alignment and other formatting on-screen before printing a document.

Key Terms and Operations

Key Terms
bold
formatting
indentation
italic
justified
line spacing
margin
Spelling Checker
style
Thesaurus

underline
WYSIWYG

Operations
Align paragraphs
Apply bold, underline, and italic
    character styles
Center text
Check spelling
Indent a paragraph
Set margins

Study Questions

Multiple Choice

1. Formatting refers to:
    a. varying line spacing.
    b. justifying paragraphs.
    c. changing margins.
    d. applying character styles.
    e. All of the above.

2. The left- and right-margin markers appear in:
    a. the status bar.
    b. the menu bar.
    c. the Toolbar.
    d. the ruler.
    e. All of the above.

3. Text aligned on both sides is:
    a. justified.
    b. left-aligned text.
    c. right-aligned text.
    d. centered.
    e. All of the above.

4. The Page Setup command from the File menu can be used to:
    a. set margins.
    b. indent text.
    c. change line spacing.
    d. justify text.
    e. All of the above.

5. Which character style causes the text to slant to the right?
   a. bold
   b. underline
   c. italic
   d. strikethrough
   e. All of the above.

6. *Vacetion* is an example of a word that is mispelled. To correct this, you would use the:
   a. Thesaurus.
   b. File menu.
   c. Format menu.
   d. Spelling Checker.
   e. The Correct command from the Error menu.

7. A document needs to have 2 inches of white space on the left side. It would be best to accomplish this by:
   a. changing to left alignment.
   b. using TAB to indent each line of text.
   c. increasing the left margin.
   d. justifying all text.
   e. All of the above.

8. Which of the following elements of a term paper are usually centered horizontally?
   a. footnotes
   b. reference list or bibliography
   c. titles
   d. direct quotations exceeding three lines
   e. All of the above.

9. Which tool recommends synonyms for words that occur in a document?
   a. Spelling Checker
   b. Thesaurus
   c. Font and Style command
   d. Print Preview
   e. The Recommend command

10. Which of the following are often italicized?
    a. names of newspapers
    b. names of magazines
    c. foreign words
    d. words that need to be emphasized
    e. All of the above.

Short Answer

1. What is the default size of the left margin, in inches?

2. What is the default size of the bottom margin, in inches?

3. _____ characters slant to the right.

4. To underline existing text, you would first _____ the text and then choose the Underline command.

5. What is the default alignment for paragraphs?

6. Where are the current margin settings displayed?

7. The Save command is in the _____ menu.

8. Which menu do you use to print a document?

9. Most formatting options are in the _____ menu.

10. The Page Setup command is in the _____ menu.

For Discussion

1. What is a character style?

2. What is a paragraph format?

3. Why is Brochure a good file name for the file in this project?

4. What types of documents have justified paragraphs?

5. Why would you save a document before printing it?

Review Exercises

Creating a Restaurant Menu

You are the owner of a restaurant. Invent a name for the restaurant and then use the Word Processor tool to create a menu similar to the one in Figure 2.24.

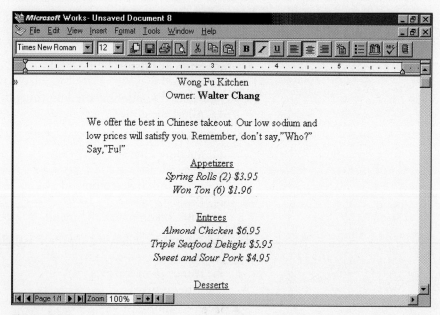

Figure 2.24

The menu should follow these guidelines:

1. At the top of the page, type and center the name of the restaurant.

2. On the second line, type `Owner:` and your name; then center the entire line.

3. Write a short paragraph describing the restaurant. Change the indentations to 1 inch from the left and right margins.

4. Justify the preceding paragraph.

5. Type the rest of the menu. Use bold, italics, and underlining somewhere in the menu. For example, in Figure 2.24 the owner's name is in bold.

6. Have at least two appetizers, three entrees, and two desserts.

7. Check the spelling of the menu.

8. Save the menu. Give it the file name *Menu*.

9. Print the menu.

Writing a Memo

Create a memo that describes bonuses for all employees of Excellent Vacations. The document should resemble the one in Figure 2.25. Be sure to include your name, the current date, and all the formatting features shown in the figure. Your memo should have three categories of bonuses: Good Attitude, Better Attitude, and Excellent Attitude. You will have to invent bonuses for Better Attitudes and Excellent Attitudes.

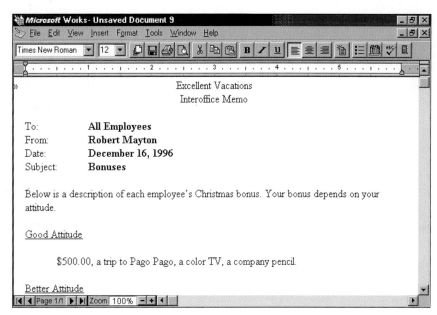

Figure 2.25

1. Save the memo. Name the file *Bonus*.

2. Preview and print the memo.

Assignments

Confirming Hotel Reservations

In Project 1 you wrote a letter canceling your newspaper delivery for the duration of your vacation. Now you need to contact the hotel in Andalusia to confirm your reservations.

Create the letter shown in Figure 2.26. Set the margins to 1¾ inches on all sides: top, bottom, left, and right. Use the Thesaurus to select an appropriate synonym for the word *best* in the first line of the body of the letter. Save the letter to the data disk with the file name *Hotel Confirmation*. Print the letter.

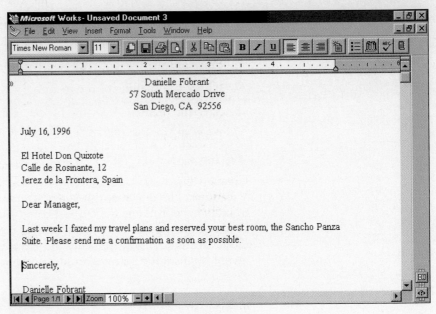

Figure 2.26

Creating a List of Favorite Items

Figure 2.27 has a list of software packages that Bill Weaver really likes. Create a list similar to this one, but choose something other than software. For example, you could write about your favorite music CDs, your favorite baseball teams, or the most interesting movies you've seen lately. Have at least three items in the document. Be sure to use left and right indentations and apply a bold character style when necessary. Your name should be at the top instead of Bill Weaver's. Save the file as *List of Favorites* and print the list.

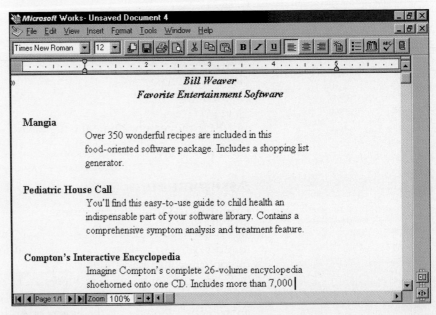

Figure 2.27

Enhancing an Existing Memo

Retrieve the file *Bad Checks* that you created in the last Assignment of Project 1. Make the following additions:

- Enter the title *Employee Memo* at the top of the page.
- Change the character style of the title to bold.
- Center the title.
- Add a new paragraph at the end of the memo explaining that automatic teller machine (ATM) cards are now available. Mention that the ATM card is free provided that a customer maintains a minimum checking account balance of $500 or a minimum savings account balance of $250. Otherwise the card is $5 per month.
- Justify all paragraphs.

Save and print the updated file as *Bank Memo*.

PROJECT 3:   ENHANCING A DOCUMENT

Objectives

After completing this project, you should be able to:

▶ Move and copy text

▶ Set and move tabs

▶ Create footnotes

▶ Change fonts

▶ Use a strikethrough character style

▶ Create headers and footers

▶ Create a hanging indentation

▶ Use Easy Formats

CASE STUDY: ENHANCING THE APPEARANCE OF THE BROCHURE

You have received a positive response to the brochure you've developed explaining the new vacation packages to Spain. However, you know you can improve the brochure's appearance as new information is added. You need to move the text around in the brochure so it is more appealing to potential customers. In addition, you need to create a table showing the price reduction of certain vacation packages. Finally, you want to add footnotes to further explain some information in the brochure. The finished brochure will look like Figure 3.1.

Excellent Vacations
3441 Drummond Street
Moreno Valley, CA 92553

Vacation Packages to Spain

Excellent Vacations is delighted to announce our exciting new
vacation packages to the regions of **Andalusia**, **Castile**, and
Catalonia.

Andalusia

> The sunny southern region of Spain, Andalusia is
> known for its sandy beaches, vast olive groves,
> and lush vineyards. Seville, an ancient city in
> the center of Andalusia, played host to Expo '92.

Castile

> Castile lies on a vast plateau that is dotted
> with ancient structures erected by the Romans and
> Moors. Madrid, a bustling city in the heart of
> Spain, is a leading European cultural center.

Catalonia

> The Mediterranean Sea brushes up against
> Catalonia's beautiful eastern coast. Barcelona,
> Spain's second largest city, was the site of the
> 1992 Summer Olympic Games.

Our vacation packages to Spain have received glowing reviews from
many leading travel magazines, including *Travel Today*. Excellent
Vacations offers the best vacation value for your dollar.[1]

Destination	Price[2]	Days	Comments
Andalusia	$~~1,234.95~~	7	Fun in the Sun
Castile	$~~2,300.00~~	14	Cultural Odyssey
Catalonia	$~~1,340.75~~	10	Scenic Coastline

Vacation Package Guidelines:

1. Make your reservations at least two months in advance. All
   reservations require a $100 deposit. Ther is a $25 processing
   charge for all refunds.

2. Pay the balance at least one month before your departure
   date. Tickets can be purchased with any major credit card
   or by check.

---

[1] *Travel Today*, June 1994, p. 57.
[2] Prices slashed to $1,000, $2,200, and $1,200.

Excellent Vacations

Figure 3.1

Designing the Solution

Look carefully at Figure 3.1 and notice how the brochure has changed.
Some of the fonts are different, additional information is included, footnotes
have been added, and a footer appears at the bottom of the page. In this
project you will enhance the appearance of the document by performing
additional formatting operations such as changing fonts and alignment,
creating a table, adding footnotes, and creating a footer at the bottom of
the brochure.

Opening an Existing Document

Because you will continue to develop the brochure you started in Project 2, you can retrieve the file from the disk and make the necessary changes.

You can open an existing file by selecting the Existing Documents tab in the Works Task Launcher. This will allow you to open the file, *Brochure,* that you created in the previous project.

To open an existing file from the Works Task Launcher:

1 Start Works.
The Works Task Launcher dialog box appears. If Works is open and you do not see the Works Task Launcher, choose New from the File menu.

2 Select the Existing Documents tab.
The screen should look like Figure 3.2. The list of existing documents may be different if you created additional files.

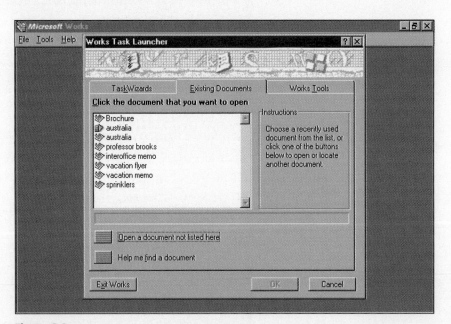

Figure 3.2

3 Select *Brochure* and then select OK to load the file.
The file is loaded into Works. If you are successful, skip the following steps.

4 If you do not see *Brochure,* select Open a Document Not Listed Here.

5 Click next to the words *Look In* at the top of the dialog box.

6 Select 3½ Floppy (A:).
If you are using drive B:, C:, or maybe something even higher, select the appropriate drive letter. The file name should appear.

7 Select *Brochure* and then select OK to load the file.
The file is loaded into Works.

8 Choose Normal from the View menu to make sure the document is displayed in normal view.

> **Getting Online Help**   If you have problems selecting a drive or do not see *Brochure* when you try to open the file, you can press F1 for Help.

CHANGING LINE SPACING

Next you will add information to the brochure. For the entire brochure to fit on one page, you will need to change the line spacing of the title so it is single-spaced.

 To change the title's spacing:

1 Select the three lines at the top of the brochure that provide the company name and address.

2 Choose Paragraph from the Format menu.

3 Select the Spacing tab.

4 Type **1** in the Line Spacing text box.
The Line Spacing text box should be set to 1 (single-spacing).

5 Select OK to apply the line spacing.

6 Click in the document to deselect the address.
The title now appears single-spaced.

> **Reminder**   For information about changing the line spacing of individual paragraphs, see the section titled "Changing Line Spacing" in Project 2.

MOVING AND COPYING TEXT

When reviewing a document, you may see sentences or paragraphs that you would like to move. In addition, a document might call for the inclusion of the same phrase or paragraph in several places. With Works, moving and copying text are easy tasks to accomplish.

Suppose you thought the brochure might be more effective if you moved the first paragraph before the last. If this change doesn't improve the effect, you can always move the paragraph back. To move a block of text, you will first select the text, choose Cut from the Edit menu, place the insertion point at the new location, and then choose Paste from the Edit menu to complete the operation.

 To move the first paragraph before the last paragraph:

1 Place the insertion point immediately *above* the letter *E* in the word *Excellent* in the first paragraph.

2 Select the first paragraph.
The selected paragraph should look like the one in Figure 3.3.

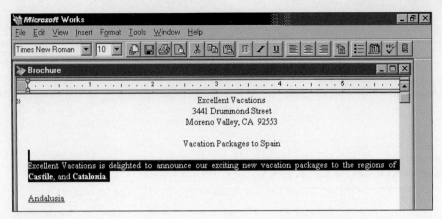

Figure 3.3

3 Choose Cut from the Edit menu to cut the text.

4 Place the insertion point right *above* the last paragraph (above the letter *O* in *Our*).

5 Choose Paste from the Edit menu to insert the text.

6 View the paragraph in its new location.

Notice that the paragraph has been moved, as shown in Figure 3.4.

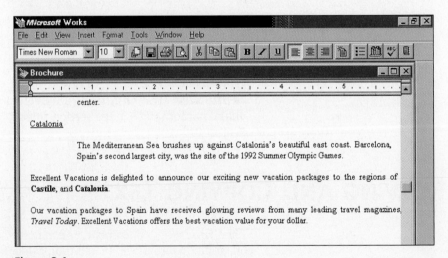

Figure 3.4

> ***Reminder*** You can select any amount of text with the mouse by dragging the pointer over the desired text.

You have decided the paragraph that you just moved was more effective in its original location. You can move the paragraph back by using the Undo command, by repeating the Cut and Paste commands, or by using the *drag-and-drop method*. Drag-and-drop allows you to highlight a selection and use the mouse to move it to a new location. You will use drag-and-drop to move the paragraph to its previous location.

To move text using drag-and-drop:

1 Place the insertion point just above the word *Excellent* in the second-to-last paragraph.

2 Select the entire paragraph.

3 Place the pointer anywhere within the selection.
Notice that the pointer has the word *DRAG* below the arrow, as shown in Figure 3.5.

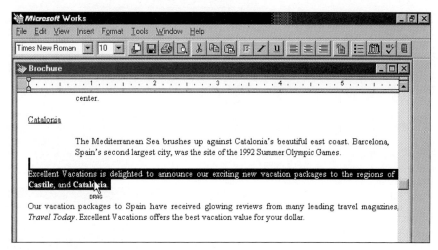

Figure 3.5

4 Hold down the left mouse button and move the mouse so the insertion point is just *above* the letter *A* in the underlined word *Andalusia*. Notice that the word *MOVE* now appears with the pointer.

5 Release the mouse button. The paragraph should be back in its original position.

Caution As you move the pointer into the ruler at the top of the Works screen, the pointer will appear as a circle with a diagonal line through it. The vertical scroll bar will continue to scroll the screen. You should keep the pointer in the ruler until the top of the document appears. Then you can place the pointer at the text's new location.

Copying text is similar to moving text. You will select the text to be copied, choose Copy from the Edit menu, place the insertion point at the desired location, and then choose Paste from the Edit menu. The copied text will be an exact duplicate of the original text.

Assume that you want to see how the company name and address would look at the bottom of the brochure. You will copy the name and address from the top to the bottom.

To copy the company name and address:

1 Select the company name and address, as shown in Figure 3.6.

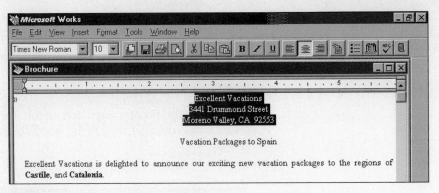

Figure 3.6

2 Choose Copy from the Edit menu to copy the text.

3 Place the insertion point below the last paragraph in the brochure.

4 Choose Paste from the Edit menu to insert the text.
A copy of the address should now appear at the bottom of the brochure, as shown in Figure 3.7.

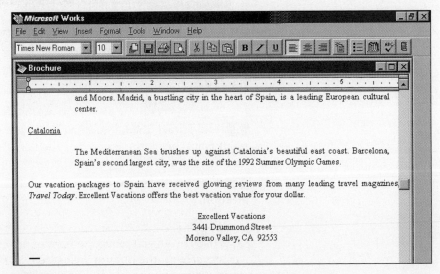

Figure 3.7

You decide you don't like the way it looks and you want to undo it.

5 Choose Undo Editing from the Edit menu.
The Undo command reverses the preceding action. The address should be gone from the bottom.

> *Tip*   The Undo command is context sensitive, which means it appears as "Undo Editing" when you want to reverse an editing change.

SETTING TAB STOPS

A *tab stop* is a set position on the ruler to which the insertion point can move in one jump. To move the insertion point to the next tab stop, you would press ⟨TAB⟩. You can use a tab to indent the first line of a paragraph or to align text more accurately than you can by pressing ⟨SPACE⟩ and "eyeballing" the position of the insertion point.

Works presets a tab stop at every ½ inch, but you can set your own tab stops by using the Tabs command in the Format menu. Preset tab stops are not visible on the ruler, but the position of any tab stop you specify will be recorded on the ruler as a mark that differs in appearance depending upon the type of tab stop. *Left* and *right tab stops* cause the text to be aligned to the left or to the right at the tab stop. *Center tab stops* cause the text to be centered at the tab stop, and *decimal tab stops* cause decimals to line up vertically. Figure 3.8 shows the effect of each type of tab stop.

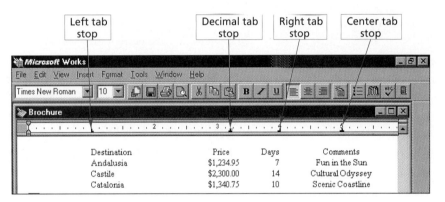

Figure 3.8

You will now add to the brochure a table that lists the prices for various vacation packages. In Works, tables are often created using tab stops, because a table contains columns that need to be positioned precisely. You could use the preset tab stops that appear at every inch, but instead you will set your own tab stops to position data with precision.

 To set a left tab stop:

1 Press ⟨CTRL⟩ + ⟨END⟩ to move to the end of the brochure.

2 Choose Tabs from the Format menu.

You should see the dialog box shown in Figure 3.9.

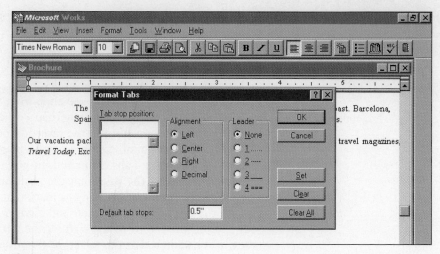

Figure 3.9

3 Place the insertion point in the Tab stop position text box.

4 Type **1** to specify a tab stop at 1 inch. Do *not* press (ENTER) after typing the number.
Notice that the Alignment in the dialog box is preset to Left.

5 Select OK to set the left tab stop.
You should see a left tab stop set at 1 inch on the ruler.

The procedure for setting decimal, right, and center tab stops is identical for each tab stop, except a different Alignment option button will be selected.

To set decimal, right, and center tab stops:

1 Choose Tabs from the Format menu.

2 Type **3.2** to specify a tab stop at 3.2 inches.

3 Select the Decimal option button under Alignment.

4 Select OK to insert the decimal tab stop.

5 Set a right tab stop at 4 inches.

6 Set a center tab stop at 5 inches.
When you are finished, the tab stop marks shown in Figure 3.10 should appear in the ruler.

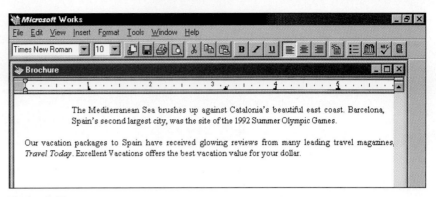

Figure 3.10

Once you have set the tab stops, you are ready to enter the contents of the table.

To enter the headings of the table:

1 Press `TAB` to place the insertion point at the left tab marker on the ruler.

2 Type **Destination** and then press `TAB`

3 Type **Price** and then press `TAB`

4 Type **Days** and then press `TAB`

5 Type **Comments** and then press `ENTER`

To enter the first row of data in the table:

1 Press `TAB` to place the insertion point at the left tab stop marker on the ruler.

2 Type **Andalusia** and then press `TAB`

3 Type **$1,234.95** and then press `TAB`

4 Type **7** and then press `TAB`

5 Type **Fun in the Sun** and then press `ENTER`

To enter the second and third rows of data:

1 Type the following two lines of data. Press `TAB` and `ENTER` where appropriate.
```
Castile $2,300.00 14 Cultural Odyssey
Catalonia $1,340.75 10 Scenic Coastline
```

2 Be sure to press `ENTER` after the words *Scenic Coastline*.
The screen should look like Figure 3.11.

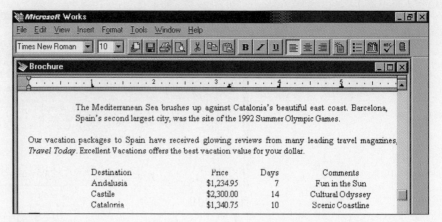

Figure 3.11

MOVING TAB STOPS

Once you have set tab stops, it is easy to move them on the ruler. The Price column will look better if moved a little to the left. You can move any tab stop by dragging it to the left or right on the ruler.

To move a decimal tab stop:

1 Place the insertion point to the left of the letter *D* in the word *Destination* and select the entire table.
You need to select the whole table so any changes in the tab stop settings affect the entire table, as shown in Figure 3.12.

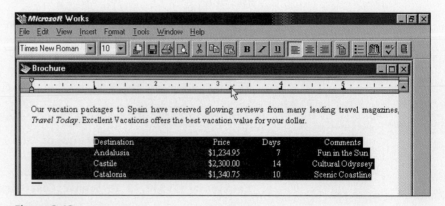

Figure 3.12

2 Place the pointer on the decimal tab stop on the ruler above the word Price, as shown in Figure 3.12.

3 Drag the tab marker to 2.5 inches on the ruler.

4 If you get a dialog box that offers Help, select OK to bypass the Help. The Price column should move a little to the left.

5 Click outside the text to deselect it.
The Days and Comments columns will look better if moved a little to the left.

To move right and center tab stops:

1 Select the entire table so any changes are reflected in the whole table.

2 Drag the right tab stop on the ruler above *Days* to 3.5 inches. The Days column should move a little to the right.

3 Drag the center tab above *Comments* to 4.5 inches. The table should look like the one in Figure 3.13.

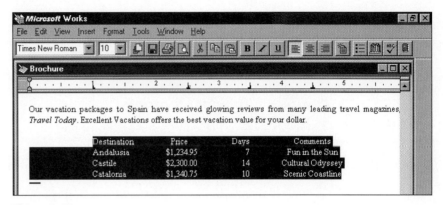

Figure 3.13

4 Click outside the text to deselect it.

Before you continue typing the rest of the document, you need to reset the tabs; otherwise, the tab stops you set for the table will be used for the rest of the document. You want the rest of the document to use the standard tab stop settings.

To reset the tabs:

1 Move the insertion point to the end of the document. The insertion point should be just below the table. If it isn't, press (ENTER) once.

2 Choose Tabs from the Format menu.

3 Select Clear All to clear all tab settings.

4 Select OK to remove the tabs you set previously.

Tab stops also can be cleared using the ruler. You can simply drag tabs off the ruler and they disappear. You would place the pointer over the tab stop and then, while holding down the mouse button, you would drag the tab stop straight down toward the main body of text. The tab stop should disappear.

EXIT If necessary, you can save your file as *Brochure,* exit Works now, and continue this project later.

USING FOOTNOTES

A *footnote* is a reference, an explanatory note, or a comment placed at the bottom of a printed page. You can use a footnote to reference a source of data. For example, if you write a term paper and include information that was derived from a book, you can give credit to the book and its author by placing a note number or symbol in the main body of the text and a corresponding number or symbol at the bottom of that page. Next to the number or symbol at the bottom of the page, you would list the book's author, title, publisher, and so on.

The brochure needs a footnote that describes the source for the quotation "the best vacation value for your dollar," which appears in the last paragraph. *Travel Today* magazine was the source for the quotation.

To add a footnote:

1 Place the insertion point just after . . . *the best vacation value for your dollar.*

2 Choose Footnote from the Insert menu and then select Insert from within the dialog box.
The screen should split into two panes, as shown in Figure 3.14. The top pane contains the main body of the text; the bottom pane is the area where you enter the footnote text.

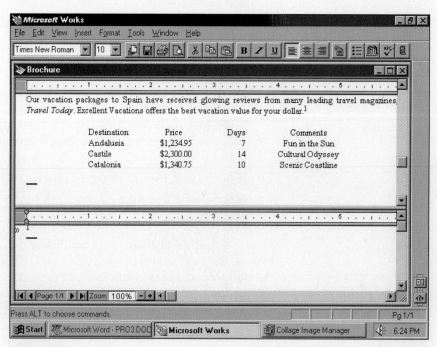

Figure 3.14

3 Type **Travel Today, June 1994, p. 57.**
Notice that the main body of text contains a superscripted 1, as does the footnote.

Tip   You can press ⑥ to move the insertion point between the text pane and the footnote pane.

To italicize the magazine title in the footnote:

1 Select the title *Travel Today*.

2 Select the Italic button on the Toolbar.
The title should look like the one in Figure 3.15.

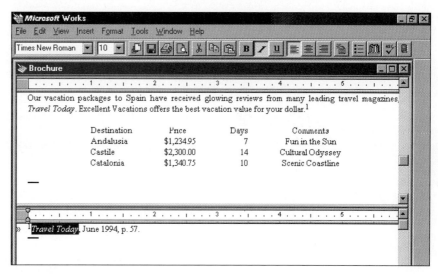

Figure 3.15

To close the footnote pane:

1 Choose the View menu.
The checkmark in front of the Footnotes option indicates that the footnote pane is displayed at the bottom of the screen. Whenever you create a footnote, a footnote pane appears, and the Footnotes option is marked automatically.

2 Choose Footnotes to close the footnote pane.
You can display the footnote again by choosing Footnotes from the View menu. For now, keep the footnote pane closed.

A print preview will give you a good idea of what the footnote will look like on the printed page.

To preview the document:

1 Select the Print Preview button on the Toolbar.
The screen should now look like Figure 3.16.

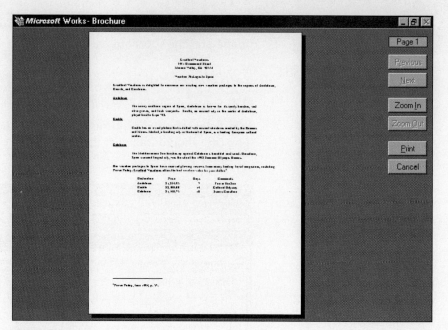

Figure 3.16

2 After examining the document, select Cancel to cancel the preview.

You need to add one more footnote to describe how prices have been reduced. The prices in the table have been slashed from $1,234.95, $2,300.00, and $1,340.75 to $1,000, $2,200, and $1,200, respectively.

To add a second footnote:

1 Within the table, place the insertion point to the right of the letter *e* in the word *Price*.

2 Choose Footnote from the Insert menu and then select Insert. The screen splits into two panes.

3 Type **Prices slashed to $1,000, $2,200, and $1,200.**
Notice that the main text contains a superscripted 2, as does the footnote.

To close the footnote pane:

1 Press (F6) to return to the main text pane.

2 Choose Footnotes from the View menu to close the footnote pane.

To preview the document:

1 Select the Print Preview button on the Toolbar.
You should see two footnotes at the bottom of the page.

2 After examining the document, select Cancel to cancel the preview.

USING FONTS

In Project 2 you used several character styles, including bold, italics, and underline. Character styles are just one aspect of the *font,* or design, of a character. A character's font is identified by its typeface, size, position, and style.

A *typeface* is a collection of characters and symbols that have a unique design. Typefaces fall into two broad categories: *serif* and *sans serif.* Serif typefaces have delicate finishing strokes called serifs at the ends of each character. Because serifs tend to make reading easier, you find serif typefaces in periodicals and books, such as the one you are reading. A typical serif typeface is Courier. The default, or standard, typeface in Works' word processor is Times New Roman.

Sans serif typefaces do not have serifs (*sans* means "without") and typically are used in headlines, advertising, and spreadsheets. A typical sans serif typeface is Arial.

The *size* or height of a character is measured in *points.* One point is 1/72 inch on the printed page. Works' default is 10-point text, which is 10/72 inch high on a printout.

Superscript and *subscript* refer to characters printed slightly above or below the normal level of a line of text. Works calls this the *position* of the characters. Superscripts are used automatically for footnote notations. In addition, you can use superscripts to create exponents, such as 5^3. Subscripts are used in math and science, such as in H_2O. You will now use a different font in the brochure for the company name and address.

To change the font:

1 Select the company name and address at the top of the page, as shown in Figure 3.17.

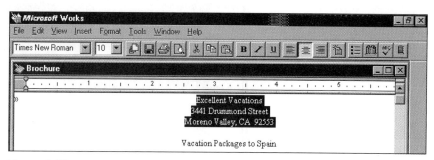

Figure 3.17

2 Choose Font and Style from the Format menu. You should see the dialog box shown in Figure 3.18.

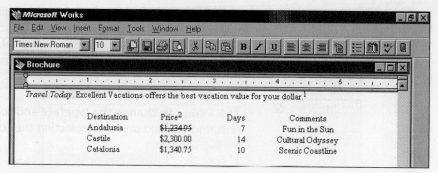

Figure 3.21

You still need to strike through the remaining prices in the table.

To apply a strikethrough style to the remaining prices:

1 Select $2,300.00.

2 Choose Font and Style from the Format menu.

3 Select the Strikethrough option.

4 Select OK to apply the style.

5 Select $1,340.75 and then apply the strikethrough style.
The table should look like the one in Figure 3.22.

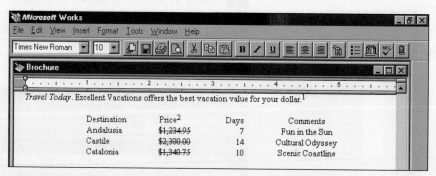

Figure 3.22

 If necessary, you can save your file as *Brochure,* exit Works now, and
continue this project later.

CREATING HEADERS AND FOOTERS

A *header* is text that appears in the top margin of every page of a document.
For example, some books have the title or the name of the current chapter
at the top of each page. A *footer* is similar to a header, except that a footer
appears in the bottom margin.

Although the document *Brochure* has only one page, you will enter a header that consists of your name. To enter a header, you will move to the top of the document where you see an H and an F. Anything you type next to the H is a header; anything typed next to the F is a footer.

To enter a header:

1 Press (CTRL) + (HOME) to move the insertion point to the top of the document.
An H and an F appear.

2 Type your name next to the H.

3 Press (↓) to move down to the letter F.

4 Type **Excellent Vacations** next to the F.
The screen should look like Figure 3.23. Of course, you will have your name, not Bob Mayton's.

Figure 3.23

To add a touch of professionalism to the brochure, you will add the date to the header. To add the current date, time, or page number to a header or footer, you can choose Date and Time or Page Number from the Insert menu.

To add the current date to the header:

1 Press (↑) to move up to the header line.

2 Press (END) to move to the end of the header line.

3 Press (TAB) once.
Notice that you are under a center tab stop. The header has two preset tab stops: center and right.

4 Press (TAB) once to move to the right tab stop.

5 Choose Date and Time from the Insert menu.
You should see a dialog box like the one in Figure 3.24. Notice that there are many date and time formats.

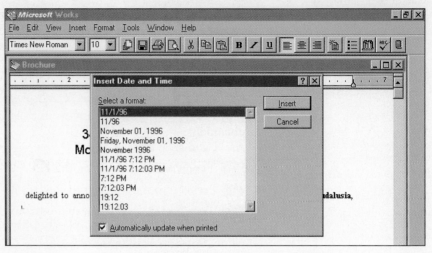

Figure 3.24

6 Select the third date format and then select the Insert button.
You should see the current date on the right side of the header. The date
will be updated every day. If you open this file tomorrow, it will have
tomorrow's date.

Previewing the document will give you a good idea of what the header
and footer will look like.

To preview the header and footer:

1 Select the Print Preview button on the Toolbar.
Notice the header and footer, as shown in Figure 3.25. Your date will be
different.

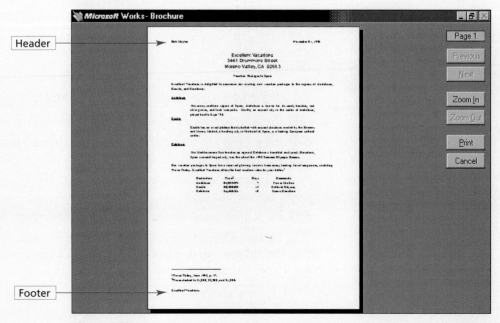

Figure 3.25

2 Select Cancel after examining the header and footer.

CREATING HANGING INDENTATIONS

In Project 2, you indented paragraphs on both sides. You can also "hang" a paragraph to the right of a number to create a ***hanging indentation.*** A hanging indentation indents every line of a paragraph except for the first line. Figure 3.26 shows two examples of hanging indentations.

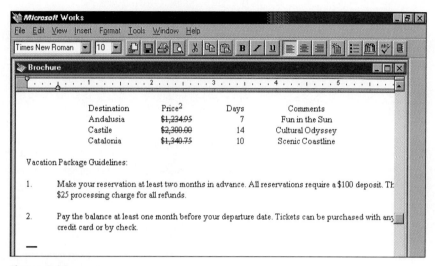

Figure 3.26

In the brochure, you need to list the steps for purchasing a vacation package. You will create hanging indentations by using the Easy Formats command from the Format menu. Easy Formats are predefined formats that provide a quick way of changing the appearance of a document.

To create a hanging indentation:

1 Press (CTRL)+(END) to move the insertion point to the end of the document.

2 Press (ENTER) to insert a blank line.

3 Type **Vacation Package Guidelines:** and then press (ENTER)

4 Press (ENTER) to insert a blank line.

5 Type **1.** and then press (TAB)

6 Type the following text:
Make your reservation at least two months in advance. All reservations require a $100 deposit. There is a $25 processing charge for all refunds.

7 Press (ENTER) twice.

8 Select the number and paragraph that you just typed.
The document should look like Figure 3.27.

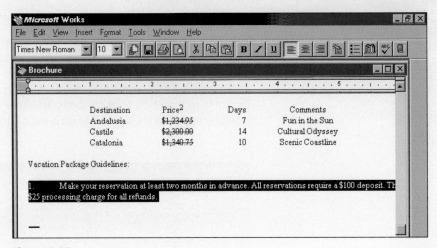

Figure 3.27

9 Choose Easy Formats from the Format menu.

10 Scroll down and then select Hanging Indent.
You should see a list of Easy Formats, as shown in Figure 3.28.

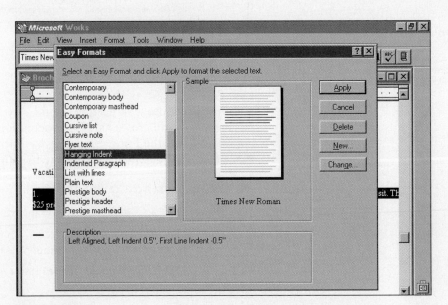

Figure 3.28

11 Select Apply to apply the hanging indentation.
The paragraph should be indented like the first one in Figure 3.26.

To enter the second hanging indentation:

1 Press $\boxed{\text{CTRL}}$ + $\boxed{\text{END}}$ to move the insertion point to the end of the document.

2 Type **2.** and then press $\boxed{\text{TAB}}$

3 Type the following text:
**Pay the balance at least one month before your departure date.
Tickets can be purchased with any major credit card or by check.**

4 Press (ENTER) at the end of the paragraph.

5 Select the number and paragraph that you just typed.

6 Choose Easy Formats from the Format menu.

7 Select Hanging Indent and then select Apply.

8 Click to deselect the text.
The paragraph should be indented like the second one in Figure 3.26.

Tip Hanging indentations also can be made using the ruler. First you would select the paragraph you want to indent. Then you would use the mouse to drag the lower triangle on the left of the ruler to the first tab position. Next, you would drag the top triangle on the left of the ruler to the left margin. Essentially, the top triangle marks the left margin of the first line of the paragraph; the bottom triangle marks the left margin of the rest of the paragraph.

SAVING AND PRINTING THE DOCUMENT

Because you have already saved this document at least once, you will not be prompted for a new file name when you save it again.

To save and then preview the document:

1 Choose Save from the File menu.

2 Choose Print Preview from the File menu.
The document should look like Figure 3.29.

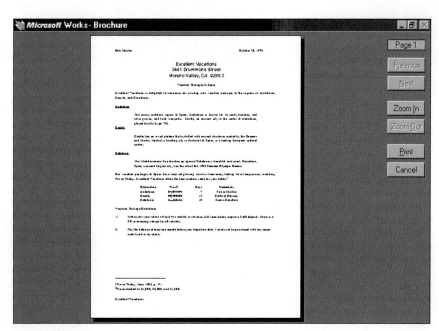

Figure 3.29

3 Select Cancel to exit the preview.

When you are satisfied that the document is ready to be printed, you can print the document.

To print the document:

1 Choose Print from the File menu.

2 Select OK to print the document.

THE NEXT STEP

The word processing skills you have learned can be applied to various documents. Works allows you a great deal of flexibility in formatting a document. By creatively using a variety of typefaces and styles in conjunction with headers and footers, you can accomplish simple desktop publishing. You might consider using Works to produce a newsletter.

This concludes Project 3. You can either exit Works or go on to work the Study Questions, Review Exercises, and Assignments or the Additional Assignment.

SUMMARY AND EXERCISES

Summary

- To move or copy text, you can use Cut or Copy from the Edit menu and then choose Paste.
- A tab stop is a set position on the ruler to which the insertion point can move in one jump.
- You can use left, right, decimal, and center tab stops to position text precisely.
- You can use footnotes to place a reference or explanatory note at the bottom of a page.
- A font is identified by its typeface, size, position, and style.
- The strikethrough character style puts dashes through characters.
- Headers and footers contain additional text that appears on every page in the top and bottom margins, respectively.
- A hanging indentation indents an entire paragraph except for the first line.

Key Terms and Operations

Key Terms
center tab
decimal tab
drag-and-drop method
font
footer
footnote
hanging indentation
header
left tab
points
position

right tab
sans serif
screen font
serif
size
strikethrough
subscript
superscript
tab stop
TrueType font
typeface

Operations
Change font style,
 size, and
 typeface
Copy text
Create a hanging
 indentation
Create footnotes
Create headers
 and footers
Cut text
Paste text
Set tab stops

Study Questions

Multiple Choice

1. The overall design and shape of a set of characters is called the:
   a. type style.   c. boldface.
   b. superscript.   d. typeface.

2. Character style refers to:
   a. the position of a character on the page.
   b. bold, italics, underline, and strikethrough.
   c. the height of a character.
   d. the use of a character in a header or footer.

3. To add a reference or explanatory note in a document you would use a:
   a. footnote.
   b. different typeface.
   c. header or footer.
   d. title.

4. To indicate that a portion of text is no longer needed in a document, you would use:
   a. a superscript.
   b. a subscript.
   c. the strikethrough style.
   d. the underline style.

5. Which type of tab is used to align decimal points in numbers in a table?
   a. decimal tab
   b. left tab
   c. center tab
   d. right tab

6. To move a paragraph to a new location, you would use which of the following commands?
   a. Cut
   b. Paste
   c. Copy
   d. At least two of the above.

7. After selecting text and then using the Copy command, you can copy the selected text to another location by using the _____ command.
   a. Put
   b. Paste
   c. Place
   d. Move

8. Which of the following appears at the top of every page?
   a. footer   c. footnote
   b. endnote   d. header

9. Which of the following appears at the bottom of every page?
   a. header   c. footer
   b. footnote   d. subscript

10. Which of the following would be the best way to emphasize a document's title?
    a. Use a superscript.
    b. Center and boldface the title.
    c. Use a subscript.
    d. Center the title and use a smaller point size.

Short Answer

1. Headers have preset tab stops in the center and _____ positions.

2. The Easy Format command in the _____ menu has many predefined formats such as a hanging indentation.

3. The Font Name and Font Size buttons on the _____ are shortcuts for changing the typeface and character size.

4. To move text, you first choose the Cut command from the _____ menu.

5. A(n) _____ character style is used to indicate that text is no longer needed but has yet to be deleted.

6. To move a tab stop, you drag it on the _____.

7. A point size of 12 is _____ inch(es) on the printed page.

8. When you enter Works, there are preset tabs every _____ inch(es).

9. Because _____ typefaces tend to make reading easier, you usually find them in books and periodicals.

10. To open and close a footnote pane, you choose the _____ command from the View menu.

For Discussion

1. What is the purpose of a footnote?

2. What kind of information is displayed in a header or footer?

3. List three font styles commonly used and the purpose of each.

4. In Works, a character's font is identified by what four characteristics?

5. What typefaces are available on the computer you are using? (Hint: Choose the Font and Style command from the Format menu.)

Review Exercises

Creating a Table of Rapid Transit Systems

1. Create the document shown in Figure 3.30. You will need to set tab stops and apply a sans serif character style. The title is set to bold italics and the column headings are underlined.

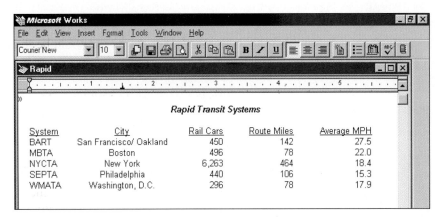

Figure 3.30

2. Save the document as *Rapid.*

3. Print the document.

Creating a Table of Ancient Greek Battles

1. Create a document like the one shown in Figure 3.31. You will need to use hanging indentations.

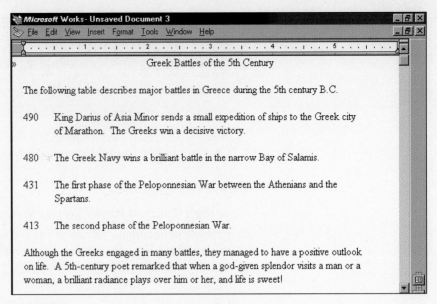

Figure 3.31

2. The last sentence in the document is a paraphrase of two lines written by Pindar in his *Pythian Odes*, lines 96 and 97. Create a footnote that credits Pindar for this thought.

3. Save the document as *Fifth Century Greece*.

4. Print the document.

Assignments

Creating a List of Instructions

You need to describe to someone how to create Figure 3.32. Figure 3.32 is a list of bulleted items. Essentially, you will first tell the user to type the text that describes the cities. Next, the user will select the text and then select the Bullets button on the Toolbar. Notice that the cities are in a bold character style; this should be in your instructions as well. Also, be sure to tell the user to save and print the document. Your step-by-step instructions should be in the form of hanging indentations, numbered 1, 2, 3, and so on.

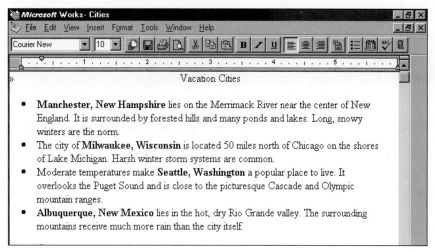

Figure 3.32

Creating a Flyer for a Ticket Office

You have been hired by a ticket office in Orange County, California, to create a flyer describing entertainment ticket prices. In the flyer, include a name, address, and phone number for the ticket office; a short description of the ticket office; and a list of upcoming concerts including dates and ticket prices. Also include the table in Figure 3.33. Notice that the Location column was lined up with a center tab stop. Use a sans serif typeface for the flyer. Save and print your work.

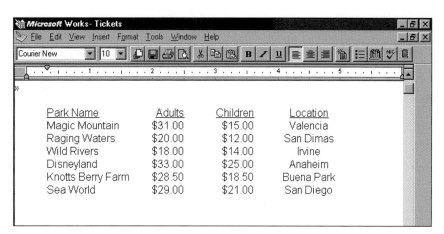

Figure 3.33

Creating a List of Famous Operas

You work for the Paris Opera House and a person named John Garcia has written to you for a description of some famous operas. Write a letter to John that includes the list in Figure 3.34. To create the hanging indentations, use Hanging Indents from the Easy Formats dialog box. Afterward, you also will have to move the left triangles on the ruler to match the triangles in the figure.

At the bottom of your letter, tell John that it is easiest to get to the opera house by getting off at the Madeleine Metro stop and then walking. Sign the letter with your name.

Add the header *Opera House, Place de l'Opera, Paris, France.* The header should be in italics. Save and print your work.

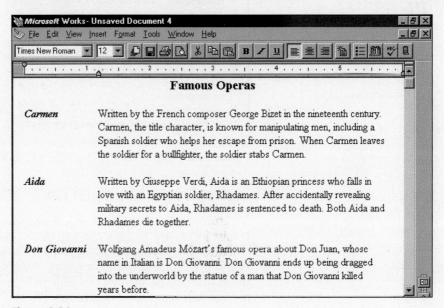

Figure 3.34

ADDITIONAL ASSIGNMENTS

CREATING A RÉSUMÉ

A résumé is a brief summary of education, experience, skills, and any other activities you want to bring to the attention of a prospective employer or an organization in which you have an interest. Although there is no precise format for creating a résumé, there are some basic guidelines.

- Try to keep a résumé short and easy to read. One page is usually sufficient.
- To create a professional appearance, make sure the résumé does not contain misspelled words.
- Use action verbs, such as *supervised, coordinated,* and *prepared,* in your job descriptions.
- Stress positive qualities and downplay negative ones.
- List job descriptions in reverse chronological order. Be specific about dates, job titles, responsibilities, and so on.

You will use a Works TaskWizard to create a résumé, but also be sure to draw upon all your word processing skills.

To open the résumé template:

1 Start Works.

2 In the Works Task Launcher dialog box, select the TaskWizards tab.

3 Under Common Tasks, select Résumé (CV) and then select OK.

4 Select Yes to run the TaskWizard.

5 Select Next to create a chronological résumé template.

6 Select Headings and then place a checkmark next to Objective, Summary, Work History, Education, Interests & Activities, and Awards Received. If you wish to include Computer Skills and Licenses & Certificates, check them as well.

7 Select OK to complete the command.

8 Select Create It!

9 Select Create Document to create the résumé.
The screen should look like Figure 3.35.

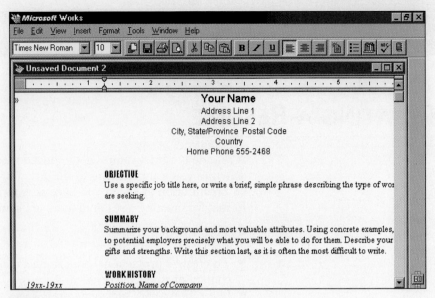

Figure 3.35

10 Change all the information in the résumé so it pertains to you.

11 Save the file as *Résumé*.

12 Print your work.

A résumé is usually accompanied by a cover letter that serves to introduce you and elicit an interview. You will create a cover letter in Part V, "Integrating the Tools," when you use all the Works tools together.

TERM PAPER PROJECT

DEVELOPING A DOCUMENT THAT DESCRIBES THE ISLAND OF SVENLAND

At the end of each major part of this book, you will create one piece of a typical college term paper. In Part V, "Integrating the Tools," you will combine all the pieces into one large term paper.

You are registered in a sociology class titled Comparative Cultures, SOC 301. The professor has assigned a term paper in which you are to describe any island in the world. You choose the fictitious island of Svenland. Use the following guidelines to create and format the term paper.

The main text for the term paper is shown in Figure 3.36.

```
Introduction
     On the northern edge of the Norwegian Sea lies the
cold, windswept island of Svenland.  Straddling the Arctic
Circle between Iceland and Norway, Svenland was settled
nearly a thousand years ago by Vikings. After centuries of
moderate Danish rule, the 120-square-mile island gained
total independence in 1948 and entrance into the United
Nations in 1954. Today Svenland is a leading exporter of
fish and sheep products.

Economy
     The deep blue seas surrounding Svenland provide 87% of
the island's income. Although intensive harvesting in the
early 1980s severely depleted the supply of cod, the main
fish export, recent efforts to allow stocks of cod to
replenish themselves have been successful. In 1992, the
United States, Britain, and France purchased large amounts
of cod along with smaller amounts of haddock, redfish,
catfish, and the Arctic halibut.
     Archeological remains indicate that sheep have been
present since the time of the earliest settlers. Today sheep
outnumber residents by three to one. Sheep products include
wool, meat, and lightweight leather.

History
     Svenlanders, as the inhabitants are known, descend from
twelfth-century Viking settlers. When the original 200
homesteaders discovered the island in 1187, they found its
rocky shores deserted except for a wide variety of birds.
Subsequent settlers from Norway and Denmark swelled the
population to roughly 3,500 by the early fourteenth century.
Recurring epidemics kept the number of Svenlanders in check
until after World War II, when improved supplies of medicine
and trained physicians pushed the population up to the
current 25,000 inhabitants.

Sports and Recreation
     Sports enthusiasts pursue skiing, mountain climbing,
and golf. At night, the stars that fill the sky feed
the Svenlanders' passion for astronomy. Since 1873, Svenlanders
have discovered seven inportant stars.
     Although the winters are long and harsh, the local
residents consider their island to be a tiny oasis of
serenity on the outermost edge of society. Inhabitants
consider the quality of life second to none.
```

Figure 3.36

To open Svenland and create a title page:

1 Open the student data file called *Svenland*. If you do not have this file, create the document shown in Figure 3.36.
The title page will be on a page separate from the main text of the term paper.

2 Choose Normal from the View menu.

3 Place the insertion point at the top of the document.

4 Press (ENTER) 10 to 12 times to place a series of blank lines on the title page.

5 Press (CTRL) + (ENTER)
A dotted line should appear on the screen. Everything above the line is on one page; everything below the line is on the next page.

6 Move the insertion point to the beginning of the first page, but not in the header area.

7 Center the following text on the first page, the title page. If necessary, insert more blank lines. Type your name instead of Wanda Chang.
```
Svenland:
Island on the Arctic Circle

Wanda Chang
SOC 301
''Comparative Cultures''
```
The title page will have no page number. The first page of the main term paper will be page number 1. You can suppress the page number on the title page by choosing the Page Setup command.

 To create a footer with page numbers:

1 Choose Page Setup from the File menu.

2 Select the Other Options tab.

3 Change the starting page number to 0.
The title page will be page 0 and the first page of the term paper will be page 1.

4 Select No Footer on First Page.
This will suppress the printing of a footer on the first page.

5 Select OK to complete the command.

6 In the footer area of the first page of the term paper, type `Svenland: Island on the Arctic Circle`

7 Press (TAB) on the footer line.

8 Choose Page Number from the Insert menu.
All pages will be numbered in the printout except for the title page.

You will double-space all text in the term paper. The title page should remain single-spaced.

 To double-space the term paper:

1 Place the pointer in the left margin.
The pointer should point to the right.

2 While holding down (CTRL), click the mouse button once.
All text in the term paper should be selected.

3 Choose Paragraph from the Format menu, and then change the line spacing to 2.
Notice that the title page is also double-spaced.

4 Select all the text in the title page, and then choose the appropriate command to single-space the text.

Use the Thesaurus to help improve your writing by investigating words that might be more suitable than the ones you have used.

To use the Thesaurus:

1 Place the insertion point in the word *cold* in the first paragraph.

2 Choose Thesaurus from the Tools menu.

3 Select an appropriate synonym for *cold*.

4 Use the Thesaurus to replace the word *blue* in the second paragraph.

The information in the second-to-last paragraph—the statement about Svenlanders discovering seven stars—was taken from the book *Nordic Stargazers*, by Bjorn Borgenson. You will create a footnote to give this book credit.

To create a footnote:

1 Type the following text to create the footnote. The footnote number should appear at the end of the sentence that states that Svenlanders have discovered seven stars.
`Bjorn Borgenson,` *`Nordic Stargazers`* `(Reykjavik, Iceland: Surtsey Press, 1979), p. 237.`

The headings "Introduction," "Economy," and so on should appear in a bold character style.

To apply a bold character style:

1 Individually select each heading.

2 Choose the appropriate command to apply a bold character style to each heading.

Correctly spelled words are essential in any document, especially a term paper.

To spell-check, save, preview, and print the term paper:

1 Spell-check the entire document.

2 Save the term paper; give it the name *Svenland*.

3 Preview and then print the term paper.

PART II

Spreadsheets

A traditional ***spreadsheet,*** also called a ***worksheet,*** is a grid of columns and rows printed on a sheet of paper. The intersection of each column and row is called a ***cell.*** Typically, the flow of goods and money in an organization is tracked by using a pencil to enter text and numbers into cells. Some of the numbers are the results of calculations. A checkbook register is an example of a spreadsheet that you probably use on a regular basis. Each financial transaction occupies a ***row*** in the spreadsheet, and a description of each transaction and its dollar amount are placed into ***columns.*** The current balance is also entered into a column and is often computed with the aid of a calculator, as shown in Figure 1.1.

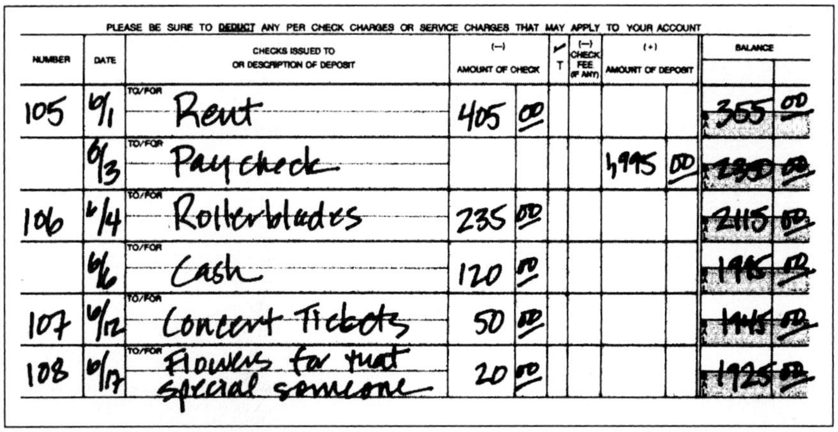
PLEASE BE SURE TO DEDUCT ANY PER CHECK CHARGES OR SERVICE CHARGES THAT MAY APPLY TO YOUR ACCOUNT

NUMBER	DATE	CHECKS ISSUED TO OR DESCRIPTION OF DEPOSIT	(−) AMOUNT OF CHECK	✓ T	(−) CHECK FEE (IF ANY)	(+) AMOUNT OF DEPOSIT	BALANCE
105	6/1	TO/FOR Rent	405 00				355 00
	6/3	TO/FOR Paycheck				1,995 00	2350 00
106	6/4	TO/FOR Rollerblades	235 00				2115 00
	6/6	TO/FOR Cash	120 00				1995 00
107	6/12	TO/FOR Concert Tickets	50 00				1945 00
108	6/17	TO/FOR Flowers for that special someone	20 00				1925 00

Figure 1.1

Electronic spreadsheets enable you to create spreadsheets using a computer instead of relying on paper, pencil, and a calculator to build financial models. The Works Spreadsheet tool is a straightforward electronic spreadsheet that enables you to create a wide variety of financial and nonfinancial spreadsheets.

The terms *spreadsheet* and *worksheet* are usually used interchangeably. Because Works uses the term *spreadsheet,* this module uses *spreadsheet.*

Objectives

After completing this project, you should be able to:

▶ Create a spreadsheet

▶ Use the mouse or keys to move around in a spreadsheet

▶ Enter text and numbers

▶ Wrap text within a cell

▶ Align cell contents

▶ Enter a simple formula

▶ Edit the contents of a cell

▶ Save and print a spreadsheet

CASE STUDY: CALCULATING GROSS PROFITS

As the president of Excellent Vacations, you have decided to carry a small line of merchandise to sell to customers departing on your company's vacations. You desire a simple method of determining gross profits on a monthly basis, and you are aware that electronic spreadsheets can automate this kind of routine task. Building an electronic spreadsheet usually involves entering the appropriate text, numbers, and formulas into individual cells. Once this data is entered, you can edit the spreadsheet to enhance its appearance and improve its readability.

Designing the Solution

When developing a spreadsheet, it is good to keep the overall design in mind. Where you place the text and numbers will determine how easily the spreadsheet is understood. If you want to determine the gross profit for the current month, you would enter the sales figures. Textual descriptions of each sales category should accompany the numbers. A formula will add the sales in each category to calculate a monthly total. You will create, edit, and print a spreadsheet like the one shown in Figure 1.2.

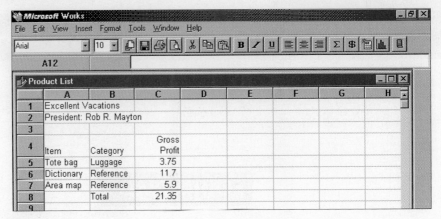

Figure 1.2

CREATING A NEW SPREADSHEET

To create a spreadsheet, you need to open the Works Spreadsheet tool.

To create a new spreadsheet:

1 Start Works, or, if you are already in Works, choose New from the File menu.
The Works Task Launcher appears, as shown in Figure 1.3.

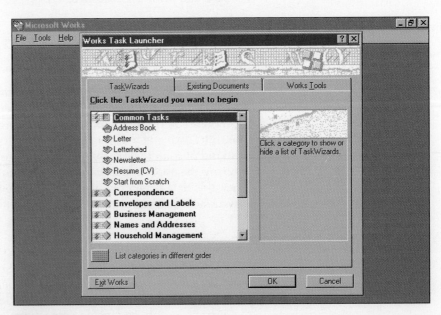

Figure 1.3

2 Select the Works Tools tab from within the Works Task Launcher.

3 Select the Spreadsheet icon to create a new spreadsheet.

UNDERSTANDING THE SPREADSHEET SCREEN

When you select the Works Spreadsheet tool, a blank spreadsheet resembling the one shown in Figure 1.4 appears. Note the features that distinguish a spreadsheet from a word processing document.

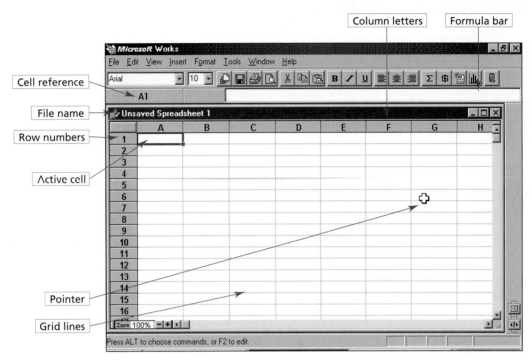

Figure 1.4

The spreadsheet has the generic file name Unsaved Spreadsheet 1, which you can change when you save the file. In the same way that Works adds a special file icon to all files created using the Word Processing tool, a spreadsheet icon is added to spreadsheet files when they are saved. To the right of the title bar are the Minimize and Maximize buttons, which are used to change the size of the active spreadsheet displayed in the document window.

The spreadsheet area is framed on the top by column letters and on the left side by row numbers. There are 256 columns labeled A through Z, AA through AZ, BA through BZ, and so on up to IV. The rows are numbered from 1 to 16,384. *Grid lines* differentiate individual cells in a spreadsheet.

The cell that has a heavy border around it is known as the *active cell* (it's also called the current cell, the selected cell, or the cell pointer). The ***active cell*** is the place where data will be entered, edited, or formatted. You can make any cell or group of cells active using the mouse or keyboard. When you create a new spreadsheet, cell A1 is the default active cell. The status bar shows the ***cell reference,*** which is the column letter and row number of the active cell. The cell reference in Figure 1.4 is A1.

The contents of the active cell appear in the ***formula bar.*** A cell can contain text, numbers, or formulas. *Text* refers to letters of the alphabet or a combination of letters and numbers. For example, *Profit* and *1st Quarter* are text entries. *Numbers* are any digits, such as 12, 36.7, and 0.034. *Formulas,* which always start with an equal sign (=), are made up of numbers, operators, and cell references. Equations, such as $=10+A4$ and $=D7-D8$, are examples of formulas.

MOVING AROUND IN THE SPREADSHEET

You can navigate within a spreadsheet using either the mouse or the keyboard. The mouse works well to select cells within the visible portion of a spreadsheet. However, you'll find that you will frequently use the arrow keys (←, ↑, →, ↓) to move around a spreadsheet.

To use the mouse to move from one cell to another, you will simply position the pointer and click. Table 1.1 describes the keys you will use to accomplish tasks in a spreadsheet.

Table 1.1

Key(s)	Action
← or →	Moves active cell one cell left or one cell right.
↓ or ↑	Moves active cell one cell down or one cell up.
HOME	Moves active cell to the first cell in a row.
END	Moves active cell to the last cell that contains a value in a row.
PGUP	Moves active cell one screen up.
PGDN	Moves active cell one screen down.
CTRL + HOME	Moves active cell to cell A1 (A1 is called the **home cell**).
CTRL + END	Moves active cell to the lowest-right cell that contains a value.
TAB	Moves active cell one cell right.
SHIFT + TAB	Moves active cell one cell left.
F5	Displays a dialog box in which you can specify a cell by entering a cell address such as A23 (F5 is called the *GoTo key*).
F2	Allows the contents of the active cell to be edited (F2 is called the **Edit key**).

To select cell C3:

1 If you are using the numeric keypad, make sure NUM LOCK is off.

2 Press CTRL + HOME to select cell A1.

3 Press ↓ twice.

4 Press → twice.

Notice that the status bar shows *C3,* the location of the current cell.

To move down one screen at a time:

1 Press PGDN

Notice that the row numbers have changed to reflect the fact that the active cell is one screen down from where it was before.

2 Press PGDN several times to see the effect.

To move up one screen at a time:

1 Press (PGUP)

2 Press (PGUP) until cell C1 is selected.

You can use the GoTo key, (F5), to jump quickly to any cell in the spreadsheet.

To go to cell T32:

1 Press (F5), the GoTo key.

You should see the dialog box shown in Figure 1.5.

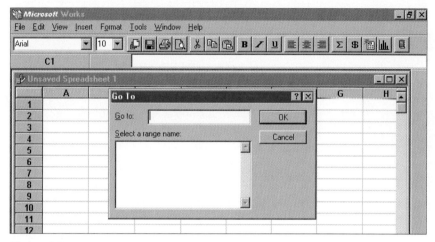

Figure 1.5

2 Type **T32** and then press (ENTER) or select OK.

To go to cell IV16,384 and then return to cell A1:

1 Press (F5) to open the Go To dialog box.

2 Type **IV16384** and then press (ENTER)

IV16,384 is the last cell in the spreadsheet area. As you can imagine, very few people create a spreadsheet large enough to include cell IV16,384.

3 Press (CTRL) + (HOME) to return to cell A1.

ENTERING TEXT

To enter text, you will select the desired location and then type the text. As you type, the text will appear in the active cell and in the formula bar. Works will automatically align the text on the left side of the cell.

The default typeface in Works' Spreadsheet tool is 10-point Arial. Make sure your default is also 10-point Arial; otherwise, your screens may look different from the ones in this book.

Excellent Vacations sells various vacation items, including tote bags, Spanish/English dictionaries, and maps of Spain. You need to create a spreadsheet that keeps track of the profits earned from the sale of these items. Figure 1.6 shows the text you'll need to enter.

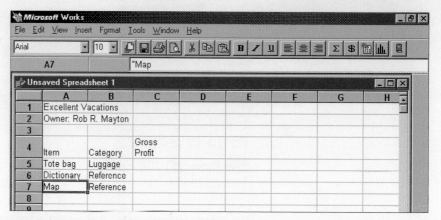

Figure 1.6

After you have typed text into a cell, you must tell Works to accept the entry. One method is to press ⊕, which in one motion enters data into a cell and moves the active cell downward. You can also press (ENTER) to enter data, but doing so does not change the active cell.

To enter text:

1 Select cell A1.

2 Type **Excellent Vacations** and then press (ENTER)
Each cell is, by default, 10 characters wide. If a string of text is wider than the active cell, the text spills over to the adjacent empty cell(s). Notice that the text *Excellent Vacations* has spilled over to cell B1, as shown in Figure 1.7.

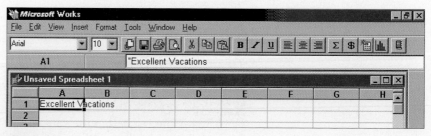

Figure 1.7

3 In cell A2, type **Owner:** followed by your name and then press ⊕ twice.

4 In cell A4, type **Item** and then press ⊕

5 In cell A5, type **Tote bag** and then press ⊕

6 In cell A6, type **Dictionary** and then press ⊕

7 In cell A7, type **Map** and then press (ENTER)
The spreadsheet should look like Figure 1.8.

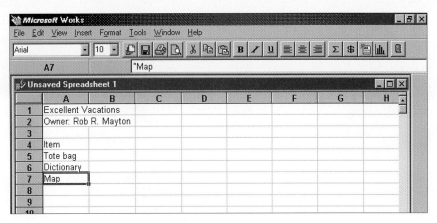

Figure 1.8

Tip If you make a mistake entering data, you can select the cell with incorrect data, retype the data, and then press (ENTER) to put the new data in the cell. You can also press (F2), the Edit key, to correct the contents of a cell.

Next you will add text to describe categories for items.

To enter additional columns of text:

1 Select cell B4.

2 Type **Category** and then press ⊕

3 In cell B5, type **Luggage** and then press ⊕

4 In cell B6, type **Reference** and then press ⊕

5 In cell B7, type **Reference** and then press (ENTER)
The screen should look like Figure 1.9.

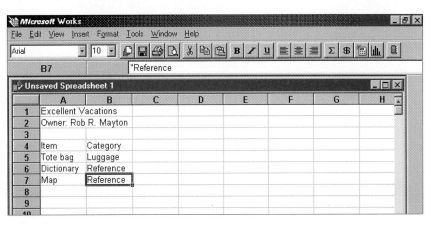

Figure 1.9

The last column heading, *Gross Profit,* will wrap around within a cell. If you don't want a long text entry to spill over into adjacent cells, you can wrap it within one cell.

To wrap a long text entry in one cell:

1 Select cell C4 and then type **Gross Profit** and press ⟨ENTER⟩

2 Choose Alignment from the Format menu.

3 Select Wrap Text.

You should see a dialog box like the one in Figure 1.10. A checkmark appears next to the Wrap Text option.

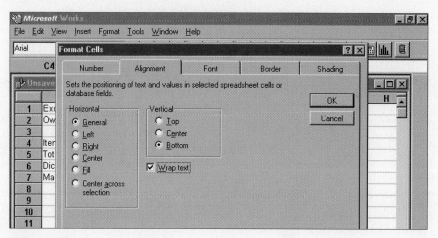

Figure 1.10

4 Select OK to complete the command.

Notice that *Gross Profit* wraps around in one cell, as shown in Figure 1.11.

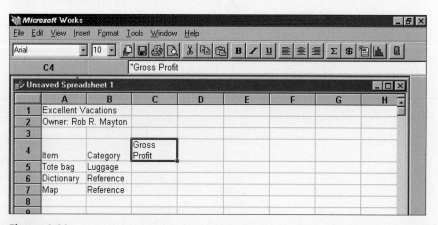

Figure 1.11

ENTERING NUMBERS

You will use the same method to enter numbers that you used to enter text. The main difference in the process of entering numbers and text is that descriptive text is automatically aligned on the left, whereas numbers are automatically aligned on the right.

You will now enter the gross profit for each item sold in cells C5 through C7.

To enter numbers in the spreadsheet:

1 Select cell C5.

2 Type **3.75** and then press ⊕

3 In cell C6, type **11.70** and then press ⊕
Notice that although you typed *11.70,* the cell contains *11.7.* Works automatically omits trailing zeros.

4 In cell C7, type **5.9** and then press (ENTER)
The spreadsheet should look like Figure 1.12.

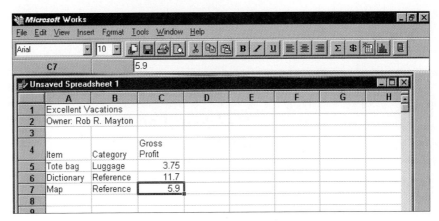

Figure 1.12

 If necessary, you can save your spreadsheet as *Product List,* exit Works now, and continue this project later.

ALIGNING TEXT

Left-aligned text is especially suitable when it appears in a column, such as the columns of text in Figure 1.12. If text is serving as a heading over a column of numbers, however, the text may look better if it is aligned to the right. For example, in Figure 1.12, the column heading *Gross Profit* would look better if it were aligned on the right with the numbers.

When you change the horizontal alignment of text, you are changing the format of the text. The Alignment command in the Format menu displays the dialog box shown in Figure 1.10 with six options for aligning text: General, Left, Right, Center, Fill, and Center Across Selection. The default, General, will align text on the left and numbers on the right.

To align text on the right, you must first select the *range* of cells that contains the text. A **range** is a group of adjacent cells that you can work on as a whole. To refer to a range, you would separate its starting and ending points with a colon (:). For example, the range of cells A3 through A10 is referred to as A3:A10.

You can select cells by using the mouse or by using various key combinations. Table 1.2 summarizes how text can be selected.

Table 1.2

Area to Select	Using the Mouse	Using the Keyboard
A cell	Click the cell.	Use ⬆, ⬇, ⬅, or ➡ to select the cell you want.
A row	Select the row number.	Select any cell in the row and press CTRL + F8.
A column	Select the column letter.	Select a cell in the column and press SHFT + F8.
A group of adjacent cells	Click and drag the area you want to select.	Select the cell in the upper-left corner and press SHFT + ⬆, ⬇, ⬅, or ➡ to select in the appropriate direction (you can press F8 instead of SHFT).
The entire spreadsheet	Select the box above row 1 and to the left of column A.	Press CTRL + SHFT + F8.

To align text on the right:

1 Select cell C4.

2 Choose Alignment from the Format menu.
The Wrap Text box should be checked.

3 Select the radio button for Right and then select OK to complete the command.
The text *Gross Profit* should be aligned on the right, as shown in Figure 1.13.

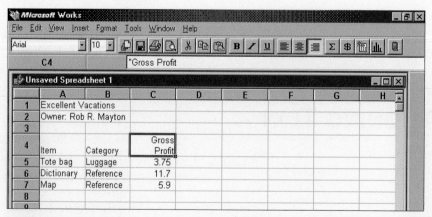

Figure 1.13

Tip You can align text to the right, in a single cell or in multiple cells, by selecting the cell(s) and then selecting the Right Align button on the Toolbar.

ENTERING A SIMPLE FORMULA

Formulas, which always begin with an equal sign (=), are used to create a new value from new and/or existing values. Figure 1.14 shows the formula for adding the range C5:C7. Notice that the formula bar shows the actual formula and that spreadsheet cell C8 shows the result of the formula. The formula tells Works to take the values in cells C5, C6, and C7 and add them together.

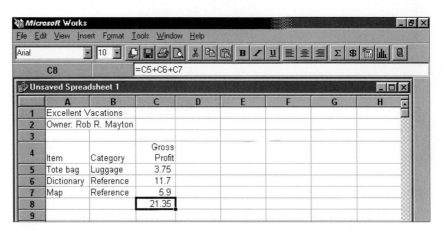

Figure 1.14

 ## To calculate the sum of C5:C7:

1 Select cell C8, because this is where you want the result of the formula displayed.

2 Type **=C5+C6+C7** and then press (ENTER)
Your formula should look like the one in the formula bar in Figure 1.14.

Tip You can also use the pointing method to construct formulas. To create the formula =C5+C6+C7 using the pointing method, you would select cell C8 and type =. Then you would select cell C5, type +; select cell C6, type +; and select cell C7 and press (ENTER).

 ## To enter the text Total in cell B8:

1 Select cell B8.

2 Type **Total** and then press (ENTER)
In the formula bar of Figure 1.15, notice that the text *Total* is preceded by a double quotation mark ("). Works automatically inserts a double quotation mark before text to distinguish text from numbers and formulas. The double quotation mark appears only in the formula bar and not in the spreadsheet.

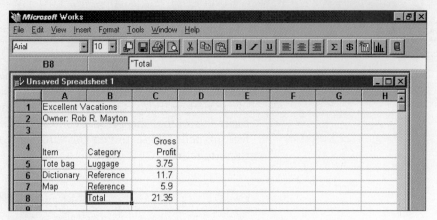

Figure 1.15

At times you will want to place a line under a column of numbers to indicate that you are adding the column together. The Border command from the Format menu lets you place lines across the top, bottom, left, or right of a cell. Figure 1.16 shows a dialog box with Works' different line styles.

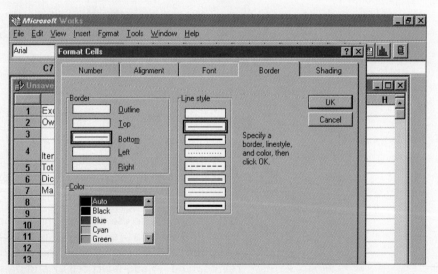

Figure 1.16

To add a border across the bottom of a cell:

1 Select cell C7.

2 Choose Borders from the Format menu.

3 Select Bottom.

To select Bottom, make sure you click the box to the left of the word *Bottom*. The line that is currently selected under Line Style is now set to appear at the bottom of cell C7.

4 Select OK to apply the line style.

There should be a line at the bottom of cell C7. It will be more apparent when you print the spreadsheet.

EDITING THE CONTENTS OF A CELL

To modify the contents of a cell, you can either retype or edit data. Retyping a cell entry replaces the previous contents of a cell with the newly typed data. Editing a cell entry allows you to change a portion of the existing cell contents without having to retype the entire entry. Typically, unless you are entering a small amount of text, you will edit the contents of a cell.

To edit the contents of a cell, you can select the cell and then either click the formula bar or press (F2), the Edit key. You can also double-click the cell to edit it.

The cell contents of A7 should be *Area map* instead of *Map*. You can use the Edit key to insert the text *Area*.

To insert the text Area into cell A7:

1 Select cell A7.

2 Press (F2), or click the formula bar.

3 Move the cursor to right after the double quotation mark (").

4 Type **Area** right before the word *Map* and after the double quotation mark.

5 Insert a space between *Area* and *Map*.

6 Delete the letter *M* in *Map* and type **m**

7 Press (ENTER) to confirm the entry.
Cell A7 should look like cell A7 in Figure 1.17.

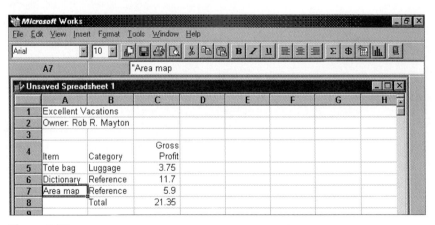

Figure 1.17

Next you notice that cell A2 contains inaccurate information. The word *Owner* should be *President*.

To delete Owner and insert President in cell A2:

1 Select cell A2.

2 Press (F2) to edit the cell contents.

3 Change the word *Owner* to *President*.
The spreadsheet should look like Figure 1.18.

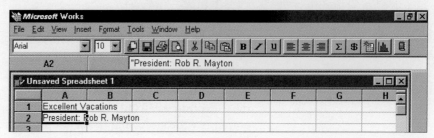

Figure 1.18

SAVING A SPREADSHEET

A new spreadsheet is automatically named Unsaved Spreadsheet 1 until you change that name. When you save a spreadsheet the first time, you can use a name that is more meaningful.

To save the spreadsheet:

1 Choose Save from the File menu.
The first time you save a spreadsheet, the dialog box shown in Figure 1.19 appears.

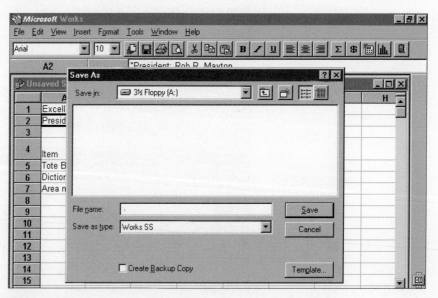

Figure 1.19

2 If necessary, select drive A: in the Save In list box.
If you want to save your work somewhere other than drive A:, select the appropriate drive.

3 Place the insertion point in the File Name box.

4 Type **Product List** and then press (ENTER)
Product List is an effective file name because it describes the document and follows the rules for naming a file.

PREVIEWING AND PRINTING A SPREADSHEET

You can use the preview feature to see the overall format of a spreadsheet.

To preview a spreadsheet on the screen:

1 Choose Print Preview from the File menu.

2 Select Zoom In twice to get a close look at the spreadsheet.
The screen should look like Figure 1.20. Notice that the grid lines you see on-screen don't appear on the printout.

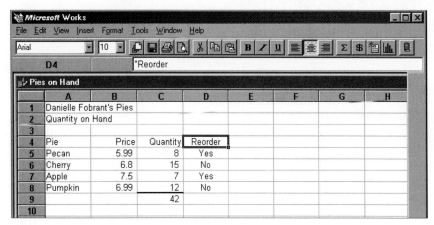

Figure 1.20

3 Select Cancel to return to the spreadsheet.

Once you are satisfied that the spreadsheet is ready to be printed, you should make sure the computer is attached to a printer (or that the proper network printer has been selected if you are working in a networked computer lab). Then you can print your work.

To print the document:

1 Choose Print from the File menu.
The Print dialog box defaults to 1 copy of all pages.

2 Press (ENTER) to print the spreadsheet.

> **Reminder** You can select the Print button on the Toolbar to print a document. If you select the Print button, you will not be prompted to verify the number of pages or print range.

THE NEXT STEP

You have used the Spreadsheet tool to create a spreadsheet that calculates gross profits from a line of merchandise by totaling the profit for three items. The formula you entered is simple in comparison to the complex formulas that can be created with Works, but it can be used to easily calculate the total of a column of numbers.

Text is also an important part of any spreadsheet because it enhances the readability of the spreadsheet. As you think of other spreadsheets you could create to add a series of numbers, envision how the placement of text labels can enhance the look of a spreadsheet.

This concludes Project 1 with the Works spreadsheet component. You can either exit Works or go on to work the Study Questions, Review Exercises, and Assignments.

SUMMARY AND EXERCISES

Summary

- A spreadsheet is a grid of rows and columns that is used to manipulate numeric information.
- The intersection of a row and a column is called a cell.
- Electronic spreadsheets enable you to create spreadsheets on a computer.
- A bold outline indicates the active cell.
- You can use the mouse or arrow keys to change the active cell.
- You can press (F5), the GoTo key, to move quickly to a specific cell.
- Text is automatically left-aligned in a cell.
- Numbers are automatically right-aligned in a cell.
- Formulas, which display the results of calculations, begin with an equal sign.
- You can press (F2), the Edit key, to edit the contents of a cell.

Key Terms and Operations

Key Terms
active cell
cell
cell reference
column
Edit key
formula
formula bar
GoTo key
grid lines

home cell
range
row
spreadsheet
worksheet

Operations
Align cell contents
Edit cell contents
Wrap text in a cell

Study Questions

Multiple Choice

1. In the Spreadsheet tool, the intersection of a column and a row is called a:
   - a. row.
   - b. column.
   - c. cell.
   - d. formula.

2. A selected group of adjacent cells is called a(n):
   - a. formula.
   - b. block.
   - c. area.
   - d. range.

3. Numbers entered into a spreadsheet appear:
   - a. left-aligned.
   - b. center.
   - c. right-aligned.
   - d. without any alignment.

4. When you print a spreadsheet, you do not see:
   - a. the column letters at the top of the spreadsheet.
   - b. the row numbers on the left side of the spreadsheet.
   - c. grid lines.
   - d. All of the above.

5. Text entered into a spreadsheet appears:
   - a. left-aligned.
   - b. center.
   - c. right-aligned.
   - d. without any alignment.

6. In a Works spreadsheet, what appears in the formula bar?
   - a. the name of the current spreadsheet
   - b. the contents of the active cell
   - c. Shortcut buttons for common Works commands.
   - d. the name of the default printer

7. The default spreadsheet name is:
   - a. Unsaved Spreadsheet 1.
   - b. SHEET1.
   - c. Save Me Now.
   - d. SPREADSHEET__1.

8. Which of the following begins with an equal sign (=)?
   - a. a range
   - b. a cell reference
   - c. column name
   - d. formula

9. What is normally displayed in a cell containing a formula?
   - a. the formula as it appears in the formula bar
   - b. the results of a calculation
   - c. text, such as *1st Qtr*
   - d. a range reference, such as A1:B6

10. What happens when you press the Edit key?
    - a. The entire cell is deleted.
    - b. The contents of the cell can be changed without deleting the entire cell.
    - c. The previous contents are placed on the clipboard.
    - d. The cell contents are copied to a new location.

Short Answer

1. Another term for spreadsheet is _____ .

2. You can enter text, numbers, and _____ into a spreadsheet cell.

3. _____ are(is) automatically aligned on the right in a cell.

4. _____ are(is) automatically aligned on the left in a cell.

5. A _____ is made up of the column letter and row number.

6. To align text on the right, you must choose _____ from the Format menu.

7. A bold outline indicates the _____ cell.

8. Works automatically inserts a(n) _____ at the beginning of all text entries.

9. To change the contents of the active cell without retyping everything, press the _____ key.

10. To wrap text in a cell, you must choose _____ from the Format menu.

For Discussion

1. What is a spreadsheet?

2. Why is a checkbook register an example of a spreadsheet?

3. If the active cell displayed *1979,* how could you tell if it was text, a number, or the result of a calculation?

4. Describe how to select the range A4:C16.

5. Write a Works formula to calculate the sum of cells C3, C4, C5 and C6.

Review Exercises

Creating a Spreadsheet for a Bakery

1. Create the spreadsheet shown in Figure 1.21 to keep track of the quantity of pies available at a bakery. The column headings Price and Quantity are right-aligned. Text in the Reorder column is centered.

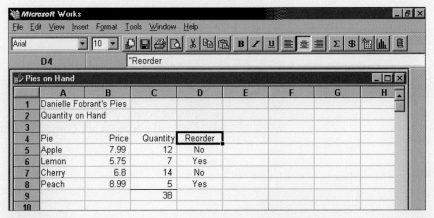

Figure 1.21

2. Place a line under the Quantity column.

3. Create a formula to sum the Quantity column.

4. Edit the cell that contains the name of the bakery so Danielle Fobrant's name is deleted and your name is inserted.

5. Save the spreadsheet, assigning it the file name *Pies on Hand*.

6. Preview and then print your work.

Creating a Class Schedule

1. Create the spreadsheet shown in Figure 1.22, which describes a student's class schedule. Use your name instead of Danielle Fobrant's, enter your school instead of Fallbrook Technical College, and enter your schedule instead of the one shown in the figure. Align the column heading Units on the right.

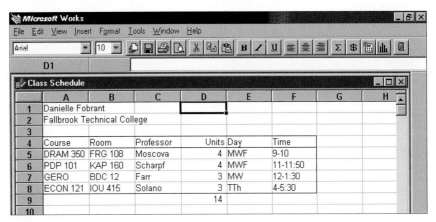

Figure 1.22

2. Add a formula in cell D10 that sums the units.

3. For extra credit, see if you can place borders around the schedule as shown in Figure 1.22.

4. Save the spreadsheet, assigning it the file name *Class Schedule*.

5. Print the spreadsheet.

Assignments

Tracking Fruit and Vegetable Profits

You run a fruit and vegetable stand, and you want to build the spreadsheet shown in Figure 1.23. Align to the right any column headings that are above numbers. Place borders around the fruits and vegetables as shown in the figure. Include a formula to calculate the total number sold of all items in the lists. Place a double line under the total number sold. Save the spreadsheet as *Fruits and Veggies*. Print the spreadsheet.

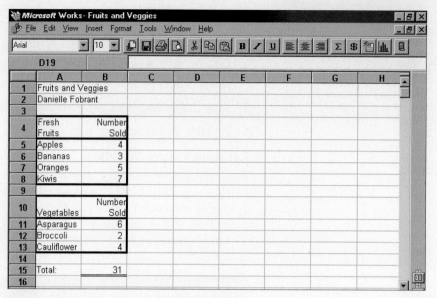

Figure 1.23

Calculating Shipping Expenses

Create the spreadsheet shown in Figure 1.24. Be sure to correctly align cells as they appear in the figure, and include the necessary formulas (formulas that total the values in each column). Save the spreadsheet as *Shipping Expenses*. Print the spreadsheet.

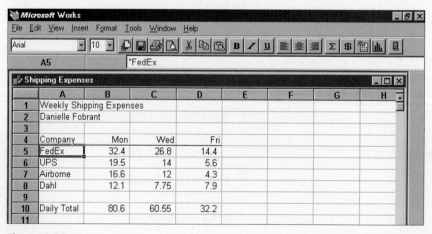

Figure 1.24

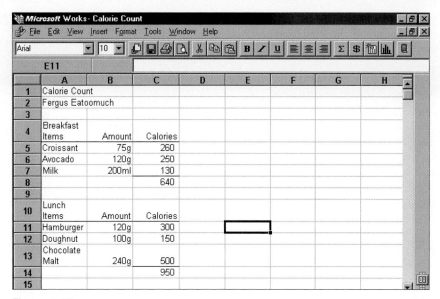

Figure 1.25

Counting Calories

Create a spreadsheet that keeps track of calories consumed for breakfast, lunch, and dinner (Figure 1.25 shows just breakfast and lunch). You will have to invent data for dinner. Align text, create formulas, and insert lines in the appropriate cells in the spreadsheet, as shown in Figure 1.25. Be sure to use your name and not Fergus's. Save the spreadsheet as *Calorie Count*. Print your work.

PROJECT 2: REVISING AND ENHANCING A SPREADSHEET

Objectives

After completing this project, you should be able to:

▶ Open an existing spreadsheet

▶ Clear an individual cell and a range of cells

▶ Move data

▶ Format numbers

▶ Adjust column widths

▶ Enter formulas

▶ Understand how a formula is calculated

▶ Copy formulas

CASE STUDY: ENHANCING THE LOOK OF A SPREADSHEET

The spreadsheet you developed in Project 1, *Products List,* provides basic information about gross profits, but it is lacking in several respects. A spreadsheet usually presents information so that information is easily understood. The numbers that represent dollar amounts should have dollar signs and a specific number of decimal places. In addition, the unit cost and quantity sold help the reader to know how profitable the business really is, so this data should be added also.

Designing the Solution

You will enhance the spreadsheet you created in Project 1 to make it easier to interpret. If you widen columns, change values to Currency format, and provide additional information, the spreadsheet will communicate more information to the reader. The enhanced spreadsheet you will create in this project will look like Figure 2.1.

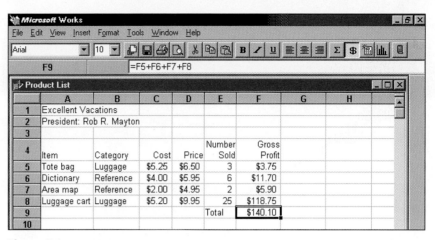

Figure 2.1

OPENING AN EXISTING SPREADSHEET

Once a Works file has been saved to disk, the file can be retrieved using the Works Task Launcher. To work on the file *Product List,* you need to open it.

To open an existing spreadsheet:

1 If you are currently in Works, choose New from the File menu; otherwise, start Works.
The Works Task Launcher appears.

2 Select the Existing Documents tab.
The screen should resemble Figure 2.2 (your list of files may be different). If you do not see *Product List,* select Open a Document Not Listed Here. In the List In box, select drive A: or the appropriate drive.

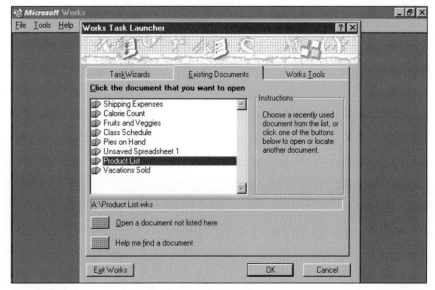

Figure 2.2

3 Select the file *Product List*, as shown in Figure 2.2.

4 Select OK to open the file.

The spreadsheet should look like Figure 2.3, except that your name should appear as the president. Also, your active cell may be different.

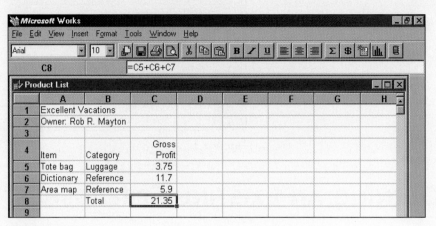

Figure 2.3

CLEARING CELLS

The Gross Profit column currently contains a list of numbers that indicate the profit for the current month. Assume that you need a detailed account of how these numbers were derived. You will first clear, or delete, the current profit data and any cells associated with this data. Next you will enter formulas for determining the profit.

You can clear either a single cell or a range of cells. You will start by individually clearing the cells B8 and C8.

To clear cells B8 and C8:

1 Select cell B8.

2 Press (DEL) to clear the word *Total*.

3 Select cell C8.

4 Press (DEL) to clear the formula.

The spreadsheet should look like Figure 2.4.

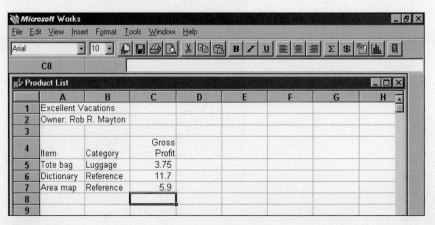

Figure 2.4

> ***Quick Fix*** If you ever accidentally press ⌐DEL¬, you can recover the cleared data by choosing the Undo Clear option from the Edit menu. However, the Undo command only works for the last command that was executed.

To clear a range of data, you will select the range and then press ⌐DEL¬.

To clear the range C5:C7:

1 Select cell C5.

2 While holding down the mouse button, drag the pointer to cell C7. The range C5:C7 should be selected.

3 Press ⌐DEL¬ to clear the data in the selected cells.

You also need to remove the border at the bottom of cell C7. You will use the Border command from the Format menu.

To remove a border:

1 Select cell C7.

2 Choose Border from the Format menu.

3 Select a blank line style (the blank box at the top of the line styles).

4 Double-click the box to the left of Bottom.
The line should disappear from the Bottom box, as shown in Figure 2.5.

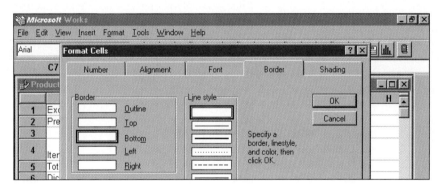

Figure 2.5

5 Select OK to complete the change.
The line should be gone from cell C7.

MOVING DATA

When you are revising a spreadsheet, you often will need to move data. You will use the ***drag-and-drop*** method to move the contents of cell C4 to cell F4. You will simply drag data from one place and drop it in another.

To move the contents of cell C4 to cell F4:

1 Select cell C4.

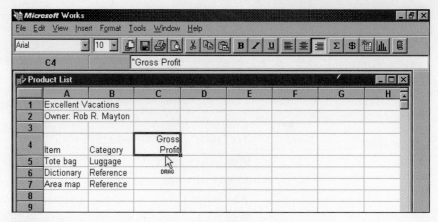

Figure 2.6

2 Place the pointer on the edge of the cell.
The pointer should say *DRAG,* as shown in Figure 2.6.

3 While holding down the mouse button, drag the cell outline to F4.
The pointer should say *MOVE.*

4 Release the mouse button to drop the text in cell F4.
The spreadsheet should look like Figure 2.7.

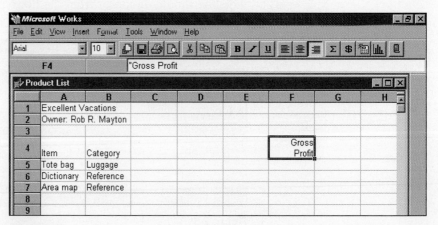

Figure 2.7

The revised spreadsheet will contain three new column headings: *Cost, Price,* and *Number Sold.*

To enter the new column headings:

1 Type **Cost** in cell C4.

2 Type **Price** in cell D4.

3 Type **Number Sold** in cell E4.
You will align the three new column headings on the right, because each one will be above a column of numeric data. Also, you will wrap the text in cell E4.

To align and wrap the text in the new column headings:

1 Select the range C4:E4.

2 Choose Alignment from the Format menu.

3 Select the Right button for right alignment.

4 Select Wrap Text.
A checkmark should appear beside the Wrap Text option.

5 Select OK to complete the formatting.
The spreadsheet should look like Figure 2.8.

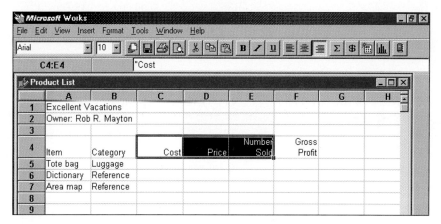

Figure 2.8

FORMATTING NUMBERS

The Number command in the Format menu provides various options that determine how numbers appear on the screen (see Figure 2.9).

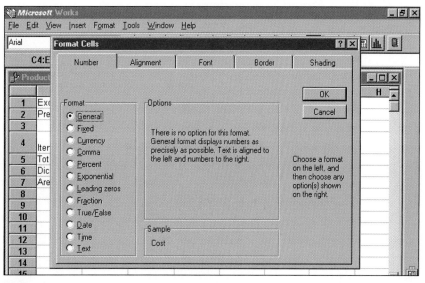

Figure 2.9

For example, the *Currency format* sets the number of decimal places, inserts a dollar sign ($) just before the number, and inserts commas if necessary. If you enter the number 5600.70 and then apply the Currency format, the number will appear in the spreadsheet as $5,600.70. Table 2.1 describes some of the available formats.

Table 2.1

Format	Number	Result	Comments
General	4.70	4.7	Default format; no trailing zeros.
Fixed	4.70	4.70	Sets number of decimal places but does not insert commas.
Currency	5600.70	$5,600.70	Sets number of decimal places; inserts commas and dollar signs.
Comma	5600.786	5,600.79	Sets number of decimal places and inserts commas.
Percent	0.09	9.00%	Sets number of decimal places, multiplies number by 100, and inserts a percent symbol.

The default number of *decimal places* for the Fixed, Currency, Comma, and Percent formats is 2, but you can adjust this from 0 to 7. Numbers that do not fit within the set number of decimal places are rounded off. For example, when the Comma format with two decimal places is applied to 5600.786, Works rounds the number to 5,600.79. Although Works displays the number as 5,600.79, Works uses the number you originally entered, 5600.786, when the cell is used in calculations.

When you enter a negative number, you must precede it with a minus sign (−). The minus sign is displayed on the screen, except when the number is formatted with the Currency or Comma format. The Currency and Comma formats place parentheses around negative numbers. For example, a number input as −560.45 is displayed as ($560.45) when the Currency format is applied to it.

Figure 2.10 shows the numbers you will enter and format. Use this figure as the source for the numbers for the Cost, Price, and Number Sold columns.

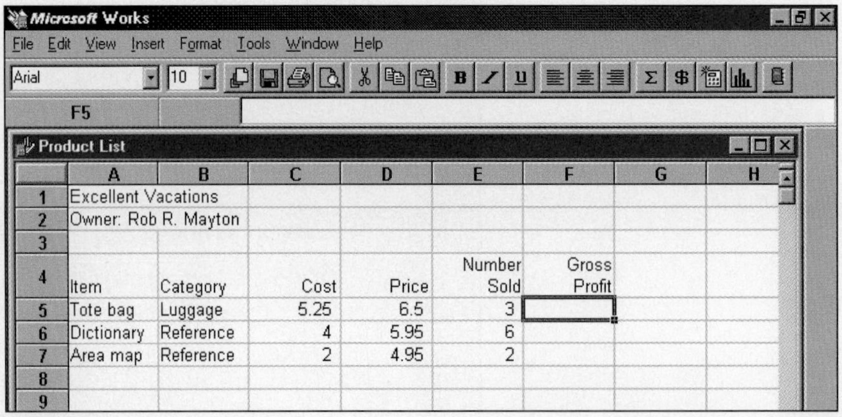

Figure 2.10

To enter numbers and apply the Currency format:

1 Enter all the numbers in the Cost column.

2 Select the range C5:C7.

3 Choose Number from the Format menu.

4 Select the radio button for Currency format.
Notice that the default number of decimal places is 2.

5 Select OK to apply the format.

The spreadsheet will look like Figure 2.11. Works will show the 4 that you entered in cell C6 as $4.00. The cell contents will remain 4, as shown in the formula bar when cell C6 is selected; the cell format will affect only how the number is displayed in the spreadsheet. If you choose a different format, the cell contents will remain the same, and only the display will change.

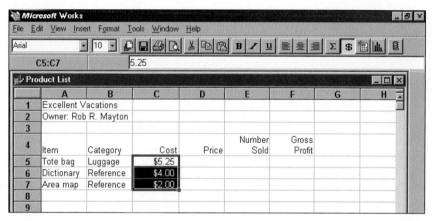

Figure 2.11

To enter numbers into the Price and Number Sold columns:

1 Enter all the numbers in the Price column, as shown in Figure 2.10.

2 Select the cells in the Price column.

3 Apply a Currency format to the Price column.
The spreadsheet should look like Figure 2.12.

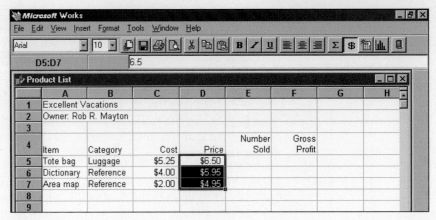

Figure 2.12

4 Enter all the numbers in the Number Sold column, as shown in Figure 2.10.

No formatting is necessary because the default General format works well with these numbers.

ADJUSTING COLUMN WIDTHS

If text is too wide to fit in a column, the entry will spill over into adjacent cells. This is fine, provided that neighboring cells do not contain data. For example, in Figure 2.12, the title "Excellent Vacations" has filled cell A1 and spilled over into cell B1.

There is one more item, a luggage cart, for which you need to enter data. The words *Luggage cart* are too long to fit in cell A8. Because the adjacent cells will contain data, you will need to widen column A to accommodate the new text.

> **Reminder** The default font used in the figures is 10-point Arial. If you are using a different font, the screen will look different from the ones shown here.

 To enter a new item:

1 In cell A8, type **Luggage cart**

2 In cell B8, type **Luggage**

3 In cell C8, type **5.2**

4 In cell D8, type **9.95**

5 In cell E8, type **25**

6 Move the active cell back to cell A8.

The screen should look like Figure 2.13. Notice that because cell A8 is too narrow to accommodate the text *Luggage cart,* the text *Luggage ca* is displayed instead.

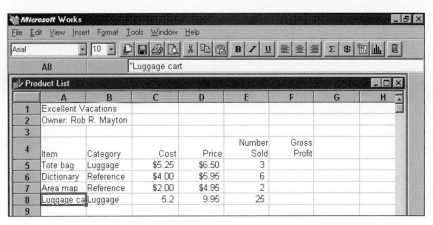

Figure 2.13

To widen column A, you will place the pointer on the border between columns A and B and then drag the border to the right.

To widen column A:

1 Place the pointer on the border that separates the tops of columns A and B.
The pointer should change shape and say *Adjust*, as shown in Figure 2.14.

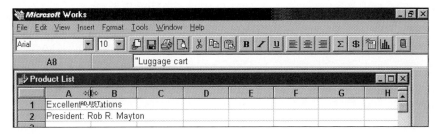

Figure 2.14

2 Drag the border a little to the right until *Luggage cart* is completely visible, and then release the mouse button.

Tip You can change the width of several columns at one time. To do so, you must first select the columns and then choose the Column Width command from the Format menu. Next, you would type in an exact numeric width for the columns.

This spreadsheet has a couple of columns that can be narrowed somewhat and still be readable. Spreadsheets have a tendency to get rather wide, so it is a good idea to keep columns as narrow as possible.

To set the widths of columns C and D to 7:

1 Select any cells in columns C and D.
Cells C4 and D4 are selected in Figure 2.15.

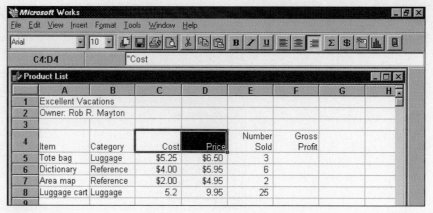

Figure 2.15

2 Choose Column Width from the Format menu.
Notice that the default column width is 10.

3 Type **7** and then select OK to complete the command.
You still need to change the widths of columns E and F.

To set the widths of columns E and F to 7:

1 Select any contiguous cells in columns E and F.
Make sure to select both columns E and F, even though there are currently
no numbers in column F.

2 Choose Column Width from the Format menu.

3 Type **7** as the column width and then select OK to complete the
command.

> **Tip** The column width can be set to the width of the widest entry
> automatically. To do this, you would select the Best Fit check box in the
> Column Width dialog box.

Next you need to change the Cost and Price columns for the luggage
cart to Currency format so they show dollar signs and two decimal places.

To format cells C8 and D8 to Currency:

1 Select cells C8 and D8.

2 Apply a Currency format to cells C8 and D8.
The spreadsheet should look like Figure 2.16.

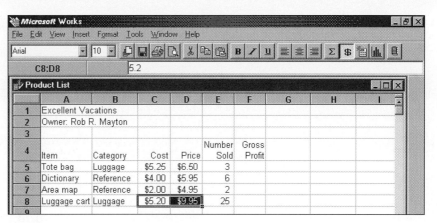

Figure 2.16

 EXIT   If necessary, you can save your spreadsheet as *Products List,* exit Works now, and continue this project later.

ENTERING FORMULAS

In Project 1, you got your first taste of a formula when you developed an equation to add a column of numbers. As you can see in the formula bar in Figure 2.17, the formula in cell F5 is somewhat more involved.

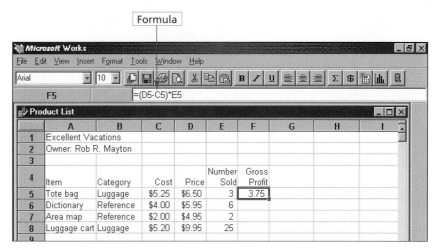

Figure 2.17

The formula $=(D5-C5)*E5$ calculates the gross profit for the tote bags that have been sold. The cost that Excellent Vacations pays for each tote bag is \$5.25 (cell C5), but the price to the public is \$6.50 (cell D5). Therefore, the profit on each tote bag is \$1.25, or price (cell D5) minus cost (cell C5). When profit is multiplied by the number sold (cell E5), in this case, 3, the result is gross profit, or 3.75.

The equation for finding the gross profit for each item is

```
Gross Profit = (Price - Cost) * Number Sold
```

or, stated in terms of a Works formula,

```
=(D5-C5)*E5
```

Notice that the equation and the formula contain parentheses. The following numbered steps will show you what happens if you leave out the parentheses. Normally, you will not enter incorrect formulas, but in this case, doing so will help you understand and avoid a common pitfall in developing formulas.

To enter an incomplete formula in cell F5:

1 Select cell F5.

2 Type **=D5-C5*E5**

3 Press (ENTER) to place the formula in cell F5.

> **Quick Fix** Formulas always start with an equal sign and can contain parentheses to indicate which calculations to perform first. Notice that the result in cell F5, −9.25, is incorrect because the formula is incomplete.

The result in cell F5 shown in Figure 2.18 is incorrect because Works multiplied C5 by E5 and then subtracted this total from D5. To fix this formula, you need to understand the hierarchy of operators.

	A	B	C	D	E	F	G	H	I
1	Excellent Vacations								
2	President: Rob R. Mayton								
3									
4	Item	Category	Cost	Price	Number Sold	Gross Profit			
5	Tote Bag	Luggage	$5.25	$6.50	3	-9.25			
6	Dictionary	Reference	$4.00	$5.95	6				
7	Area map	Reference	$2.00	$4.95	2				
8	Luggage cart	Luggage	$5.20	$9.95	25				

Figure 2.18

USING THE HIERARCHY OF OPERATORS

Symbols such as −, +, and * are known as *operators*. When a formula contains multiple operations, Works evaluates the formula based on the hierarchy, or order, of each operator. Table 2.2 shows this hierarchy.

Table 2.2

Operator	Operation
^	Exponentiation
−	Negation
* /	Multiplication and division
+ −	Addition and subtraction

For example, the operators * (multiplication) and / (division) are evaluated before + (addition) and − (subtraction). The following example explains how Works evaluates a typical formula. The operation that is highest in the order of operators is underlined. When two operations have the same hierarchical level, the operations are performed from left to right.

$$=5-6*2+\underline{4^2}/8+7$$

$$=5-\underline{6*2}+\underline{16}/8+7$$

$$=5-12+2+7$$

$$=2$$

You can override the Works hierarchy of operators by inserting parentheses. Works will perform the operations in parentheses first. For example, the algebraic equation

$$\frac{16 - 10}{5 + 7}$$

must be entered as:

(16-10)/(5+7)

and not

16-10/5+7

The first example correctly represents the algebraic equation and evaluates to .5. The second example evaluates incorrectly to 21.

For this spreadsheet to calculate profit correctly, you must insert parentheses into the formula in cell F5. The correct formula is $=(D5-C5)*E5$.

To use parentheses to override the hierarchy of operators:

1 Select cell F5.

2 Press (F2) to edit the cell.

3 Type an opening parenthesis right before D5 and a closing parenthesis right after C5.

4 Press (ENTER) to complete the formula.
The formula should look like the one in the formula bar in Figure 2.19.

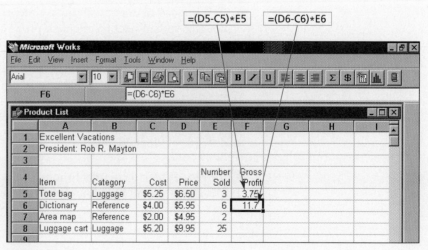

Figure 2.19

You now have the correct formula and the correct result in cell F5. When you enter formulas in the future, be sure to consider how Works will evaluate the formula and insert parentheses as needed.

COPYING FORMULAS: RELATIVE REFERENCING

Now that you have the correct formula in cell F5, you can copy the formula down to the range F6 through F8. When you copy a cell formula, Works adjusts the cell references to correspond to the new location of the formula. For example, if you copy the formula $=(D5-C5)*E5$ down one cell, the cell references change to $=(D6-C6)*E6$, as you can see in Figure 2.20. A cell reference that adjusts itself is called a ***relative reference***. If the cell references did not change in F6, both the cell formula, $=(D5-C5)*E5$, and the result, 3.75, would be incorrect.

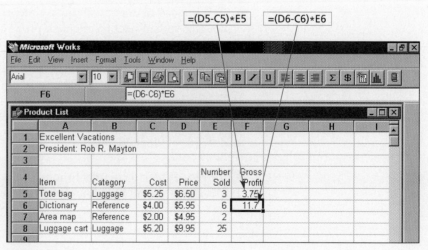

Figure 2.20

You can copy text, numbers, or formulas into contiguous cells by dragging the active cell. In the bottom-right corner of the active cell is a little black box. When you place the pointer over the box, the pointer changes to a cross with the word *FILL* underneath, as shown in Figure 2.21. When you drag this pointer to the right or downward, the adjacent cells are filled with text, numbers, or formulas.

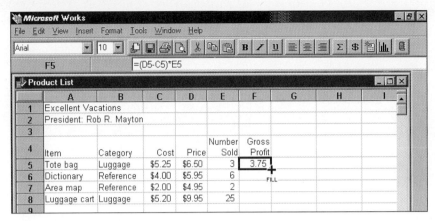

Figure 2.21

To copy the formula in cell F5 to the range F6:F8:

1 Place the pointer in the bottom right of cell F5.
The pointer should change to a cross with the word *FILL* underneath.

2 Drag downward to cell F8 and then release the mouse button.
The formula is copied down the selected range.

3 Select cell F6 to examine its formula.
Notice that the cell references in the formula bar reflect the cell references of the original formula, except that the row references have changed. This changes because the cell references in the formula are relative.

Using the Copy command in the Edit menu is another way to copy data, and the only way if the destination range, the range that will receive the copied data, is not adjacent to the source cell, the cell that has the original data. For example, if you were to copy a formula from cell F5 to the range F20:F25, you would need to use the Copy command. In most situations, you'll be able to fill ranges of cells as you did in the preceding numbered steps.
You still need to apply the Currency format to the range F5:F8.

To apply the Currency format to the range F5:F8:

1 Select the range F5:F8.

2 Apply the Currency format.
Notice that cell F8 contains a series of pound signs (#), as shown in Figure 2.22. This indicates that the column is too narrow to display the formatted answer.

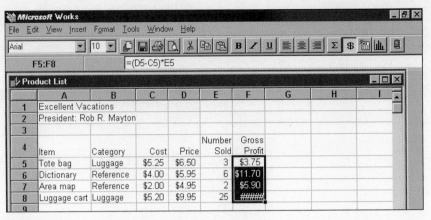

Figure 2.22

3 Click the letter *F* at the top of the column.
The entire column should be selected.

4 Choose Column Width from the Format menu.

5 Select Best Fit.
The Best Fit option adjusts the column width to fit the longest entry in the column. The spreadsheet should now look like Figure 2.23.

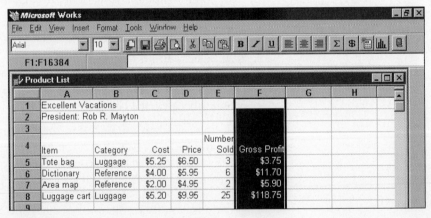

Figure 2.23

6 Click to deselect the range.

You have almost finished the spreadsheet. You still need to place a line under the Gross Profit column and add data in cells E9 and F9. When you are finished, the spreadsheet will look like Figure 2.24.

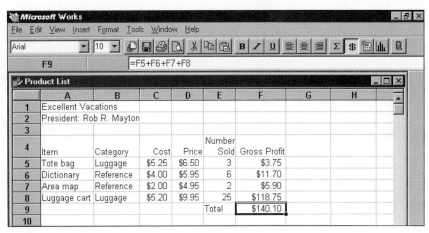

Figure 2.24

To place a line under the Gross Profit column:

1 Make cell F8 the active cell.

2 Choose Border from the Format menu.

3 Select the Bottom option and then select OK to apply a bottom border.
A line should appear on the screen.

To enter text in cell E9 and a formula in cell F9:

1 In cell E9, type **Total**

2 In cell F9, enter a formula that sums the Gross Profit column, as shown in the formula bar in Figure 2.24.

3 Apply the Currency format with two decimal places to cell F9.
The completed spreadsheet should look like Figure 2.24.

SAVING, PREVIEWING, AND PRINTING A SPREADSHEET

This spreadsheet is currently titled *Product List*. Because you have already saved the spreadsheet at least once, you will not be prompted for a file name when you save it again.

To save and then preview the spreadsheet:

1 Choose Save from the File menu to save the spreadsheet.

2 Choose Print Preview from the File menu.

3 When you are satisfied that the spreadsheet is ready to be printed, print the spreadsheet.

THE NEXT STEP

In this project you edited the spreadsheet you created in Project 1 by changing number formats and column widths and by building more complex formulas. These skills enable you to create spreadsheets that provide the reader with information that is more easily understood than a spreadsheet like the one you created in Project 1. For example, most financial reports display numbers in Currency format and have columns wide enough to show all pertinent cell information. The skills learned in this project will assist you in building more complex spreadsheets.

This concludes Project 2 using the Works Spreadsheet tool. You can either exit Works or go on to work the Study Questions, Review Exercises, and Assignments.

SUMMARY AND EXERCISES

Summary

- To clear the contents of a cell, you can select the cell and press (DEL).
- To clear a range of cells, you can select the range and then press (DEL).
- To move data, you can use Works' drag-and-drop feature.
- The format of a number determines how it appears on the screen. There are several formats, including General, Currency, and Percent.
- Some formats set the number of decimal places. Numbers that do not fit within a set number of decimal places are rounded off.
- Columns can be widened or narrowed to accommodate data.
- Works evaluates a formula according to the hierarchy, or order, of operators. Multiplication and division are evaluated before addition and subtraction.
- Parentheses can be used to override the hierarchy of operators.
- When you copy a formula, the cell references in the formula are adjusted to reflect the new position of the formula. This is known as relative referencing.
- A formatted number that is too wide to fit in a cell will appear in the spreadsheet as a string of pound signs.

Key Terms and Operations

Key Terms	Operations
Currency format	Adjust column widths
decimal places	Clear a range of cells
drag-and-drop	Copy formulas
operator	Format numbers
relative reference	Move data

Study Questions

Multiple Choice

1. What appears in a cell if the column width is too narrow to display a value?
   a. the word *ERROR*
   b. a series of question marks (?)
   c. a series of pound signs (#)
   d. Nothing. The cell appears as blank.

2. All of the following are valid numeric entries except:
   a. 100.00.
   b. "100.
   c. =100.
   d. −100.

3. In Works, what is the result of $=4+3*5+2$?
   a. 37
   b. 21
   c. 49
   d. None of the above.

4. In Works, what is the result of $=(4+3)*5+2$?
   a. 37
   b. 21
   c. 49
   d. None of the above.

5. In Works, what is the result of $=(4+3)*(5+2)$?
   a. 37
   b. 21
   c. 49
   d. None of the above.

6. When you drag the active cell downward to copy data, the pointer becomes a cross. What word appears below the pointer?
   a. FILL
   b. COPY
   c. MOVE
   d. RELOCATE

7. What happens when the formula $=(A1*12)$ is copied one cell downward?
   a. It changes to $=(A2*12)$.
   b. It changes to $=(A2*13)$.
   c. It changes to $=(B2*12)$.
   d. None of the above.

8. What kind of cell entries can be copied?
   a. numbers
   b. text
   c. formulas
   d. All of the above.

9. The value $5,600.79 appears in a cell. What is its number format?
   a. Percent
   b. Decimal
   c. Money
   d. Currency

10. The default (standard) number format is:
   a. General.
   b. Currency.
   c. Fixed.
   d. Decimal.

Short Answer

1. To clear a range of cells, select the range and press the _____ key.

2. The _____ format omits trailing zeros.

3. The _____ format sets the number of decimal places and inserts a dollar sign in front of the number.

4. Use _____ in a formula to change the normal order of operations.

5. The operator for exponentiation is _____.

6. To move the contents of cell A1 to cell D1, use the _____ feature.

7. To recover data that you just deleted by mistake, choose the _____ command from the Edit menu.

8. To format a column so that the longest entry will be displayed, choose the _____ button in the Column Width dialog box.

9. To work on an existing spreadsheet, choose the _____ tab in the Works Task Launcher dialog box.

10. To change a formula that has already been entered without retyping the entire entry, press the _____ key.

For Discussion

1. What steps must you perform to make a cell containing .075 display 7.50%?

2. Why would you align text so it appears on the right in a column?

3. How is the algebraic equation $\dfrac{360 - 23}{14 * 3^2}$ written as a Works formula?

4. Describe how formulas change when copied to other locations in the spreadsheet.

5. What happens when the number in a cell is too wide to be displayed as formatted?

Review Exercises

Creating a List of Guests at a Resort

1. Create the spreadsheet shown in Figure 2.25, which consists of a list of patrons who are guests at a resort. Enter your name instead of Todd Leykis'. Use the Currency format where needed. Make sure column headings over numbers are right-aligned. Save your spreadsheet as *Resort Guests*.

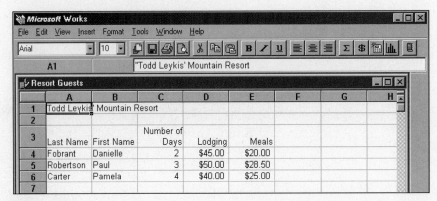

Figure 2.25

2. Create an additional column (shown in Figure 2.26), called *Amount Due*, that will determine the amount due for each patron. The formula for finding the amount due is:

```
Number of Days * (Lodging + Meals)
```

Be sure to use parentheses where appropriate. Lodging and meals should be added together before they are multiplied by number of days. Use the data in Figure 2.26 to create the formula for Danielle only, not for the other guests.

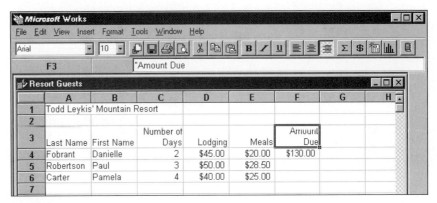

Figure 2.26

3. Apply the Currency format to Danielle's amount due.

4. Copy the formula for the amount due to all the appropriate cells in the Amount Due column.

5. Add three guests of your own choosing. You can invent information for each column, but be sure to copy the formula for the Amount Due column and to format the currency amounts.

6. Save the spreadsheet as *Resort Guests*.

7. Print the spreadsheet.

Tracking Student Grades

1. The spreadsheet shown in Figure 2.27 keeps track of grades. Create the spreadsheet, but enter your name instead of Neeraj Chari's. Also, widen column A to accommodate all the names, and make sure the appropriate column headings are right-aligned.

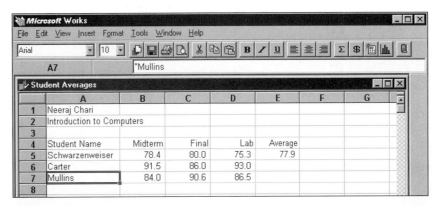

Figure 2.27

2. Display all numbers in Fixed format with one decimal place.

3. Add three students. Apply the appropriate format to all numbers.

4. Create a formula to determine the average. The midterm, final, and lab scores are each worth one-third of the total grade. For example, Schwarzenweiser's average is 77.9. Create the formula just for Schwarzenweiser, and then copy it downward. Apply the Fixed format, with one decimal place, to all numbers in the Average column.

5. Save the spreadsheet as *Student Averages*.

6. Print the spreadsheet.

Assignments

Calculating Long-Distance Charges

You want to use the Spreadsheet tool to find out whether the long-distance charges appearing on this month's phone bill are correct. Create, save, and print the spreadsheet shown in Figure 2.28. Be sure to use formulas in column E. Also, use your name at the top of the spreadsheet. Save the spreadsheet using the name *Phone Bill*.

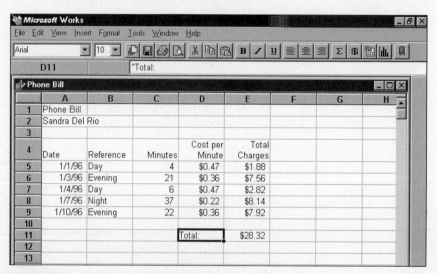

Figure 2.28

Calculating Sales Commissions

As owner of your own bicycle store, you want to easily calculate the commission the sales staff earns each week. Create the spreadsheet shown in Figure 2.29. Employees are paid a 13 percent commission on total sales. Put your name in the spreadsheet instead of Bob Kline's. Save the spreadsheet as *Bike Sales*. Print the spreadsheet.

6 In cell D9, type `Catalonia`

7 In cell E9, type `Total Sales`

8 Choose Alignment from the Format menu.

9 Select Wrap Text and then select OK.
Total Sales should be wrapped.

10 In cell F9, type `Bonus`

All the column headings will appear over numeric data except for *Travel Agents*. Column headings over numeric data should be right-aligned.

To align the column headings on the right:

1 Select the range B9:F9.

2 Select the Right Align button on the Toolbar.

3 Press any arrow key to deselect the range.
The spreadsheet should look like Figure 3.3.

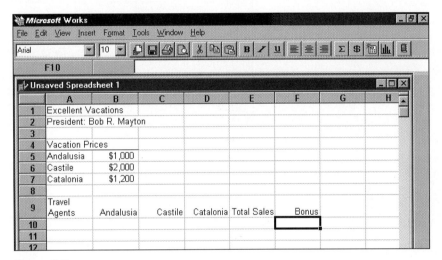

Figure 3.3

You can place a line underneath all column headings by using the Border command.

To create a line beneath the column headings:

1 Select the range A9:F9.

2 Choose Border from the Format menu.

3 Select Bottom and then select OK.

4 Press any arrow key to deselect the range.
The spreadsheet needs another line across it in row 12.

To place a line across row 12:

1 Select the range A12:F12.

2 Choose Border from the Format menu.

3 Select Bottom and then select OK.

4 Press any arrow key to deselect the range.
The spreadsheet should look like Figure 3.4.

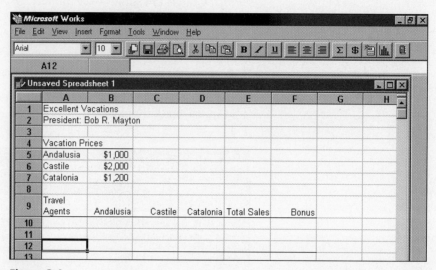

Figure 3.4

You still need to enter employee names and sales data.

To enter employee names and sales data:

1 Use Figure 3.5 as a guide to entering the names and sales data. When you have finished, the spreadsheet should look like Figure 3.5.

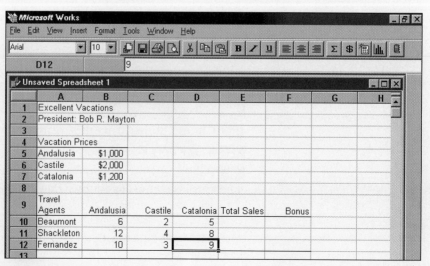

Figure 3.5

COPYING FORMULAS: ABSOLUTE REFERENCING

Copying formulas in Works can be a great advantage. For example, if a formula is complicated, you can create it only once and then you can copy it to other cells. As you learned in Project 2, Works automatically adjusts the cell references in a copied formula to correspond to the formula's new position in the spreadsheet.

Sometimes cell references should *not* be changed when they are copied. A cell reference that does not change when it is copied is called an ***absolute reference.*** You can create an absolute reference by placing a dollar sign in front of the row number and/or the column letter in the cell reference. For example, in Figure 3.6 the formula =B$2*B5, which multiplies price by the number sold, has been copied down one cell. Notice that, because the cell reference B$2 contains a dollar sign in front of the row number, the row number was not changed when the formula was copied. B5 did change to B6, however, because it is a relative reference.

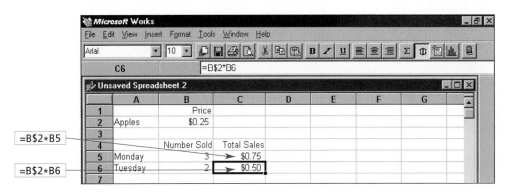

Figure 3.6

A ***mixed reference,*** like =B$2, contains an absolute reference to only either the column or the row. Mixed references are useful when either the column or the row reference must remain absolute. Table 3.1 shows the four types of cell references.

Table 3.1

Reference	Example
Absolute column, absolute row	A1
Absolute column, relative row	$A1
Relative column, absolute row	A$1
Relative column, relative row	A1

In Figure 3.6, if you did not place a dollar sign before the row number to make it an absolute reference, what would happen? When you copied the formula down from cell C5 to the next row, the cell reference for the price would change to B3, which does not contain a value. Therefore, the result would be incorrect, as shown in Figure 3.7.

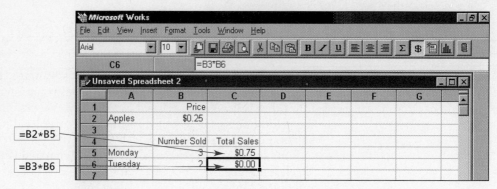

Figure 3.7

Note that a dollar sign in a cell reference such as B$2 has nothing to do with currency. It is just a signal to Works that the row number or column letter is an absolute reference and should not be changed when copied. A formula can contain more than one absolute reference.

In this spreadsheet, to find the total sales for each travel agent, you need to multiply the number of trips sold by the price. For example, Beaumont sold six trips to Andalusia for $1,000 each, two to Castile for $2,000 each, and five to Catalonia for $1,200 each. To get the total sales of $16,000, you will use the equation:

    6 * 1,000 + 2 * 2,000 + 5 * 1,200

Stated in terms of a Works formula, this equation is:

    =(B10*B5)+(C10*B6)+(D10*B7)

This formula needs dollar signs for its absolute references. The correct formula is =(B10*B$5)+(C10*B$6)+(D10*B$7). According to the hierarchy of operators, the parentheses are optional, but they do make the formula easier to read.

To enter the formulas to find the total sales:

1 In cell E10, type **=(B10*B$5)+(C10*B$6)+(D10*B$7)**
You should see 16000 in cell E10, as shown in Figure 3.8.

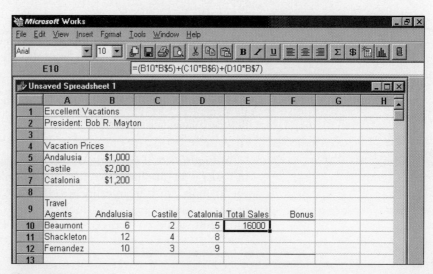

Figure 3.8

2 Place the pointer on the bottom-right corner of E10.
You should see the pointer in the shape of a cross with the word *FILL* underneath.

3 Drag the cell downward to cell E12.
The Total Sales column should be filled with results, as shown in Figure 3.9.

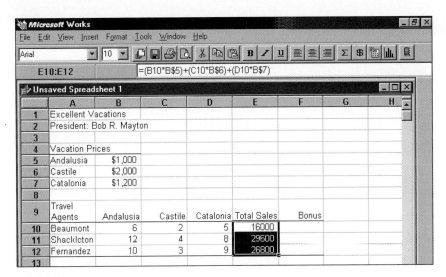

Figure 3.9

4 Place a line across the bottom of cell E12 (the previous line disappeared when you copied the formula down).

5 Select the range E10:E12.

6 Choose Number from the Format menu.

7 In the Number dialog box, select the radio button for Currency.

8 Type **0** for the number of decimal places and then select OK.
The spreadsheet should look like Figure 3.10.

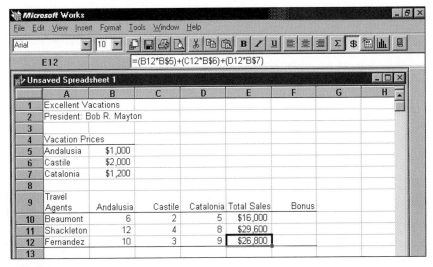

Figure 3.10

USING THE SUM AND AVG FUNCTIONS

Works has many built-in *functions* that perform a wide variety of standard spreadsheet calculations. Functions often serve as shortcuts in formulas. For example, the SUM function adds a series of numbers. In Figure 3.11, the Total Sales column is added by using the function =SUM(E10:E12) instead of the formula =E10+E11+E12.

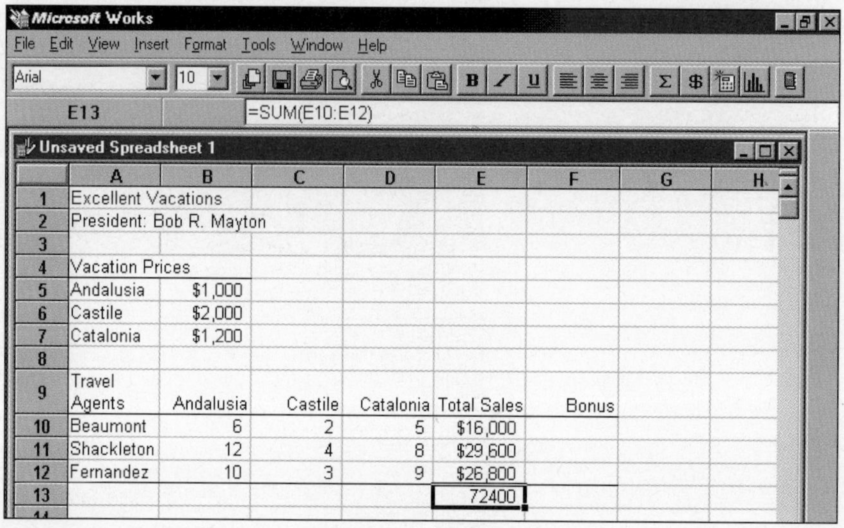

Figure 3.11

The order in which you enter characters in a formula or function is called the *syntax*. If you enter incorrect syntax, Works will give you an error message. If a function appears at the beginning of a cell entry, the function must start with an equal sign, just like a formula. Following the equal sign is the name of the function and the argument(s) of the function surrounded by parentheses, as in =SUM(E10:E12).

Arguments are the values that functions use in their calculations. In the previous SUM function, the argument is the range E10:E12. The formula will sum all data within the argument, or, in this case, within the range E10 to E12. The colon (:) separates the beginning of the range from the end of the range.

In Works, functions can be grouped into several broad categories, such as statistical, logical, date, and financial. Table 3.2 shows some commonly used statistical functions.

Table 3.2

Function	Result
AVG	Averages a range of numbers.
COUNT	Counts the number of entries in a range.
MAX	Finds the maximum value in a range.
MIN	Finds the minimum value in a range.
SUM	Adds a range of numbers.

You will use the SUM function to determine the total sales for all employees.

To calculate and format the total sales for all employees:

1 In cell D13, type **Total**

2 In cell E13, type **=SUM(E10:E12)**
Cell E13 should contain the sum, 72400.

3 Choose Number from the Format menu and then select Currency.

4 Type **0** and then select OK.
Cells D13 and E13 should look like the ones in Figure 3.12.

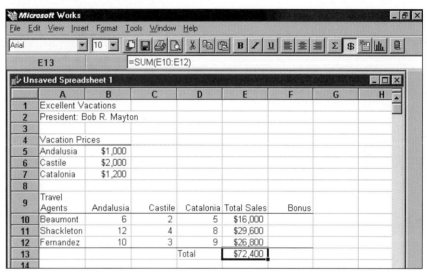

Figure 3.12

Tip   You can select the AutoSum button on the Toolbar to sum a range of cells. This button is labeled with a Greek capital Sigma (Σ), a traditional mathematical symbol to indicate summation.

You will use the AVG function to find the average sales of the employees.

To calculate and format the average sales for all employees:

1 In cell D14, type **Average**

2 In cell E14, type **=AVG(E10:E12)**
Cell E14 should contain the average, 24133.333.

3 Choose Number from the Format menu and then select Currency.

4 Type **0** and select OK.
The spreadsheet should look like Figure 3.13.

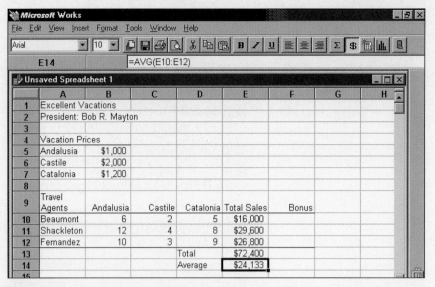

Figure 3.13

EXIT If necessary, you can save your spreadsheet as *Sales Data,* exit Works now, and continue this project later.

USING THE IF FUNCTION

Logical functions return one value if a comparison is true and another if a comparison is false. Operators that are used in logical comparisons are called *relational operators.* Table 3.3 describes the relational operators available in Works.

Table 3.3

Operator	Meaning
=	Equal to
<	Less than
>	Greater than
<>	Not equal to
<=	Less than or equal to
>=	Greater than or equal to

A typical logical function compares two cells, in a statement such as A2 > B5. If the condition is true, the function returns a certain value; if it is false, the function returns a different value.

Works offers several logical functions, but only one is used on a regular basis: the IF function. The basic syntax for the IF function is

```
IF(condition,result if true,result if false)
```

All travel agents at Excellent Vacations earn a bonus. If an agent's sales are $25,000 or more, the agent's bonus is 9 percent of his or her total sales.

If an agent sells less than $25,000, the bonus is 5 percent of the total sales. You can enter 9 percent as .09 or 9%. If you enter 9%, Works will convert it to .09. Because the value appears in a formula, how you enter the value does not affect how it is displayed. The cells containing the formula will be changed to Currency format.

To enter the IF function to find the bonuses:

1 In cell F10, type `=IF(E10>=25000,E10*.09,E10*.05)` and then press ENTER.

The result is 800. Because the condition E10>=25000 is false, Works evaluated E10*.05 to determine the bonus.

2 Copy the contents of cell F10 to cells F11 and F12.

3 Apply the Currency format, without decimal places, to the range F10:F12.

4 Select cell F12.

5 Choose Border from the Format menu.

6 Select Bottom and then select OK.

The Bonus column should look like the one in Figure 3.14.

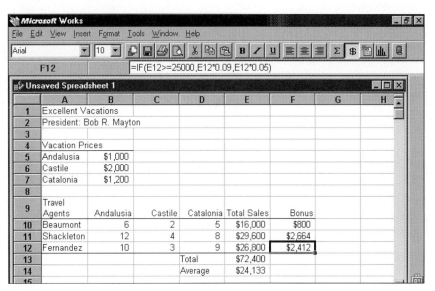

Figure 3.14

Caution When entering numbers in a cell, never add a dollar sign or comma to the number. These characters are reserved for use in formulas.

USING RANGE NAMES IN FUNCTIONS

If you plan to use the same range several times, it is a good idea to give the range a name. A *range name* is used to refer to a specified area of the spreadsheet. For example, if you are going to refer repeatedly to the range

E10:E12 (the range for the total sales), you can give the range a name such as *Sales*. From then on you can refer to the range by the name *Sales* instead of by the reference E10:E12. Once you have named a range, you don't have to worry about remembering the exact location of its beginning and end, because you can always refer to it by name.

To assign a name to a range, you will use the Range Name command in the Insert menu.

To assign the name Sales to the range E10:E12:

1 Select the range E10:E12.

2 Choose Range Name from the Insert menu.
The Range Name dialog box appears. Note that Works assumes that you want to use the column heading as the range name. You will type a new name.

3 Type **Sales**
The screen should look like Figure 3.15.

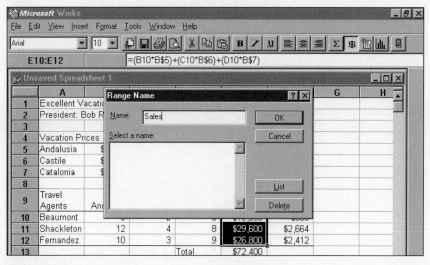

Figure 3.15

4 Select OK to complete the command.

You can now use the range name in a function. You will use the MAX statistical function, which finds the maximum value in a range, to determine the highest number in the Sales range.

To find the highest value in the Sales range:

1 In cell D15, type **Highest** and press (ENTER)

2 In cell E15, type **=MAX(Sales)** and press (ENTER)
The spreadsheet should look like Figure 3.16.

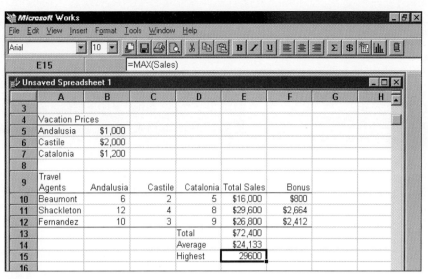

Figure 3.16

Next you will use the MIN statistical function to find the lowest, or minimum, value in the Sales range.

To find the lowest value in the **Sales range:**

1 In cell D16, type `Lowest`

2 In cell E16, type `=MIN(Sales)`

To apply a Currency format:

1 Select cells E15 and E16.

2 Apply a Currency format, without decimal places.
The screen should look like Figure 3.17.

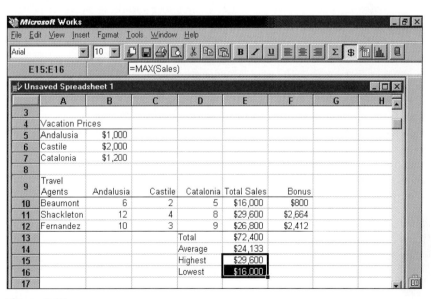

Figure 3.17

The Bonus column can also be given a range name, which can then be used in a function. For example, you can use the appropriate function with the range name to find the total, average, highest, and lowest bonuses.

To create the range name Bonuses:

1 Select the range F10:F12.

2 Choose Range Name from the Insert menu and then type **Bonuses**
The screen should look like Figure 3.18.

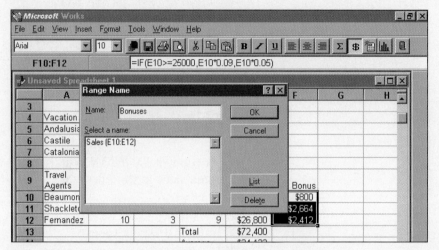

Figure 3.18

3 Select OK to complete the command.

To enter several functions and then format a range:

1 In cell F13, enter the correct function to sum the Bonuses range.
The spreadsheet should look like Figure 3.19. Notice the function in the
formula bar.

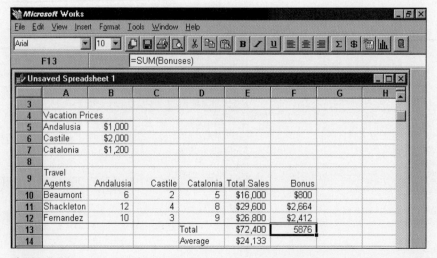

Figure 3.19

2 In cell F14, use the AVG function to average the Bonuses range.

3 In cell F15, use the MAX function to find the highest bonus.

4 In cell F16, use the MIN function to find the lowest bonus.

5 Apply the Currency format, without decimal places, to the range F13:F16.

The spreadsheet should look like Figure 3.20.

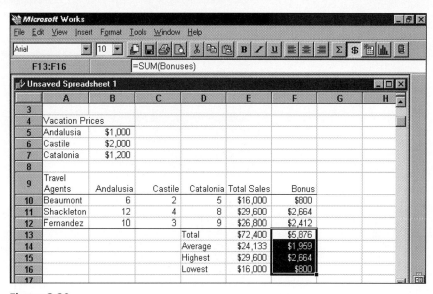

Figure 3.20

ASKING WHAT-IF QUESTIONS

Look at Figure 3.20. The number of Castile vacations sold seems a little low when compared to the number of Andalusia and Catalonia vacations. This could be due to the price of the Castile vacation, which is currently $2,000. You have taken a survey of potential customers and have concluded that if you were to lower the price of the Castile vacation to $1,800, you could double the number of vacations sold. Now you want to find out how this would affect your profit.

Works is the perfect platform for asking *"what-if" questions.* In the current example, you need only to change a few values to get the answer, because Works will automatically recalculate all the pertinent values for you. If you were to do this sort of experimentation manually, you would need to perform many time-consuming calculations.

Before asking "what if?" you should save the spreadsheet. By saving the file first, you can easily return later to an original copy of the spreadsheet.

To save the spreadsheet:

1 Choose Save from the File menu.

2 Type **Sales Data** as the file name and select OK.

The total sales for all travel agents, $72,400, is shown in cell E13. You will investigate whether this total increases if you lower the price of the Castile vacation to $1,800 and double the number of Castile vacations sold.

To calculate the Castile vacation changes:

1 In cell B6, type **1800**

2 In cell C10, type **4**

3 In cell C11, type **8**

4 In cell C12, type **6**

Look at the new total in cell E13. The amount has increased by $14,400, from $72,400 to $86,800, as shown in Figure 3.21.

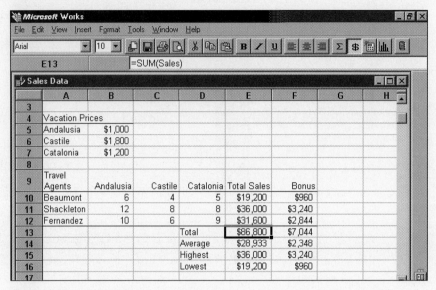

Figure 3.21

As the president of Excellent Vacations, you might strongly consider reducing the price of the Castile vacation. For the moment, however, you will change the data back to the original figures.

To reenter the original data:

1 In cell B6, type **2000**

2 In cell C10, type **2**

3 In cell C11, type **4**

4 In cell C12, type **3**

PRINTING IN LANDSCAPE MODE

The spreadsheet is rather wide and may look better if you place it sideways on the printed page. *Landscape orientation* refers to a printout that is turned sideways. The standard, vertically-oriented printout is referred to as *portrait orientation.*

To change the printing orientation to landscape:

1 Choose Page Setup from the File menu.

2 Select the Source, Size & Orientation tab.

3 Select Landscape.
The screen should look like Figure 3.22.

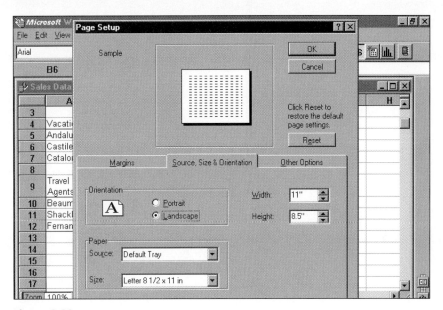

Figure 3.22

4 Select OK to complete the command.

Now you will preview and then print the spreadsheet in the new orientation.

To preview and then print the spreadsheet:

1 Choose Print Preview from the File menu.
Notice the new orientation, as shown in Figure 3.23.

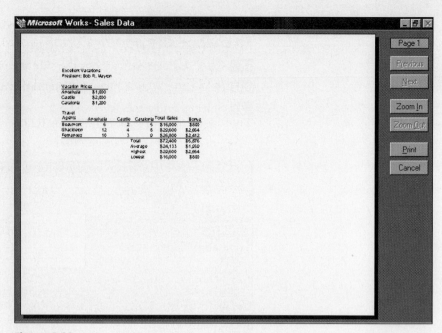

Figure 3.23

2 Select Print.

3 Select OK to print the spreadsheet.

SHOWING FORMULAS IN A PRINTOUT

So far, whenever you have printed your work, you have printed only the spreadsheet and not the underlying formulas. There may be times when you want to see all the formulas in a spreadsheet without having to separately select each cell containing a formula and display the formula in the formula bar. It is possible to show the formulas in a spreadsheet by choosing the Formulas command in the View menu.

To display cell formulas in a printout:

1 Choose Formulas from the View menu.
Notice that all the columns get wider to display the formulas. Some columns, such as E and F, still need to be a little wider.

2 Use the scroll bar or press ⊙ several times to examine the entire spreadsheet.

3 Set the widths of columns E and F to 35, as shown in Figure 3.24.
By widening columns E and F to 35, you can see the complete formulas in both columns. (Be sure to change these two columns back to 20 before you turn off the Formulas option.)

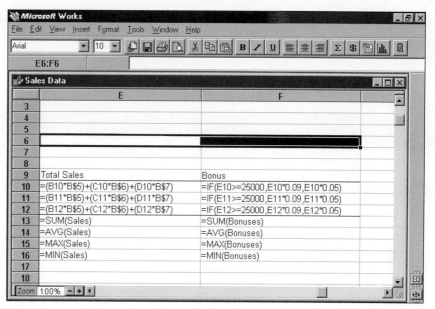

Figure 3.24

4 Print the spreadsheet.
The printout of the spreadsheet will show the cell formulas. Expect more than one page.

To turn off the Formulas option:

1 Reset the widths of columns E and F to 20.

2 Choose Formulas from the View menu.
The screen should now show the usual spreadsheet display.

3 Choose Save from the File menu to save the file.

THE NEXT STEP

In this project you have applied some advanced spreadsheet concepts. Absolute references are used in spreadsheets that contain many formulas that reference a single cell, such as an amortization schedule, which is used for finding loan payments. What-if questions can be used in spreadsheets where you want to see how certain changes will affect other values in the spreadsheet. For example, a spreadsheet designed to display a student's current grade-point average (GPA) could contain IF functions to determine how changes in one or more grades would change the GPA.

This concludes Project 3 with the Spreadsheet tool. You can either exit Works or go on to work the Study Questions, Review Exercises, and Assignments.

SUMMARY AND EXERCISES

Summary

- To create an absolute cell reference in a formula, you would place a dollar sign before the row number or column letter.
- Works offers several built-in statistical functions. SUM adds a range, AVG averages a range, MAX finds the maximum value in a range, and MIN finds the minimum value in a range.
- Logical operators are operators used in logical comparisons.
- The IF logical function returns one value if a condition is true and another value if the condition is false.
- Range names, which are used to refer to a specified area or range of the spreadsheet, can be used in a function.
- Works provides an effective means for answering what-if questions because it automatically recalculates the spreadsheet each time you change a value.
- As with most Windows programs, Works lets you print sideways to better accommodate your work. This is called landscape orientation.
- To display formulas in a spreadsheet, you can use the Formulas command in the View menu.

Key Terms and Operations

Key Terms
absolute reference
argument
function
landscape orientation
logical function
mixed reference
portrait orientation

range name
relational operator
syntax
what-if question

Operations
Name a range
Show cell formulas
Use functions

Study Questions

Multiple Choice

1. Which of the following symbols is not a relational operator?
   a. <
   b. >
   c. =
   d. /

2. Which function is used to determine the average of a series of values?
   a. AVERAGE
   b. AVER
   c. SUM
   d. AVG

3. To show formulas in a spreadsheet, you choose Formulas from the _____ menu.
   a. Format
   b. Edit
   c. Tools
   d. View

4. Which of the following is a logical function?
   a. MIN
   b. IF
   c. MAX
   d. SUM

5. The formula =IF(E11<=1000,E11*.05,E11*.1) will:
   a. Add 1000 to the value in cell E11.
   b. Multiply the positive value of cell E11 by 1000 and then multiply this total by 5 percent.
   c. Evaluate the value in cell E11 and multiply E11 by 10 percent if that value is not less than 1000.
   d. Multiply 1000 by 5 percent, then multiply this total by 10 percent, and finally add 1000 to the total.

6. The formula =MIN(Sales)+E16*B$3 contains:
   a. an absolute reference.
   b. a relative reference.
   c. a range name.
   d. All of the above.

7. Which of the following cell values is formatted to Currency with no decimal places?
   a. $5,000   c. 1,000
   b. 7,550   d. 900

8. Which of the following formulas contains an absolute reference?
   a. =MIN(A11:A14)*A$1   c. =AVG(A11:A14)
   b. =MAX(F22:F64)   d. =SUM(F22:F64)*A1

9. Which feature in Works provides an effective means of asking what-if questions?
   a. Print Preview
   b. automatic recalculation
   c. Currency format
   d. Show Formulas

10. Assume that the formula =A5*C1 appears in cell A1. What appears when the formula is copied to cell A2?
    a. =B5*C1   c. =B6*C2
    b. =A6*D2   d. =A6*C1

Short Answer

1. The symbol that "locks" the row number or column letter in a formula so that it does not change when copied is the _____.

2. If only the column letter or row number is absolute, but not both, then it is called a(n) _____ reference.

3. The _____ function finds the lowest value in a range.

4. The values that functions use in their calculations are called _____.

5. Operators that are used to compare one value to another are called _____ operators.

6. A specified area of the spreadsheet that has been given a name is a(n) _____.

7. The operator that means *not equal to* is _____.

8. The _____ function calculates the number of entries in a range.

9. The order in which you enter characters in a formula or function is called the _____.

10. _____ orientation refers to a sideways printout.

For Discussion

1. Under what circumstances should you give a range name to a group of cells?

2. Why is an electronic spreadsheet more appropriate than a paper spreadsheet for a what-if analysis?

3. Why is it easier to average a column of 100 numbers with the AVG function rather than a formula?

4. Write a Works formula that would give a result of 0 if cell A9 was greater than 10, and a result of 1 if it was not.

5. Describe some of the ways what-if analyses can be useful when calculating your personal budget.

Review Exercises

Tracking a Stock Portfolio

Danielle Fobrant uses Works to keep track of her stock portfolio. Use the spreadsheet in Figure 3.25 and the following steps to create a display of your own portfolio.

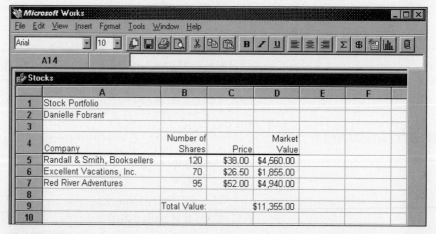

Figure 3.25

1. Enter all the text in the spreadsheet. Use your name, not Danielle Fobrant's. Column A needs to be widened to accommodate the names of all the companies. Be sure to enter the line that appears under the column headings.

2. Align on the right all column headings that are over numeric data.

3. Enter the numbers for the Number of Shares and Price columns.

4. Find the market value by multiplying the number of shares by the price. Copy the formula downward.

5. Use the SUM function to determine the total market value.

6. Format all numbers that need it.

7. Add three companies of your own choosing. They can be real or invented companies. Make sure to enter and format all the information for the Number of Shares, Price, and Market Value columns.

   To insert the company names, place the active cell in row 8. Choose Insert Row from the Insert menu. Repeat this command until you have inserted three blank rows.

   Type the company names, stock data, and the market value formulas.

8. Assign a range name to the market value formulas (you should select six cells).

9. Use the range name, along with the MAX and MIN functions, to find the maximum and minimum values of the Market Value column.

10. Save the spreadsheet, assigning it a name of your own choosing.

11. Print the spreadsheet.

12. Print the cell formulas of the spreadsheet.

Tracking Profits for a Small Business

Danielle Fobrant has a small business that specializes in cappuccino cheesecakes. The spreadsheet for keeping track of profits is shown in Figure 3.26.

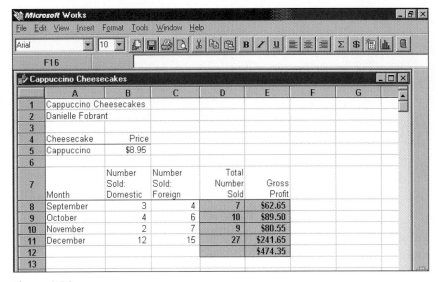

Figure 3.26

1. Create the spreadsheet in Figure 3.26, but use your name instead of Danielle Fobrant's. Type everything except what is in the shaded area.

2. Enter a formula in cell D8 to find the total number sold for September. Copy the formula downward to cells D9 through D11.

3. Enter a formula in cell E8 to find the gross profit for September. This cell will contain =B5*D8. Somewhere in this formula you will have to enter one or more dollar signs. Copy the completed formula downward to cells E9 through E11.

4. Enter a function in cell E12 to find the total of the Gross Profit column.

5. Format all numbers that need it.

6. Add borders (lines) where necessary. You do not need to shade any cells like the range D8 to E12.

7. Save the spreadsheet as *Cappuccino Cheesecakes*.

8. Print the spreadsheet sideways.

9. Print the cell formulas of the spreadsheet.

Assignments

Calculating Utility Increases

After staying constant for three years, gas, electric, and water charges will increase beginning next month. Design the spreadsheet shown in Figure 3.27 to determine how the increase will affect you. When you are finished, save the spreadsheet as *Utilities*, print the spreadsheet, and then print the spreadsheet formulas.

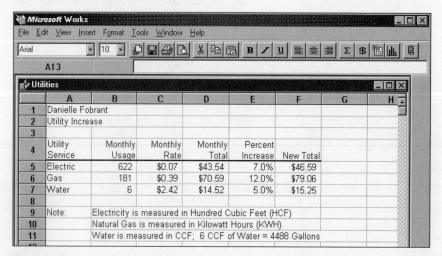

Figure 3.27

Determining Quantity Pricing

As the owner of a bicycle store, you want to make quantity pricing available to your customers. Create the spreadsheet shown in Figure 3.28. Use your name instead of Bob Kline's. Use borders and appropriate formatting. Enter the values of the range B8 to B11. Use formulas in cells C8 through

F11. Name the file *Pricing Table*. Print the spreadsheet twice, once the standard way and once with formulas displayed.

Extra credit: When you create the spreadsheet, enter the formula only once and then copy it to the rest of the table. That is, enter a formula in cell C8 and then copy it to cells D8 through F8. Next, copy cells D8 through F8 downward to row 11.

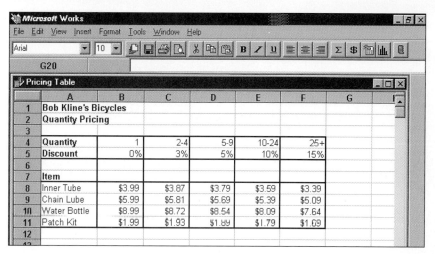

Figure 3.28

Objectives

After completing this project, you should be able to:

▶ Use the NOW, DATE, and TIME functions

▶ Enter a complex formula

▶ Use the PMT financial function

▶ Create an amortization schedule

▶ Freeze titles

CASE STUDY: BUILDING AN AMORTIZATION SCHEDULE

As president of Excellent Vacations, sometimes you need to borrow money from a bank to make purchases. In this case, assume you need to buy a new car for the company. Loans are typically issued for a specific amount (the *principal*), at a specific interest rate, to be repaid over a fixed time period (the *term*). A spreadsheet can be used to calculate the loan repayment information. Such a document is called an *amortization schedule*.

Designing the Solution

When you repay a car loan, every month you write a check to the bank. Part of the monthly payment goes toward paying off the loan and part goes toward interest. You will create a spreadsheet called an amortization schedule, which will provide a detailed description of the repayment of the car loan over the course of its term. The loan principal, interest rate, and term will be used to calculate the monthly payment. You will use the PMT function to perform the calculation. Once a few formulas are defined, you will copy them down the spreadsheet to display all loan repayment information. The completed spreadsheet will consist of several screens of information. The first screen will resemble Figure 4.1.

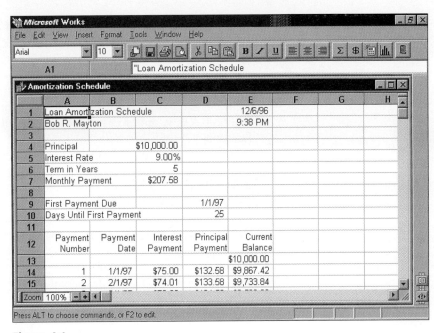

Figure 4.1

CREATING A NEW SPREADSHEET

To create an amortization schedule you will need to start a new document.

To create and title a new spreadsheet:

1 Start Works and then choose the option to create a new spreadsheet.

2 In cell A1, type the title `Loan Amortization Schedule`

3 In cell A2, type your name.

USING THE NOW FUNCTION

All computers that use Windows 95 have a built-in clock that maintains the date and time. The computer's date and time, which can be set from within the Control Panel, can be displayed in a spreadsheet with the numerous date and time functions that Works offers. For example, suppose that on November 10 you buy a sofa for which you must make three equal payments: the first in 30 days, the second in 60 days, and the last in 90 days. You can use the DATE function to determine when each payment is due. Or, suppose you work in the Payroll Department of a company and need to calculate employee salaries. You can use the TIME function to determine the daily number of hours worked by each employee.

Dates and times appear as numbers in the spreadsheet, so you can perform calculations on them. The DATE and NOW functions display the number of days that have passed since a standard reference point: December 31, 1899. For example, to represent the date October 15, 1996, you would enter =DATE(96,10,15) and you would see the number 35353 in the spreadsheet. This means that 35,353 days would have passed since December 31, 1899. Notice that the format for the DATE function is DATE(year,month,day).

The TIME function displays the time as a fraction of a 24-hour period in which midnight is the starting point. To enter 6:00 A.M., you would type =TIME(6,0,0) and you would see .25. The decimal form .25 indicates that 6:00 A.M. is one-quarter of a 24-hour period. The format for the TIME function is TIME(hours,minutes,seconds).

The NOW function displays both the current date and time. If the current date is October 15, 1996, and the current time is 6:00 A.M., NOW( ) will display 35353.25.

On-screen numbers such as 35353 and .25 do not mean much to the average person in terms of date or time. The Date and Time options in the Number command enable you to display dates and times in a more meaningful manner. Table 4.1 shows several date and time functions, their results in a spreadsheet, and their appearance after formatting. Note that the number 35400 refers to December 1, 1996.

Table 4.1

Function	Result	Formatted Result	Description
=DATE(96,12,1)	35400	12/1/96	Displays a date.
=TIME(18,0,0)	.75	6:00:00 PM	Displays a time.
=NOW( )	35400.75	12/1/96	Displays current date (formatted with a date format).
=NOW( )	35400.75	6:00:00 PM	Displays current time (formatted with a time format).
=DAY(35400)	1	1	Extracts day of the month.
=MONTH(35400)	12	12	Extracts month.
=YEAR(35400)	96	96	Extracts year.

The Number command in the Format menu contains numerous options for formatting a variety of numeric data, including dates and times. The dialog box shown in Figure 4.2 displays some of the available formats for dates.

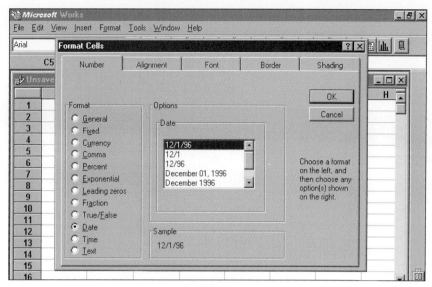

Figure 4.2

Figure 4.3 shows the formats for times.

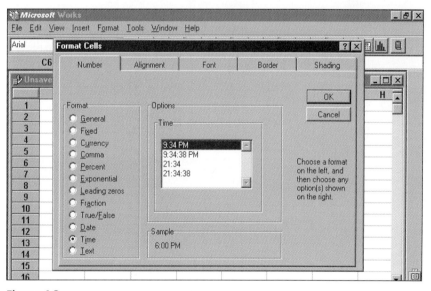

Figure 4.3

You will use the date and time functions mentioned above throughout this project. The first one you will use is the NOW function to enter the current date and time in the upper-right corner of the spreadsheet.

To enter the current date and time:

1 In cell E1, type =NOW( )

2 In cell E2, type =NOW( )

If you see a series of pound signs (#), this indicates that the column is too narrow to display the current value. If necessary, widen column E to view the current date and time.

Both cells will now have a number that reflects the current date. Figure 4.4 shows 35405.902, which corresponds to December 6, 1996. The actual number that appears on the screen will depend upon the current date logged in the computer's system clock.

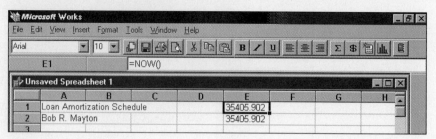

Figure 4.4

Next you need to format both cells, the first with a date format and the second with a time format.

To apply a date format to cell E1:

1 Select cell E1.

2 Choose Number from the Format menu.

3 Select the radio button for Date.
Notice that there are many date formats.

4 Select the first format in the list (it should already be selected).

5 Select OK to complete the command.
The date should now be formatted. The number 35405.902 would appear as 12/6/96, as in Figure 4.5. Your date, of course, will be different.

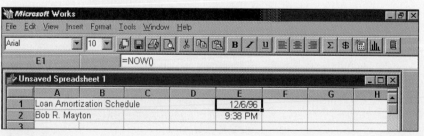

Figure 4.5

To apply a time format to cell E2:

1 Select cell E2.

2 Choose Number from the Format menu.

3 Select the radio button for Time.
You should see several time formats.

4 Select the first format in the list (it should already be selected).

5 Select OK to complete the command.
The time should now be formatted. The time appears as 9:38 PM, as shown in Figure 4.5 (your time will be different).

If you load this spreadsheet on a subsequent day, the spreadsheet will display a new date in the upper-right corner. The time will also change much more frequently, because Works will update the current time every time you enter new data or execute a command.

ENTERING A COMPLEX FORMULA

You plan to buy a new car for $15,000, and you have $5,000 as a down payment. You will get the balance, $10,000, from a lending institution that offers a 5-year repayment schedule at an interest rate of 9.0 percent. If you obtain a $10,000 loan for a term of 5 years at an interest rate of 9.0 percent, what is your monthly payment?

To find the monthly payment, you will create a complex formula.

To begin the car loan spreadsheet:

1 In cell A4, type `Principal`
Do not widen any columns. The term *principal* refers to the loan amount.

2 In cell A5, type `Interest Rate`

3 In cell A6, type `Term in Years`

4 In cell A7, type `Monthly Payment`

5 In cell C4, type `10000`

6 In cell C5, type `.09`

7 In cell C6, type `5`

Reminder   You can enter 9 percent as either .09 or 9.00%. If you enter .09, you will need to format the number as a percent. If you enter 9.00%, the number is automatically formatted as 9.00%.

To apply the Currency format to cell C4:

1 Select cell C4.

2 Choose Number from the Format menu.

3 Select the radio button for Currency.

4 Select OK to complete the command.
If cell C4 is filled with pound signs, this indicates that the number $10,000.00 is too wide for the current cell. If necessary, widen the column until you see the number.

To apply the Percent format to cell C5:

1 Select cell C5.

2 Choose Number from the Format menu.

3 Select the radio button for Percent.

4 Type `2` for the number of decimal places.

5 Select OK to complete the command.
Cell C5 should show the formatted number 9.00%. The spreadsheet should look like Figure 4.6.

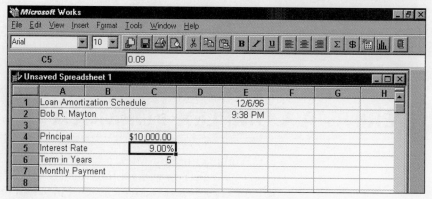

Figure 4.6

To display the monthly payment in cell C7, you have the option of entering a complex formula or using a built-in *financial function.* In this project, you will do both. First you will get more practice in developing complex formulas, and then you will see how easy it is to use a built-in function to find the monthly payment.

The formula for finding the monthly payment on a loan is

$$\text{Monthly Payment} = \text{Principal} * \frac{\text{Interest Rate}/12}{1 - (1 + \text{Interest Rate}/12)^{(-\text{Term}*12)}}$$

You need to convert this algebraic equation into a formula that Works understands.

To enter a formula to find the monthly payment:

1 In cell C7, type `=C4*(C5/12)/(1-(1+C5/12)^(-C6*12))` and press (ENTER)
The positions of the parentheses are critical for this formula to evaluate correctly. In cell C7 you should see the number 207.58355.

2 Choose Number from the Format menu.

3 Select the Currency radio button.

4 Select OK to complete the command.
Cell C7 should look like the one in Figure 4.7. The value $207.58 is the monthly payment for a $10,000 loan at a yearly interest rate of 9.0 percent for a term of 5 years.

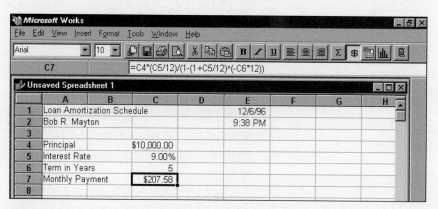

Figure 4.7

USING THE PMT FUNCTION

Finding a periodic payment, in this case, a monthly payment, for a loan is a common operation, so Works includes a built-in payment function called PMT. The PMT financial function finds the periodic payment for a loan and can serve as a shortcut to save you from having to enter the large formula you used previously. Because this periodic payment is a monthly payment, you will use the following syntax to find the payment:

```
PMT(principal,monthly interest rate,term in months)
```

To use the PMT function to find the monthly payment:

1 Make cell C7 the active cell.

2 Type **=PMT(C4,C5/12,C6*12)** and press ENTER
You should see $207.58, which is the same result as the one produced using the large formula.

Notice that in the PMT argument the yearly interest rate from cell C5 was divided by 12 to create a monthly interest rate, and the yearly term from cell C6 was multiplied by 12 to create a monthly term.

USING THE DATE FUNCTION

Now you will use the DATE function to display the date of the first loan payment. You will also use the NOW function and a formula to determine the number of days from the current date until the date of the first payment. Figure 4.8 shows how the screen will look after the two functions have done their work.

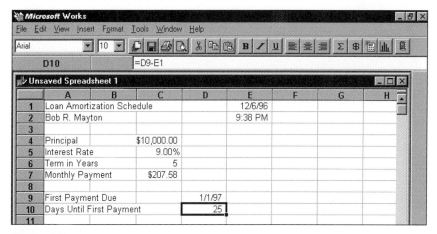

Figure 4.8

To enter text associated with the starting date:

1 In cell A9, type **First Payment Due**

2 In cell A10, type **Days Until First Payment**

The date of the first payment should be the first day of the following month. For example, in Figure 4.8, the current date was 12/6/96, so the start date should be 1/1/97. Of course, your current date will be different. You need to look at your current date and then enter a DATE function to represent the first day of the following month.

Reminder The DATE function syntax is =DATE(year,month,day).

To enter and format the date of the first payment:

1 In cell D9, use the DATE function to enter a date that is the first day of the following month.
You should see a number. For example, if you entered =DATE(97,1,1), you would see 35431. Remember, the syntax for the DATE function is =DATE(year,month,day). For example, if the date is September 3, 1996, you would enter =DATE(96,9,3).

2 Choose Number from the Format menu.

3 Select the radio button for Date.

4 Select OK to complete the command.
The date should be formatted. For example, 35431 would appear as 1/1/97.

In cell D10 you will enter a formula to show the number of days from the current date until the first payment. Then you will apply the Fixed format, without decimal places.

To enter a formula and apply the Fixed format:

1 Make cell D10 the active cell.

2 Type **=D9-E1**

3 Choose Number from the Format menu.

4 Set the format to Fixed, with 0 decimal places.
Compare your spreadsheet with the one in Figure 4.8.

If necessary, you can save your spreadsheet as *Amortization Schedule*, exit Works, and continue this project later.

CREATING AN AMORTIZATION SCHEDULE

An amortization schedule describes in detail the amount of each loan payment, the amount from each payment that is applied toward the principal, the amount that is applied toward interest, and the current balance. Other information is often displayed as well, such as the date of each payment.

This amortization schedule will have several column headings, as shown in Figure 4.9.

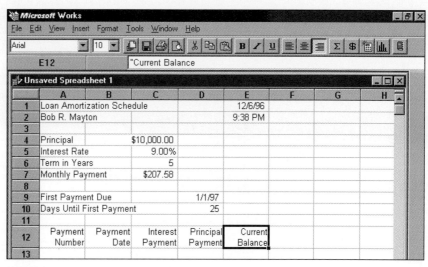

Figure 4.9

To enter and align the column headings:

1 Using Figure 4.9 as a guide, type the headings in row 12.

2 Use the Wrap Text option to wrap all text in row 12.

3 Align all the column headings to the right.
Now you need to place the starting balance in cell E14.

To enter the starting balance and apply the Currency format:

1 In cell E13, type **=C4** and press ENTER
You should see 10000. This step may look like you're copying cell C4 to cell E13, but you're not. You're just setting cell E13 equal to cell C4. If you change the contents of cell C4, the contents of cell E13 will change correspondingly.

2 Choose Number from the Format menu, and then select the Currency option.

3 Select OK to complete the command.
If you see pound signs in cell E13, widen column E. The spreadsheet should look like Figure 4.10.

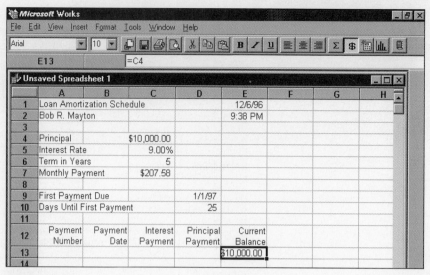

Figure 4.10

You now need to enter a detailed description of payment number 1, as shown in Figure 4.11.

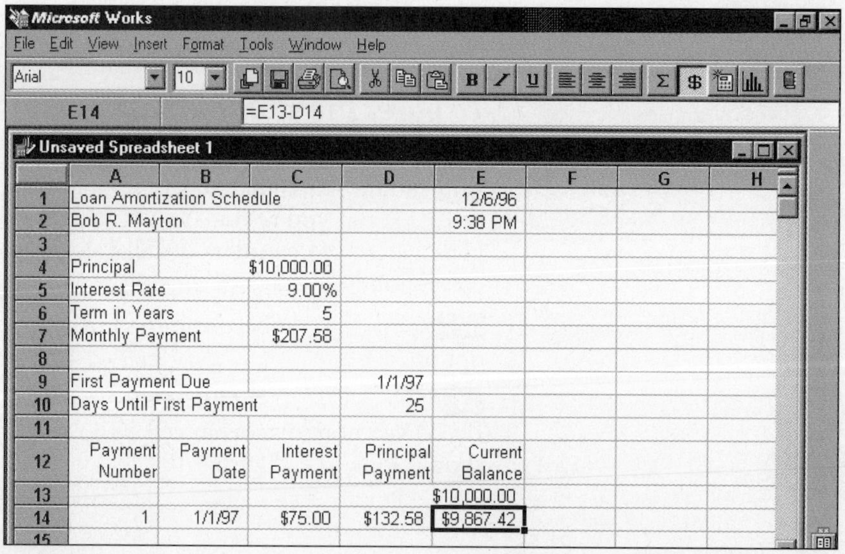

Figure 4.11

Remember, the monthly payment is $207.58. Figure 4.11 indicates that, out of $207.58, the interest that the bank receives for giving you a loan is $75.00. The amount that actually goes toward paying off the loan principal is $132.58.

The interest payment, $75.00, and the principal payment, $132.58, add up to the total monthly payment, $207.58. Out of the total monthly payment, only the principal amount is used to pay off the loan. The current balance after the first payment is the previous current balance minus the principal payment, or $9,867.42.

To enter the payment number and date:

1 In cell A14, type **1** and press (ENTER)

2 In cell B14, type **=D9** and press (ENTER)
You should see a number that represents the date of the first payment. The number needs to be formatted.

3 Choose Number from the Format menu, and change the format to Date.

4 Select OK to complete the command.
The payment date should be formatted like the one in Figure 4.11. Remember, your date will be different.

A standard method for finding the interest payment is to multiply the current balance by the monthly interest rate. You will use the current balance from the Current Balance column. To derive the monthly interest rate, you will divide the yearly interest rate in cell C5 by 12.

To calculate and format the interest payment:

1 In cell C14, type **=E13*(C5/12)** and press (ENTER)
This formula represents the current balance (cell E13) multiplied by the monthly interest rate (cell C5/12). Your interest payment should be 75.

2 Choose Number from the Format menu, and set the format to Currency with 2 decimal places.
You should see $75.00 in the spreadsheet.

A standard method for finding the principal payment is to subtract the interest payment from the monthly payment.

To calculate and format the principal payment:

1 In cell D14, type **=C7-C14** and press (ENTER)
This formula represents the monthly payment (cell C7) minus the interest payment (cell C14). The principal payment should be displayed as 132.58355, which is too wide to be shown in the cell.

2 Choose Number from the Format menu and set the format to Currency with 2 decimal places.
Cell D14 should display $132.58, as shown in Figure 4.12.

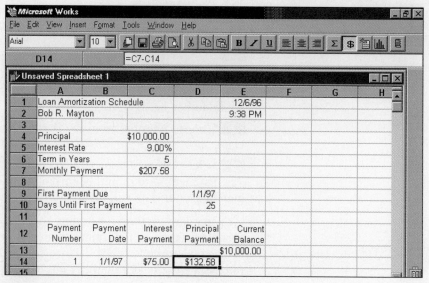

Figure 4.12

To find the current balance, you will subtract the principal payment from the previous balance.

To calculate the current balance:

1 In cell E14, type **=E13-D14** and press (ENTER)
This formula represents the previous balance (cell E13) minus the principal payment (cell D14). The current balance should be displayed as 9867.4164.

2 Set the format to Currency with 2 decimal places.
Cell E14 should display $9,867.42.

Next, you will enter and then copy down the row that describes payment number 2. Figure 4.13 shows the information about payment number 2. Payment number 2 will have a different date.

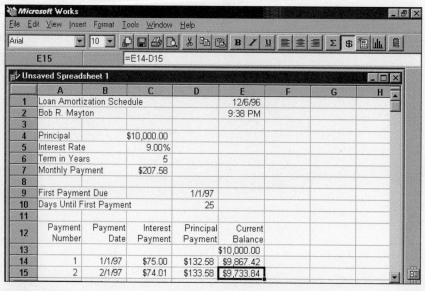

Figure 4.13

To enter the payment number and date for payment 2:

1 In cell A15, type =A14+1 and press (ENTER)

This formula adds 1 to the value in the previous cell. When copied down the spreadsheet, the formula creates a column in which each subsequent value increases by 1.

2 In cell B15, type =DATE(YEAR(B14),MONTH(B14)+1,1)

In this DATE function, the year is taken from cell B14, the month is derived by adding 1 to the previous month, and the day is set to 1. The references to cell B14 are relative, so each formula will calculate the date by adding 1 to the value in the cell above it.

3 Set the format of the cell to display the date.

The date should be formatted like the one shown in Figure 4.14.

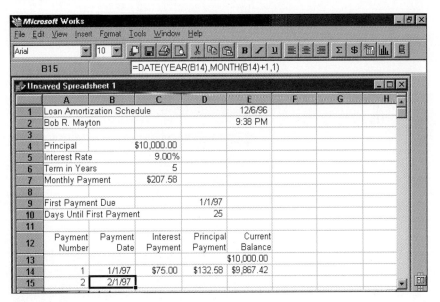

Figure 4.14

To enter and format the interest payment:

1 In cell C15, type =E14*C$5/12 and press (ENTER)

The interest payment should be displayed as 74.005623.

2 Format the number in cell C15 by applying the Currency format, with 2 decimal places.

Cell C15 should display $74.01.

Reminder In a formula, using a dollar sign before the row number prevents the row number from changing when the formula is copied downward. This is an example of an absolute reference.

To enter and format the principal payment:

1 In cell D15, type =C$7-C15 and press (ENTER)

The principal payment should be displayed as 133.57793.

2 Format the number in cell D15 by applying the Currency format, with 2 decimal places.
Cell D15 should display $133.58.

To enter and format the current balance:

1 In cell E15, type **=E14-D15** and press (ENTER)
The current balance should be displayed as 9733.84.

2 Format the number in cell E15 by applying the Currency format, with 2 decimal places.
Cell E15 should display $9,733.84.

Next you need to copy down all the formulas you created for payment number 2. Because the loan has a 5-year term, you will have a total of 60 payments (5 years times 12 payments per year). To copy down the formulas for payment number 2, you will highlight the range A15 through E73 and then use the Fill Down command in the Edit menu.

To copy down the formulas for payment number 2:

1 Select the range A15:E73.
Because this is a big range, be careful in selecting it. The screen should look like Figure 4.15.

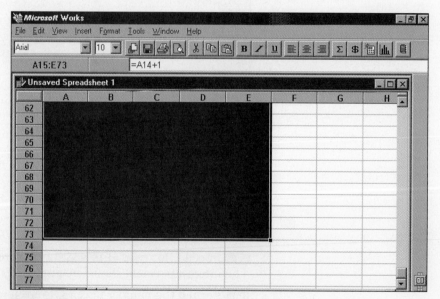

Figure 4.15

2 Choose Fill Down from the Edit menu to copy the formulas down. The spreadsheet should look like Figure 4.16. Notice that, in addition to copying the formulas, Works has also copied the cell formats.

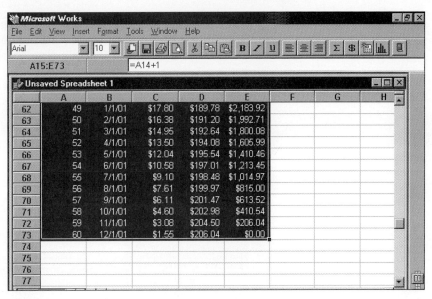

Figure 4.16

3 Click to deselect the range.

4 Move to the top of the spreadsheet.

By moving to the top of the spreadsheet, the following analysis will be easier. An amortization schedule provides a lot of information, such as payoff amounts, accrued interest, and many other details related to a loan. For example, assume that you have made 36 payments (3 years of payments) and you want to pay off the loan. To figure out the payoff amount, you would simply display payment number 36. The balance shown in Figure 4.17, $4,543.83, is the payoff amount after 36 payments.

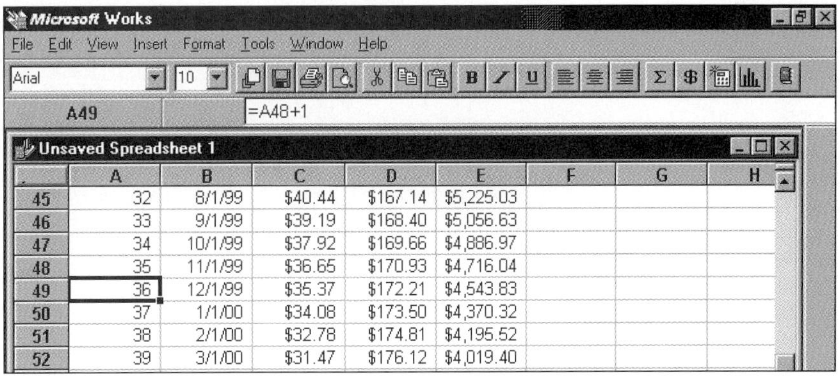

Figure 4.17

FREEZING TITLES

In Works you can *freeze titles,* or lock certain areas of a spreadsheet, such as titles or column headings. When you looked up the payoff amount, the column headings disappeared off the top of the screen. The Freeze Titles command in the Format menu will freeze the column headings on the screen. To *unfreeze titles* in a worksheet, you can choose Freeze Titles again in the Format menu to toggle the option off. This time when you glean information from the amortization schedule, the column headings will be "frozen," or locked, on the screen.

To freeze column headings:

1 Press (CTRL) + (HOME) to go to cell A1.
Cell A1 should be the active cell.

2 Press ⤓ until the active cell reaches A13, as shown in Figure 4.18.

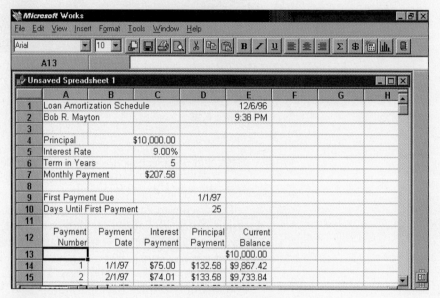

Figure 4.18

3 Choose Freeze Titles from the Format menu.
Nothing seems to happen, except that a faint line appears across the top of row 13.

4 Press ⤓ until you get to cell C74.
Notice that the column headings have remained on the screen, as shown in Figure 4.19.

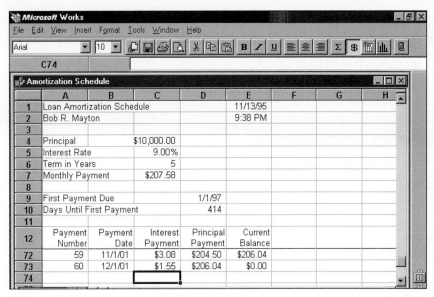

Figure 4.19

Your last task in this project is to find the total amount of interest paid over the course of the loan's term. To determine the interest paid, you will use the SUM function to add the numbers in the Interest Payment column.

To sum the Interest Payment column:

1 In cell C74, type **=SUM(C14:C73)** and press (ENTER)
You should see 2455.0131 displayed in cell C74.

2 Format the number in cell C74 by applying the Currency format, with 2 decimal places.
As shown in Figure 4.20, you will have paid **$2,455.01** in interest after paying off the loan in 5 years.

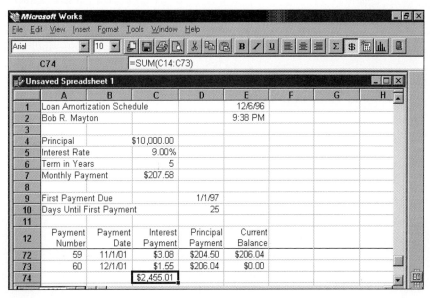

Figure 4.20

SAVING AND PRINTING A SPREADSHEET

Now you will save and print the spreadsheet. Because this is a large spreadsheet, it will print on several pages. Also, all the column headings that you have frozen on the screen will appear at the top of each printed page.

To save and print the spreadsheet:

1 Save the spreadsheet and give it the file name *Amortization Schedule*.

2 Print the spreadsheet.

If you have trouble printing, you may need to widen one or more columns. If so, first preview the document to see which columns need widening. Next, widen the columns. Last, print the spreadsheet again.

Your spreadsheet was saved with Freeze Titles active. This means that the next time you open the file, this option will still be active, which in this case is fine. If you ever want to unfreeze an area, you have to deactivate Freeze Titles.

To deactivate Freeze Titles:

1 Choose Freeze Titles from the Format menu.
The line above row 13 should disappear.

THE NEXT STEP

In this project, you have created a very practical spreadsheet, because you can use an amortization schedule to evaluate many types of loans, from car loans to home loans. To use this amortization schedule for any type of loan, you would enter the principal, interest rate, and term in the appropriate cells. The spreadsheet will automatically display the monthly payment. Next, you would copy the formulas for payment number 2 the appropriate number of times, as you did in this project. For example, if the loan will be paid off in 36 months, you would include 36 payments.

This concludes Project 4 with the Spreadsheet tool. You can either exit Works or go on to work the Study Questions, Review Exercises, and Assignments, and then the Additional Assignments and the Term Paper Project.

SUMMARY AND EXERCISES

Summary

- The DATE function displays the number of days since a standard reference point: December 31, 1899.
- The TIME function displays the time as a fraction of a 24-hour period.
- The NOW function displays the current date and time as a number.
- All functions associated with dates and times can be formatted by using the Number command in the Format menu.
- Complex formulas must be entered very carefully. Usually, the position of parentheses is critical for proper evaluation.
- The PMT function finds the periodic payment of a loan.
- An amortization schedule is a detailed account of each payment of a loan over the course of its term.
- You can freeze certain areas of a spreadsheet by using the Freeze Titles command in the Format menu.

Key Terms

amortization schedule   principal
financial function   term
freeze titles   unfreeze titles

Study Questions

Multiple Choice

1. Which function is used to determine the monthly amount due on a loan?
   a. PMT   c. AMT
   b. PAY   d. AVG

2. Which of the following will correctly display 12:00 PM?
   a. =DATE(95,12,6)   c. =TIME(12,0,0)
   b. =TIME(10,0)   d. =DATE(12,6,95)

3. Which of the following is not a date or time function?
   a. NOW   c. PMT
   b. DATE   d. TIME

4. In an amortization schedule, what word describes the length of time over which the loan is repaid?
   a. rate   c. term
   b. principal   d. ending balance

5. To keep column headings from scrolling off the screen when a large spreadsheet is viewed, you can choose:
   a. Zoom from the View menu.
   b. Save Workspace from the File menu.
   c. Freeze Titles from the Format menu.
   d. Delete Page Break from the Insert menu.

6. In the formula =C4*C5/12^2-4, which operation is performed first?
   a. 12^2
   b. C5/12
   c. C4*C5
   d. 2-4

7. Which function automatically updates the value after each calculation?
   a. DATE
   b. MONTH
   c. TIME
   d. NOW

8. The amount of money borrowed that is used to determine a repayment schedule is known as the:
   a. term.
   b. rate.
   c. principal.
   d. ending balance.

9. The formula =C4*(C5/12)/(1-(1+C5/12)^(-C6*12)) contains:
   a. at least one absolute reference.
   b. two relative references.
   c. one mixed reference.
   d. no absolute references.

10. In the formula =PMT(C4,C5/12, C6*12), the number 12 refers to:
    a. a 12-hour period.
    b. an interest rate of 12 percent.
    c. 12 months in a year.
    d. a principal of $12.

Short Answer

1. The _____ function automatically checks your system clock every time you enter new data or execute a command.

2. To enter the date May 16, 1996, you type the date function _____.

3. The term _____ refers to the amount of the loan.

4. The standard reference point for all date numbers is _____.

5. The _____ command in the Format menu formats dates and times.

6. In the function =PMT(A4,A5/12,A6*12), the principal is contained in cell _____.

7. The result of the function =DAY(DATE(96,12,15)) would be _____.

8. To find out how much of your payment is applied toward the principal, you subtract the _____ payment from the total monthly payment.

9. To copy a row of formulas, you can select the range and then use the _____ command in the Edit menu.

10. At the end of the term of the loan, your current balance should be _____.

For Discussion

1. What is an amortization schedule?

2. If the function =NOW() displays a result of 34098.00, what time is it? How can you tell?

3. Describe situations where freezing titles would be appropriate.

4. If you use the function =DATE(93,5,9), what does the result 34098 indicate?

5. How would you find the total interest paid over the term of a loan? Can you think of more than one way?

Review Exercises

Tracking the Payments of a Home Loan

You are buying a new home that costs $100,000. You are putting $20,000 down and financing $80,000. Create a spreadsheet that answers the following questions.

1. What is the monthly payment on a $80,000 loan at an 8.50 percent interest rate over a 30-year term?

2. After making payments for 10 years, what would your payoff amount be? In your amortization schedule, apply a bold style to the row (payment #120) that contains the payoff amount.

3. After completely paying off the loan in 30 years, how much will you have paid in interest? Place this information at the bottom of the spreadsheet.

4. Many lending institutions offer a 15-year term. How much more is your monthly payment with a 15-year term than with a 30-year term? Place this information somewhere at the top of the spreadsheet.

5. Save the spreadsheet as *Home Loan*. Print the spreadsheet.

Finding the Best Car Loan

An alternative method for finding the total amount paid in interest on a loan is to subtract the original principal from the product of the monthly payment and the term in months:

```
Interest Paid = (Monthly Payment * Term in Months) - Original
        Principal
```

For example, if you have a loan amount of $10,000, a monthly payment of $224.98, and a term of 5 years, the formula to find the interest paid is as follows:

```
Interest Paid = (224.98 * (5 * 12)) - 10,000
            =3498.762935
            =$3,498.76
```

Assume that you need a car loan for $8,000. Various lending institutions have made the following offers.

Federal National Bank		The Credit Union	
Principal	$9,000	Principal	$9,000
Interest Rate	9.00%	Interest Rate	8.00%
Term in Years	5	Term in Years	6
Monthly Payment	?	Monthly Payment	?
Total Interest Paid	?	Total Interest Paid	?
First Payment Due	12/7/96	First Payment Due	11/28/96

Joe's Car Dealership	
Principal	$8,000
Interest Rate	14.50%
Term in Years	5
Monthly Payment	?
Total Interest Paid	?
First Payment Due	11/14/96

Notice that Joe's Car Dealership, where you will buy the car, will sell you the car for $8,000 instead of $9,000 if you take the dealership's loan at a 14.50 percent interest rate.

Use the preceding information to create a spreadsheet that answers the following questions:

1. What is the monthly payment for each loan?

2. What is the total amount of interest paid when you reach the term of each loan?

3. For each lending institution, use the DATE function to enter the first payment due.

4. Place the current date at the top of the spreadsheet by using the NOW function.

5. Is it better to take a loan from Federal National Bank or Joe's Car Dealership? Why?

6. Save the spreadsheet as *Car Loan*. Print the spreadsheet. Print the spreadsheet again, but this time display the cell formulas.

Assignments

Calculating Miles per Gallon

Create a spreadsheet that tracks miles per gallon for the current month. Place your name in cell A1, and the title "MPG Analysis" in cell A2. Enter the text "Odometer Reading:" in cell A4 and the starting number for the odometer in cell C4. Create six columns with the following headings: Date, Odometer, Gallons, Price, MPG, and $/Mile. Align all column headings to the right.

Use the DATE function to enter the current date in the first row of data. Format the date so it looks like the one in Figure 4.21. In the cell below this, create a formula that increments the date by three days. Copy the formula down the next two rows. Make sure all the dates are formatted.

	A	B	C	D	E	F	G	H
1	Robert Mayton							
2	MPG Analysis							
3								
4	Odometer Reading:		55,001.9					
5								
6	Date	Odometer	Gallons	Price	MPG	$/Mile		
7	12/4/96	55,223.6	12	1.27	18.5	0.07		
8	12/7/96	55,450.2	11	1.26	20.6	0.06		
9	12/10/96	55,600.1	13	1.28	11.5	0.11		
10	12/13/96	55,825.6	11	1.24	20.5	0.06		

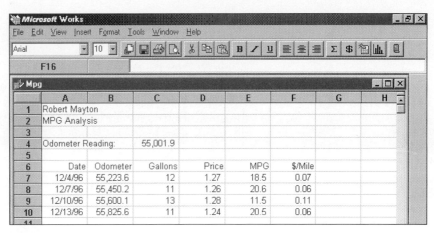

Figure 4.21

Make up odometer readings, gallons, and price per gallon for all four rows of data. Create formulas in the first row of data for MPG and $/Mile and then copy the formulas down the spreadsheet. Save the spreadsheet as *MPG.* Format the spreadsheet as needed so it looks like Figure 4.21.

Calculating the Future Value of an Investment

Assume that you deposit $100 per month into a savings account. After 5 years, how much money will you have in the bank? You need to use the future value (FV) function. The syntax for FV is as follows:

```
FV(monthly investment amount,monthly interest rate,term in
    months)
```

Create the spreadsheet shown in Figure 4.22. Make sure to use your name. Save the spreadsheet as *Investment* and then print it.

	A	B	C	D	E	F
1	Danielle Fobrant					
2	Investment Return					
3						
4	Monthly Investment	$100.00				
5	Yearly Interest Rate	6.00%				
6	Term in Years	5				
7	Total Return	$6,977.00				
8						

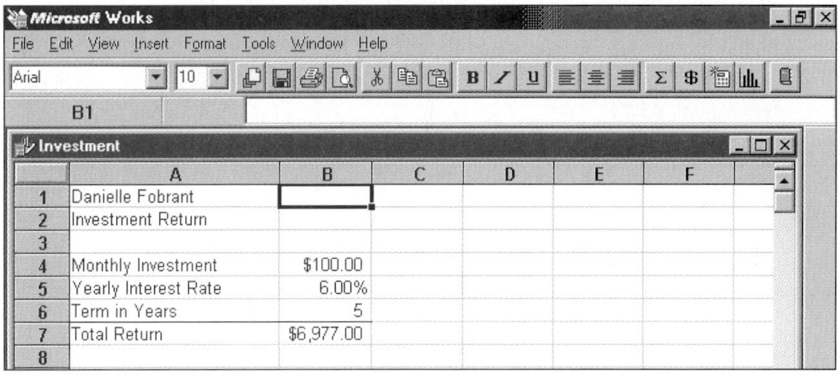

Figure 4.22

Hint: The function in cell B7 will look something like =FV(B4,B5,B6), but this function needs to be modified. The first argument is the monthly investment amount, which in this case is cell B4. The second argument is the monthly interest rate, which in this case is cell B5/12. You need to divide cell B5 by 12 so the yearly interest rate in cell B5 (6.00 percent) becomes a monthly interest rate. The third argument is the term in months, which in this case is cell B6*12. You need to multiply cell B6 (the term in years) by 12 so you get the term in months.

Modifying an Amortization Schedule

Retrieve the file *Amortization Schedule*. Enter 100,000 as the loan principal, 30 years as the term, and 8.45 percent as the interest rate. Edit the spreadsheet by copying formulas down until the loan balance is zero. Save the file as *Amortization Schedule 2*.

ADDITIONAL ASSIGNMENTS

CREATING A CHECKBOOK REGISTER

Create a checkbook register that looks like Figure 4.23.

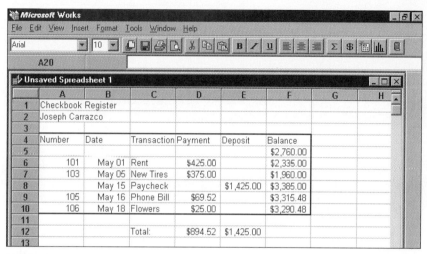

Figure 4.23

1. Use your own checkbook information if possible. Have at least five transactions.

2. Use the NOW function to place the current date in the upper-right corner (not shown in Figure 4.23).

3. Use the DATE function for the transaction dates. Reformat the numbers so they match the figure.

4. Correctly align and format all text and numbers.

5. Create all formulas.

6. Save and print your work.

FINDING CIVIC ARENA REVENUES

The Murrieta Valley Civic Arena is the site of a wide variety of events. The arena has different prices for its three seating areas: loge seats are $12 each, mezzanine seats are $10, and balcony seats are $7.50. In September the arena hosted three events. The number of seats sold in each section for each event is shown in Figure 4.24.

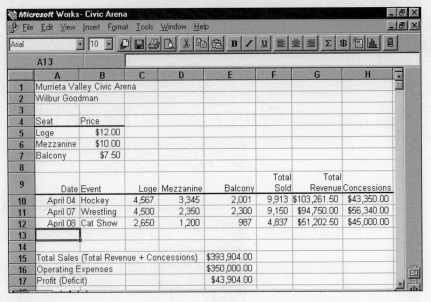

Figure 4.24

1. Create a spreadsheet based on the data in Figure 4.24 that finds the total number of seats sold for each event. Use your name. Use the DATE function for all dates. Align text. Format numbers and dates as needed.

2. Create a formula to calculate total revenues. Enter the formula for the first event and then copy the formula downward.

3. Add one more event in row 13.

4. In cell E15, create a formula to find the total revenue generated by ticket sales and concessions for the month of April.

5. Operating expenses for the month of April were $350,000. In cell E17, determine whether the civic arena made a profit.

6. Save the spreadsheet as *Civic Arena*.

7. Print the spreadsheet.

8. Print the cell formulas.

CREATING A SCHEDULE FOR ARRIVING FLIGHTS

The Ontario International Airport needs someone to develop a computerized system to keep track of arriving flights. The system should show the information provided in Figure 4.25.

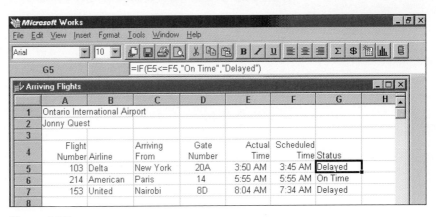

Figure 4.25

1. Create the arrival schedule. Make sure to include your name at the top. Use the TIME function to include time. Use the IF function to display "On Time" if the flight is on time and "Delayed" if the flight is delayed. Note: The IF function is displayed in the formula bar of Figure 4.25.

2. Add three more flights of your own choosing.

3. Save your work as *Arriving Flights.*

4. Print the spreadsheet.

5. Print the cell formulas.

TERM PAPER PROJECT

TRACKING SVENLAND'S FISH EXPORTS

The main source of income on the island of Svenland is the sale of fish, primarily cod, haddock, redfish, catfish, and arctic halibut. Use the following guidelines to create a spreadsheet that describes fish exports to Svenland's main trading partners, the United States, Britain, and France.

1. From the student data disk, open the spreadsheet file *Svenland*, or type the spreadsheet shown in Figure 4.26.

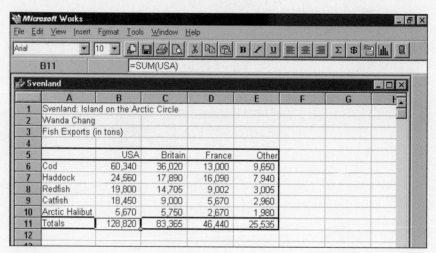

Figure 4.26

2. Use your name instead of Wanda Chang's.

3. Align all column headings on the right.

4. Apply the Comma format, without decimal places, to all numbers.

5. Widen any column that needs it.

6. Use range names to name each column of figures up to the line. You will have four range names with five cells each. For example, the first range can be named USA and would have the range B6 to B10.

7. Use the SUM function and the range names to find the totals for each column.

8. Save the spreadsheet, assigning it the name *Svenland*. You should already have the word processing file *Svenland* on your disk. Notice that you will have two files called *Svenland*. One is a spreadsheet and the other is a word processing document.

9. Print the spreadsheet.

10. To document your work, show all the formulas in the spreadsheet and then print it again.

PART III

Charting

Spreadsheet data is often more easily analyzed when it is represented graphically in a chart. Charts help you decipher trends in data and assist you in forecasting. In addition, charts make a positive impact in reports and presentations. There are several types of charts, some of which are shown in Figure 1.1.

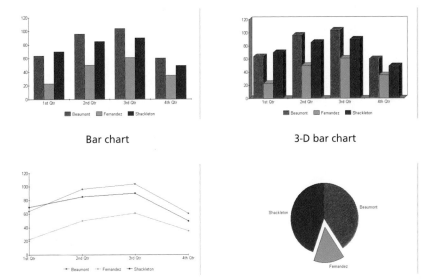

Bar chart   3-D bar chart

Line chart   Pie chart

Figure 1.1

A **bar chart** shows simple comparisons of data at different points in time or for different categories. A **3-D bar chart** is a special type of bar chart that displays data in three dimensions. Both types of bar charts are well suited for presentations, but most people prefer the 3-D bar chart because it looks more professional. A *line chart* is often used to graph the same kinds of data as a bar chart would. The line chart is useful for showing trends over a period of time. A *pie chart* compares each discrete value in a single data series in relation to the whole.

PROJECT 1:   CREATING CHARTS

Objectives

After completing this project, you should be able to:

▶ Sort data

▶ Create bar and 3-D bar charts

▶ Use a chart to ask what-if questions

▶ Name charts

▶ Create a line chart

▶ Add grid lines, data labels, and titles to a chart

▶ Create a pie chart and explode a slice

▶ Save and print charts

CASE STUDY: REPRESENTING SALES WITH CHARTS

As the president of Excellent Vacations, you are always looking for new ways to understand the dynamics of your business. Charts are an effective way of showing relationships among numeric data so the data can be more easily interpreted.

In Works, charts are produced from spreadsheet data. Assume that you have a spreadsheet (see Figure 1.2) that contains the number of vacations sold for three sales associates: Beaumont, Fernandez, and Shackleton. The spreadsheet has data for each quarter of the previous year. You would like to see in which quarter the most vacations were sold and who sold the most vacations for each quarter. You also would like to see whether the general trend is for more or fewer vacations being sold. Also, there is an employee named Fernandez who currently works part-time, and you are considering promoting her to full-time. You would like to concentrate on her data to see whether you can predict what her sales figures would be if she worked full-time.

Designing the Solution

A bar chart, the standard chart in Works, is a good place to start for getting a quick graphical representation of your data. A bar chart will give you a good idea of how many vacations were sold in each quarter and who sold the most. A line chart will show you whether the overall general trend is for more or fewer vacations being sold. A pie chart will enable you to concentrate on one particular quarter and one particular salesperson within that quarter.

All of Works' chart types can be enhanced by adding titles, changing the formatting, or performing a variety of other operations. Charts, like spreadsheets, can be previewed and printed.

OPENING AN EXISTING SPREADSHEET

There is no separate charting tool in Works, so charts are created in the Spreadsheet tool. This module is available with a student data disk. Perform the following steps only if you have access to the student data disk.

To open the student data file Vacations Sold:

1 If you haven't done so already, start Works.

2 Open the student data file *Vacations Sold*.

3 Replace Bob R. Mayton's name with your own.

4 Save the file.

Perform the following steps if you do not have the student data disk.

To create a new spreadsheet named Vacations Sold:

1 If you haven't done so already, start Works.

2 Open the Spreadsheet tool.

3 Create the spreadsheet shown in Figure 1.2. Replace Bob R. Mayton's name with your own.

4 Save the file as *Vacations Sold*.

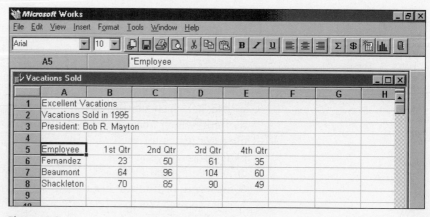

	A	B	C	D	E	F	G	H
1	Excellent Vacations							
2	Vacations Sold in 1995							
3	President: Bob R. Mayton							
4								
5	Employee	1st Qtr	2nd Qtr	3rd Qtr	4th Qtr			
6	Fernandez	23	50	61	35			
7	Beaumont	64	96	104	60			
8	Shackleton	70	85	90	49			
9								

Figure 1.2

SORTING DATA BEFORE CHARTING

Although sorting spreadsheet data is not absolutely necessary to create a chart, charted data is often clearer when placed in *ascending order* (in sequence from lowest to highest) or *descending order* (in sequence from highest to lowest).

To sort the list of employee names:

1 Select the range A6:E8, as shown in Figure 1.3.
Be sure not to select column headings when doing a sort.

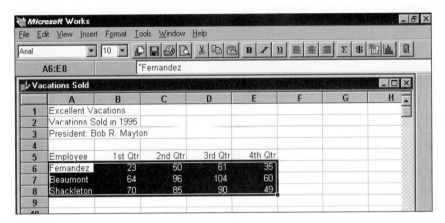

Figure 1.3

2 Choose Sort from the Tools menu.
You should see the dialog box shown in Figure 1.4. If you see a dialog box that says "First-time Help," select OK, and then you will see Figure 1.4.

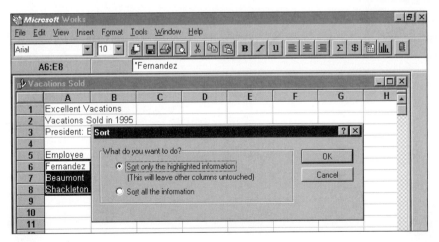

Figure 1.4

3 Select OK in the dialog box.

You should see another dialog box, as shown in Figure 1.5. Notice that the box labeled 1st Column contains the letter *A*. Works assumes that you want to sort the selected rows by column A. From this dialog box, you can also choose the sort order, either ascending or descending, and whether or not your list contains a header row (column headings).

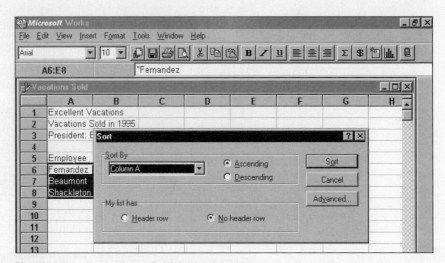

Figure 1.5

4 Select Sort to perform the sort.

The rows should now be sorted alphabetically in ascending order, as shown in Figure 1.6.

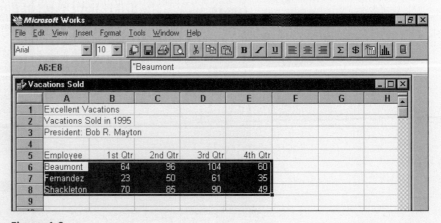

Figure 1.6

CREATING A BAR CHART

A bar chart, the default chart in Works, shows variations in data over a period of time or displays comparisons among data items. You will create a simple bar chart to display the sales figures for the three travel agents.

To create a bar chart:

1 Select the range A5:E8, which contains the data to use in building the chart.

2 Choose Create New Chart from the Tools menu.
The New Chart dialog box shown in Figure 1.7 should appear (a different chart type may be selected in the Chart Type section on the screen). If you see a dialog box that says "First-time Help," select OK, and then you will see Figure 1.7.

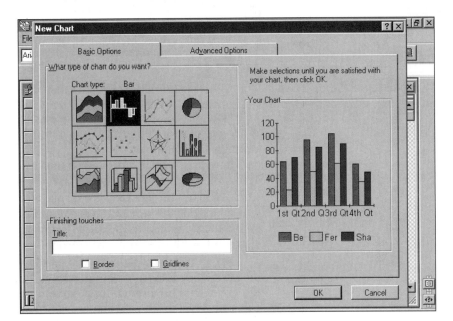

Figure 1.7

3 Make sure the selected chart type is Bar.

4 Select OK to create the chart.
You should see a bar chart like the one in Figure 1.8.

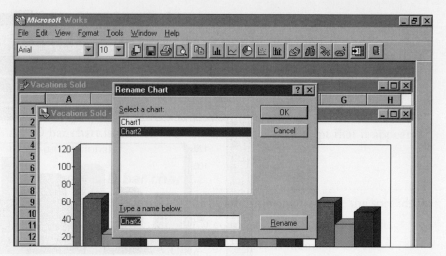

Figure 1.14

2 Select Chart1 as the chart to rename.

3 Press (TAB) to move the insertion point to where you can type a new name.

4 Type **Number Sold**
5 Select Rename to complete the command.
The first chart is now named Number Sold, as indicated in the list of charts shown in Figure 1.15.

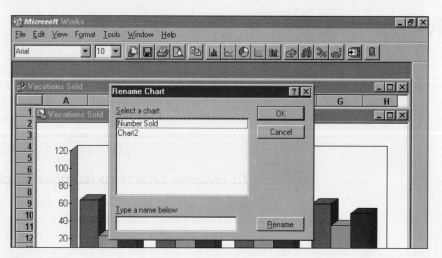

Figure 1.15

6 Select Chart2 as the next chart to rename.

7 Press (TAB) to move the insertion point into the Type a Name Below text box.

8 Type **Number Sold 3-D** and then select Rename.
You should see Number Sold 3-D in the list of charts.

9 Select OK to close the dialog box.

10 Choose Spreadsheet from the View menu to display the spreadsheet.

Creating a Line Chart

Line charts show trends or changes in data over a period of time. Line charts are better than bar charts for displaying the transition from one *data point* to another. A data point is the exact point for a single numeric quantity. In addition, line charts are effective when there are many continuous data points, because the bars in a bar chart can become very narrow and difficult to discern.

To create a line chart:

1 Select the range A5:E8, which contains the data for the chart.

2 Choose Create New Chart from the Tools menu.
The New Chart dialog box appears.

3 Select Line in the Chart Type section, as shown in Figure 1.16.

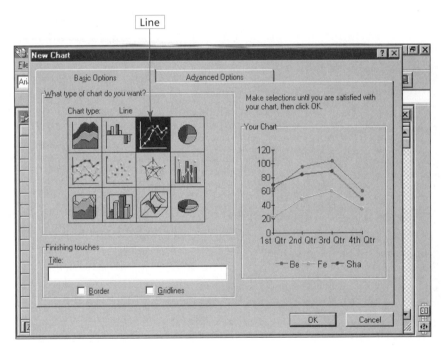

Figure 1.16

4 Select OK to create the chart.
The chart shown in Figure 1.17 appears.

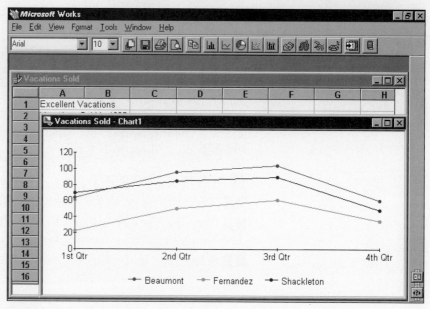

Figure 1.17

Each line in Figure 1.17 represents a row, or data series, from the spreadsheet. On a color screen, the lines will be displayed in different colors. If you are using a monochrome monitor, the lines will be all the same color, but the data points in each data series will be represented by different shapes. Notice how the lines in Figure 1.17 display the fluctuations in the number of vacations sold over the course of four quarters.

To rename the line chart:

1 Choose Rename Chart from the Tools menu.

2 Rename Chart1 *Trends* and then select OK.

ENHANCING A CHART

Works gives you a lot of control over the appearance of charts. You can use commands in the Edit and Format menus to clarify or emphasize chart data and make data analysis easier.

Adding Grid Lines

Grid lines are horizontal lines that guide your eye across the chart and make it easier to determine data point values.

To add y-axis grid lines:

1 Choose Vacations Sold-Number Sold from the Window menu. You should see a bar chart.

2 Select Vertical (Y) Axis from the Format menu. The Format Vertical Axis dialog box shown in Figure 1.18 appears. In addition to specifying grid lines, you can change the scaling of the *y*-axis. The minimum is the lowest number that is displayed on the *y*-axis, the

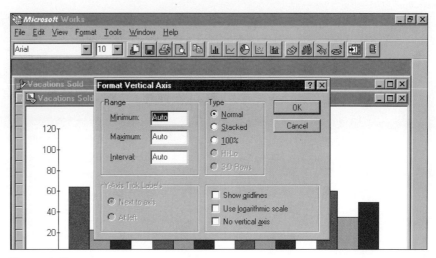

Figure 1.18

maximum is the largest number, and the interval is the amount that Works adds to each number on the scale to determine the next number.

3 Select the Show Gridlines box to add grid lines to the chart.

4 Select OK to complete the command.
You should see dashed, horizontal grid lines, as shown in Figure 1.19.

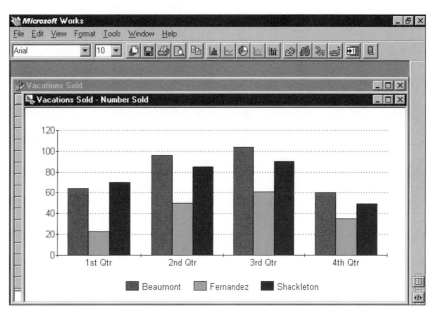

Figure 1.19

Specifying Data Labels

Data labels indicate the precise value of data points. Works places data labels above the points they identify.

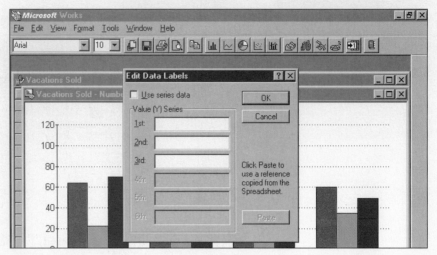

Figure 1.20

To create data labels for the first y-axis data series:

1 Choose Data Labels from the Edit menu.
The dialog box shown in Figure 1.20 appears.

2 Select Use Series Data to use the data as the labels.
A checkmark should appear and the Y series boxes should be dimmed.

3 Select OK to complete the command.
You should see data labels above all data points, as shown in Figure 1.21.

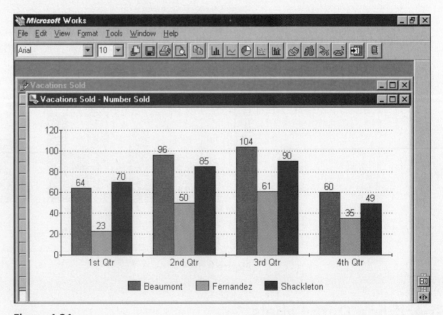

Figure 1.21

Adding Titles

When you create a chart from an area that has text in its rows and columns, Works automatically adds the text to the chart as legends and category labels. Works automatically creates a legend using the first column of the selected spreadsheet, and it creates category labels using the first row of the selected spreadsheet. You also can add text such as a chart title, a subtitle, an *x*-axis title, and a *y*-axis title.

To add titles to a chart:

1 Choose Titles from the Edit menu.
The dialog box shown in Figure 1.22 appears.

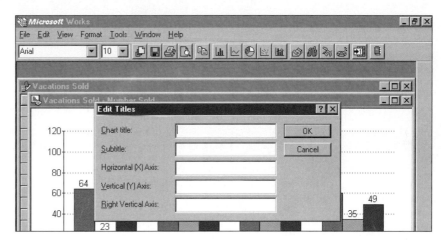

Figure 1.22

2 For the chart title, type **Excellent Vacations** and then press ⊂TAB⊃

3 For the subtitle, type **Vacations Sold in 1995** and then press ⊂TAB⊃

4 For the *x*-axis, type **Quarters** and then press ⊂TAB⊃

5 For the *y*-axis, type **Number Sold** and then select OK.
You should see a chart with four titles, as shown in Figure 1.23.

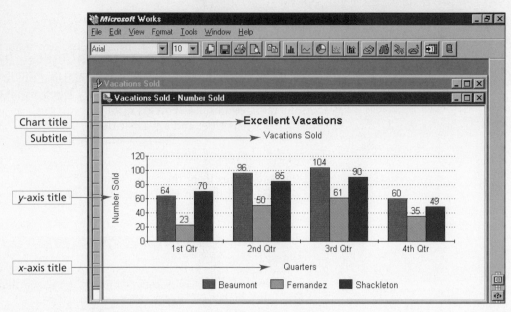

Figure 1.23

CREATING A PIE CHART

Pie charts use data from only one data series. Each individual value from the data series is represented as a slice of pie. The slices are labeled as a percentage of the whole pie. You will create a pie chart that depicts the percentage of vacations sold by each employee in the first quarter. Beaumont sold 40.8 percent of all vacations, or 64 out of 157; Shackleton sold 44.6 percent, or 70 out of 157; and Fernandez sold 14.6 percent, or 23 out of 157. You do not have to calculate the percentages yourself, because Works automatically does so when you create a pie chart.

You will specify only one data series for a pie chart. Your pie chart will show how the employee sales figures relate to each other for the first quarter.

To create a pie chart:

1 Make sure the spreadsheet is the active window.

2 Select the range A6:B8, as shown in Figure 1.24.

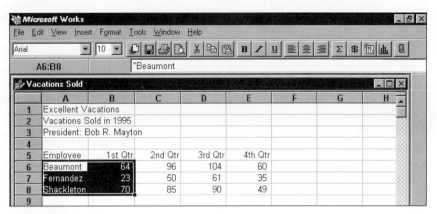

Figure 1.24

The employee names are automatically used as labels of the pie. The numbers determine how big the pie slices are. Notice that you have only one data series, the numbers from the first quarter.

3 Choose Create New Chart from the Tools menu.
The New Chart dialog box appears.

4 Select Pie from the Chart Type section, as shown in Figure 1.25.

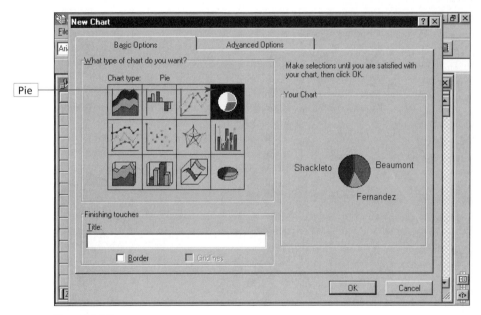

Figure 1.25

5 Select OK to create the pie chart.
You should see the pie chart shown in Figure 1.26.

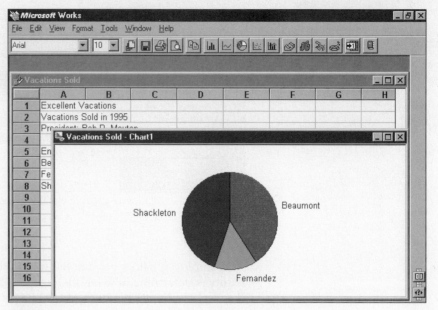

Figure 1.26

6 Choose the Tools menu and then rename the new chart *1st Qtr Sales.* The slices of the pie contain the names of the individuals, but no numbers appear. Percentages can be added by using the Format menu.

To add percentages to the pie slices:

1 Choose Chart Type from the Format menu.

2 Select the Variations tab.

3 Select the last chart option in the Chart Type section, as shown in Figure 1.27.

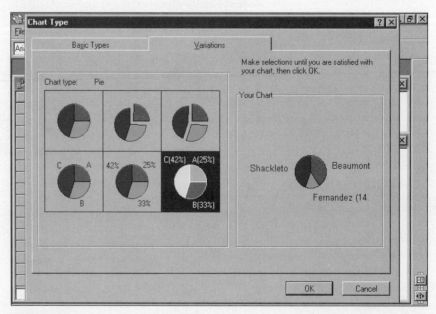

Figure 1.27

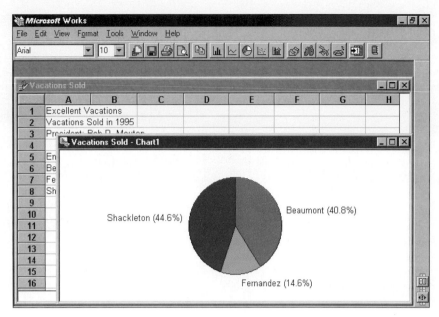

Figure 1.28

4 Select OK to complete the command.
The chart shown in Figure 1.28 appears. Notice the percentages next to each pie slice.

EXPLODING A SLICE OF THE PIE CHART

To emphasize a slice of the pie chart, you can *explode,* or pull out, a piece of pie. Usually, you will pull out only one slice of pie, but you can also explode multiple slices. Assume that you are considering giving Fernandez a raise and want to examine her sales data more closely.

To explode the Fernandez slice:

1 Choose Shading and Color from the Format menu.
You should see the dialog box shown in Figure 1.29. In addition to exploding a slice of pie, you can set a slice's color and pattern.

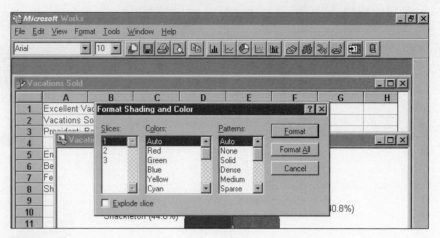

Figure 1.29

2 Select 2 in the Slices list box to explode this slice.

3 Select the Explode Slice check box.
A checkmark should appear.

4 Select Format to confirm the new format.

5 Select Close to indicate that you have finished.
Figure 1.30 shows the pie slice exploded. The exploded slice draws your attention and emphasizes Fernandez's sales figures.

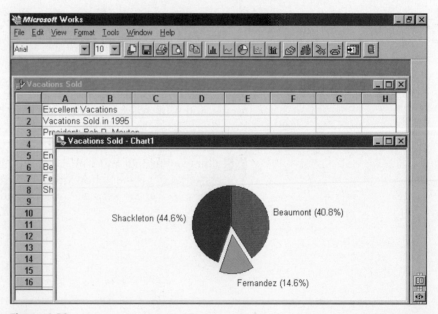

Figure 1.30

 To save all the charts along with the spreadsheet Vacation Sold:

1 Choose Save from the File menu.
All charts are saved within the file *Vacation Sold*.

PRINTING CHARTS

You know how the chart looks on the screen. Now you will get a preview of how it will appear on the printed page. Charts should be printed in landscape orientation, or sideways on a page. A portrait orientation prints charts vertically. The portrait orientation tends to abnormally stretch a chart vertically to fit the page.

To set landscape orientation:

1 Choose Chart from the View menu.

2 Select Number Sold as the active chart and then select OK.

3 Choose Page Setup from the File menu.

4 Select the Source, Size & Orientation tab.

5 Select Landscape and then select OK.
The chart will print sideways.

6 Choose Print Preview from the File menu.
A preview similar to Figure 1.31 appears.

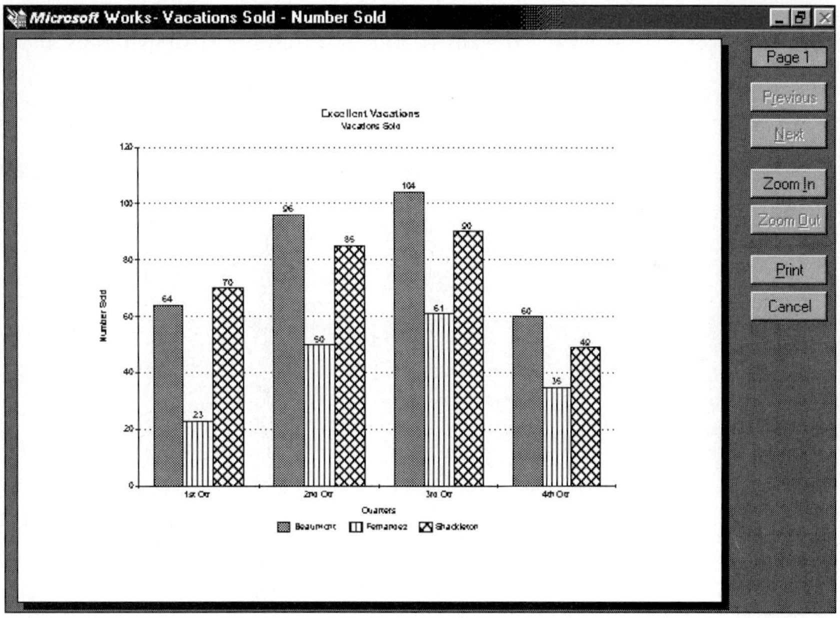

Figure 1.31

7 Select Cancel to close the preview.

If your chart looks okay, it is ready to print. If not, go back through the exercise and see whether you can identify and fix problems.

To print the chart:

1 Choose Print from the File menu.

2 Select OK to print the chart.

You also need to print the rest of the charts you created in this project. The charts should be printed in landscape mode.

To print the rest of the charts:

1 Select and print each chart.
Make sure you use landscape mode for each chart.

2 Save the spreadsheet again so you do not lose all your modifications.

3 When you have finished printing all charts, switch back to the spreadsheet.

4 Close the file using the Close command in the File menu.

THE NEXT STEP

Charting is a powerful feature of Works. Visually representing data in a chart helps readers to quickly understand relationships among numeric data. In addition, charts can be copied into Works word processing documents, giving reports another means of communicating information to readers.

As seen in this project, charts can be used to quickly conduct what-if analyses. A pie chart created from a spreadsheet of monthly expenses will allow you to see how factors such as an increase in rent or car insurance will change the percentage each consumes of your monthly income. A line chart of each semester's GPA will allow you to visually see your progress in school.

This concludes Project 1 with the charting feature. You can either exit Works or go on to work the Study Questions, Review Exercises, and Assignments and the Term Paper Project.

SUMMARY AND EXERCISES

Summary

- A bar chart is the default chart type in Works. Bar charts show variations in data over a period of time or display comparisons among data items.
- A 3-D bar chart looks three-dimensional.
- The *x*-axis is organized by categories and the *y*-axis is scaled to measure data.
- Category labels and legends are automatically displayed in a chart if you include them in the chart data range.
- Charts are saved automatically when the associated spreadsheet is saved.
- What-if questions are often more easily analyzed with charts than with normal spreadsheet data.
- Charts are automatically named Chart1, Chart2, Chart3, and so on, but you can change these names.

- You can enhance a chart by adding grid lines that guide your eye across the chart, data labels that indicate the precise value of data points, and titles that describe the chart.
- You can emphasize slices of a pie chart by exploding them.
- Many people think charts look better if printed in landscape orientation.

Key Terms and Operations

Key Terms	Operations
ascending order	Add a title
bar chart	Add data labels
category label	Add grid lines
data label	Create a bar chart
data point	Create a line chart
data series	Create a pie chart
descending order	Create a 3-D bar chart
explode (a pie slice)	Define a data series
grid lines	Explode a pie slice
legend	Name a chart
line chart	Sort data
pie chart	
3-D bar chart	
x-axis	
y-axis	

Study Questions

Multiple Choice

1. How are charts saved in Works?
   a. Charts are saved by selecting the option to save the chart.
   b. A chart is saved when it is named.
   c. Charts are automatically saved when created.
   d. Charts are saved when a spreadsheet containing any charts is updated.

2. Which type of chart is best suited for showing trends over time?
   a. pie chart
   b. area chart
   c. line chart
   d. bar chart

3. Which of the following serves as a key to identify data series of a chart?
   a. title
   b. legend
   c. label
   d. grid lines

4. Horizontal or vertical lines used to assist the reader in interpreting a chart are called:
   a. titles.
   b. legends.
   c. labels.
   d. grid lines.

5. Which type of chart can have only one data series?
   a. pie chart
   b. area chart
   c. line chart
   d. bar chart

6. Charts are named using which menu?
   a. File
   b. Edit
   c. Format
   d. Tools

7. What sort orders are available in Works?
   a. ascending
   b. descending
   c. prescending
   d. Both a and b.

8. What must be done before a chart can be created?
   a. The spreadsheet file must be saved to disk.
   b. Any other Works documents, such as those created with the Word Processing tool, must be closed.
   c. The spreadsheet must be in chart view.
   d. A range of cells must be selected.

9. Which of the following menus can be used to switch from the spreadsheet to a chart or vice versa?
   a. File
   b. Window
   c. File and Window
   d. View and Window

10. Numbers above data points are called:
    a. data series.
    b. data labels.
    c. data-point text.
    d. number points.

Short Answer

1. The vertical axis is called the _____.

2. The default chart in Works is the _____.

3. To emphasize a particular slice of a pie chart, you can _____ it.

4. When data is arranged from highest value to lowest value, it sorted in _____ order.

5. Lines added to a chart that help guide your eye across the page are called _____.

6. The _____-axis is organized by categories.

7. All charts that have been defined within the current spreadsheet are listed in the _____ menu.

8. A(n) _____ is the precise location for a single numeric quantity.

9. The first chart that you create is automatically named _____.

10. Charts generally look better if they are printed in _____ orientation.

For Discussion

1. Explain the difference between a bar chart and a 3-D bar chart.

2. When would you use a line chart?

3. Why would you want to sort data to be charted?

4. Describe how to change the scale of the axes.

5. Describe how the chart-view menus are different from the spreadsheet-view menus.

Review Exercises

Creating a Bar Chart for Motor Vehicle Production

The data shown in Figure 1.32 describes world motor vehicle production from 1989 to 1992.

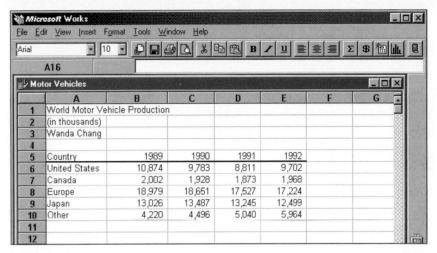

Figure 1.32

1. Create a spreadsheet that consists of the data in Figure 1.32.

2. Use your name in the spreadsheet instead of Wanda Chang's.

3. Create a bar chart.

4. Include a chart title.

5. Use your name as the subtitle.

6. Add grid lines.

7. Give the chart a name other than Chart1.

8. Save the spreadsheet.

9. Print the spreadsheet.

10. Print the chart in landscape orientation.

Creating a Pie Chart of Physician Expenses

The data shown in Figure 1.33 describes the average expenses in 1984 for self-employed physicians.

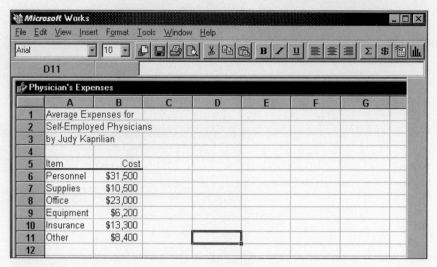

Figure 1.33

1. Create a spreadsheet of the data in Figure 1.33. Be sure to use your name instead of Judy Kaprilian's.

2. Sort the items in ascending order.

3. Create a pie chart with percentages and item names next to each slice.

4. Explode the insurance slice.

5. Modify the spreadsheet to answer this question: What if insurance were $36,000? Display the chart.

6. Change the insurance back to $13,300.

7. Give the chart a title.

8. Save the spreadsheet and chart.

9. Print the spreadsheet.

10. Print the chart in landscape orientation and then portrait orientation.

Assignments

Charting Personal Expenses

Create a spreadsheet that keeps track of your personal monthly expenses. For example, you can put down how much you spend on rent, food, leisure activities, and so on.
Create a pie chart that shows in each slice of the pie what percentage of your money goes toward rent, food, leisure, and so on. Use your name as the title of the chart.
Print and save the spreadsheet and chart.

Charting Civic Arena Revenues

Retrieve the file *Civic Arena*. Create a 3-D bar chart of the loge seats, mezzanine seats, and balcony seats for each event. Include grid lines. Name the chart *Seating Comparison*. Save the spreadsheet. Print the chart.

Charting Television Shows and Commercials

Watch a typical half-hour or one-hour television show. Use your watch to time the length of all commercials. Create a spreadsheet that displays the amount of time spent on commercials and the amount of time spent on the actual show. The total amount of time should add up to 30 minutes or 60 minutes. Create a pie chart that displays the percentage of time spent on commercials and the percentage of time spent on the actual show. Print the chart. Save the file as *Television Time*.

TERM PAPER PROJECT

CREATING CHARTS OF SVENLAND'S FISH EXPORTS

In the previous term paper project, you created a spreadsheet describing Svenland's fish exports. Now you will create a bar chart of fish exports to the United States, Britain, France, and the other trading partners. You also will create a pie chart that depicts the foreign sales of cod, Svenland's main fish export, to each country.

To create a bar chart:

1 Open the spreadsheet file *Svenland*, which you developed in the previous term paper project.

2 Create a bar chart that has the fish categories as the *x*-axis and the names of countries as legends.
You will have five *x*-axis labels, one each for five kinds of fish: cod, haddock, redfish, catfish, and arctic halibut. The legends will be *U.S.A., Britain, France*, and *Other*.

3 For the chart title, type `Fish Exports,` and for the subtitle, type your name.

4 Create appropriate titles for the *x*-axis and *y*-axis.

5 Name the chart *Fish Exports*.

6 Save the spreadsheet as *Svenland*.

7 Print the chart.

To create a pie chart:

1 Select the range of cells that consists of the column headings and the export figures for cod.
You should select a total of eight cells.

2 Create a new pie chart.

3 For the chart title, type `Cod Exports,` and for the subtitle, type your name.

4 Name the chart *Cod Exports*.

5 Save the spreadsheet as *Svenland*.

6 Print the chart.

PART IV

Database Management

Aprogram that manages databases is called a ***database management system (DBMS).*** The Database tool in Works is a DBMS that enables you to add, edit, delete, search for, and sort data. In addition, you can summarize data and print it. The Works Database tool is not quite powerful enough to manage the record-keeping tasks of a large corporation such as General Motors or Mobil, but it is well-suited for meeting the database needs of smaller organizations or individual users.

Databases are structured to allow swift access to information. A telephone directory, a list of videos in a video store, and personnel files in a payroll department are all typical examples of databases. In a telephone book, telephone numbers and addresses can be easily accessed when you understand the simple structure of the directory: People are listed alphabetically according to last name.

Figure 1.1 contains part of a database that is used by the River View Resort, a bed-and-breakfast inn, emphasizing personalized service.

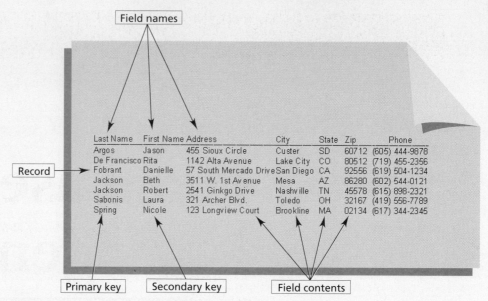

Figure 1.1

As individuals book reservations, their names are entered under Last Name and First Name. Other pertinent details are entered under adjacent headings, to create a row of data for each guest. In each column, each slot for data is called a *field*. Fields are referred to by field names, which, in Figure 1.1, are displayed as column headings. The data entered in each field are called the *field contents*. Each group of fields that share a common element—or each row, in the case of Figure 1.1—is called a *record*.

Not all collections of records are databases. A database record must include a *key*, which is a field that uniquely identifies each record—in other words, a field that identifies only one record. In Figure 1.1, the Last Name field contains data that uniquely identifies each patron. If two patrons happen to have the same last name, you can use a secondary key, such as First Name, to identify each individual.

Objectives

After completing this project, you should be able to:

▶ Use the database screen

▶ Design a form

▶ Enter and edit data

▶ Enhance the form design

▶ Add records

▶ Print a form

CASE STUDY: BUILDING A DATABASE FOR THE RIVER VIEW RESORT

The River View Resort is a small bed-and-breakfast that emphasizes personalized service. Recently a computer was purchased for the administrative office, and, as the manager, you have been instructed by the owners to design a database to keep track of each guest who visits the resort. The database needs to include name and address information and also should provide the ability to calculate the amount guests owe when they check out. Figure 1.2 shows how the first record of the bed-and-breakfast database could be placed onto an index card.

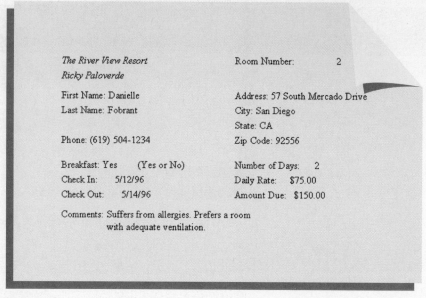

The River View Resort   Room Number: 2
Ricky Paloverde

First Name: Danielle   Address: 57 South Mercado Drive
Last Name: Fobrant   City: San Diego
                                          State: CA
Phone: (619) 504-1234   Zip Code: 92556

Breakfast: Yes   (Yes or No)   Number of Days: 2
Check In: 5/12/96   Daily Rate: $75.00
Check Out: 5/14/96   Amount Due: $150.00

Comments: Suffers from allergies. Prefers a room
                with adequate ventilation.

Figure 1.2

Designing the Solution

A database should be carefully planned to ensure that it meets your needs—both now and in the future. You should begin by determining what information is needed for each guest. In addition, you will need to consider how information from the database will be reported. For instance, if you want to print an alphabetical list of all guests by last name, Last Name will need to be a key field. Therefore, each guest's name will consist of two fields: First Name and Last Name.

Because the database will include information pertaining to the length of each guest's stay and the daily rate the guest is charged, the database can include a *calculated field,* which is a field that uses numeric data within a record to determine a value. This database will use the check-in and check-out dates to determine the length of each patron's stay. This data is multiplied by the daily rate to determine the amount due.

Finally, before data can be entered into a database, a *database structure* must be established. The database structure consists of the data fields. Data fields are usually given a field name, and a length for each field is set. After the structure is created, data can be entered into the database.

There are several ways to view a database. In *Form view,* you will see only one record on the screen at a time, much like how you view information written on a 3- by 5-inch card. *Form Design view* is the view you will use to design and edit the structure of a form.

In *List view,* Works displays multiple records on-screen in a column-and-row format, much like in the Spreadsheet tool. Figure 1.3 shows the grid that is used to designate fields and records in List view. Field names appear as column headings near the top of the screen. List view is the Works default database view. *Report view* enables you to design a report that displays data in more detail than the list in List view.

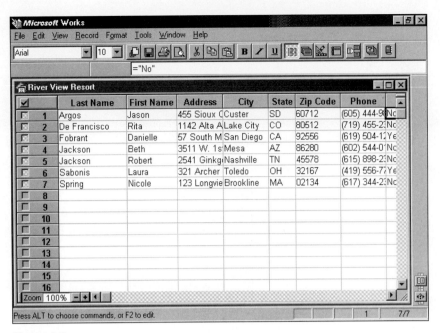

Figure 1.3

STARTING A NEW DATABASE

Assume you are the manager of the River View Resort. In this project you will create, edit, and print several records in a database of people who are planning a stay at the resort.

If at any time you are asked for First-time Help, you can select OK to bypass the dialog box. As you perform the numbered steps, you will never need First-time Help.

Getting Online Help For information about using the Works Database tool, you can choose Contents from the Help menu. Then you can choose Database and then Database Basics. Finally, you can select an appropriate topic from the list.

To create a new database file:

1 Start Works if you haven't done so already.

2 Select the Works Tools tab from within the Works Task Launcher.

3 Select the Database button.
If you get a message that asks whether you need First-time Help, select OK to bypass the message. The screen should look like Figure 1.4.

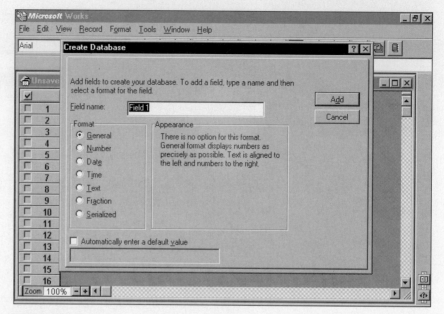

Figure 1.4

In Figure 1.4, Works is asking you to type the name of the first *field name,* or column heading, that will appear on the top of the screen. As you can see in Figure 1.3, the first field name is Last Name.

To type the first few field names:

1 In the Create Database dialog box, type `Last Name` and then press ⟨ENTER⟩
You should see *Field 2* in the dialog box.

2 Type `First Name` for Field 2 and then press ⟨ENTER⟩

3 Type `Address` for Field 3 and then press ⟨ENTER⟩
Table 1.1 contains the rest of the field names you will enter.

Table 1.1

Field	Field Name
Field 4	City
Field 5	State
Field 6	Zip Code
Field 7	Phone
Field 8	Breakfast
Field 9	Room Number
Field 10	Check In
Field 11	Check Out
Field 12	Number of Days
Field 13	Daily Charge
Field 14	Amount Due
Field 15	Comments

To type the rest of the field names:

1 Type all the field names shown in Table 1.1. Be sure to press (ENTER) after typing each name.

2 After typing the last field name, select Done.
The screen should look like Figure 1.5.

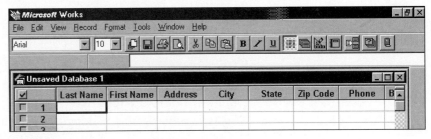

Figure 1.5

Because you have finished entering all the field names, this is a good time to save the database. The database is currently called Unsaved Database 1. You will give it a more descriptive name.

To save the database:

1 Choose Save from the File menu.

2 Within the Save In box, select drive A:.

3 For the file name, type **River View Resort** and then press (ENTER)

ENTERING DATA

After typing all the field names, you will be ready to type the field contents. Danielle Fobrant will be the first visitor at the resort.

Entering Text, Numbers, and Dates

To enter data, you will place the active cell in the desired location and then type the data.

To enter a guest's name:

1 Press (CTRL) + (HOME) to move the active cell to Record 1 under the Last Name field.

2 Type **Fobrant** and press (→)
The cell selector should have moved to the First Name field.

3 Type **Danielle** and then press (ENTER)

The screen should look like Figure 1.6. Notice in the formula bar that Works has inserted a double quotation mark (") to indicate that the field entry is text. Entering text in List view is just like entering text in a spreadsheet.

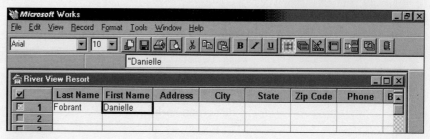

Figure 1.6

To enter Danielle's address and phone number:

1 Press ⊙ to move one cell to the right.

2 In the Address field, type **57 South Mercado Drive** and then press ⊙
Notice that this entry is so long that it spills over into the adjacent column.

3 Type **San Diego** as the city and then press (ENTER)
San Diego should cover most of the street address, as shown in Figure 1.7.
This is okay for now.

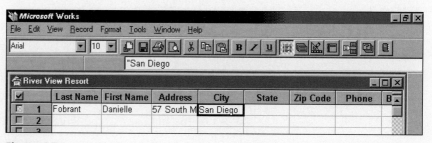

Figure 1.7

4 Press ⊙ to move to the next field.

5 Type **CA** as the state and **"92556** as the zip code.
A quotation mark precedes the Zip Code entry so the entry will be treated
as text and any leading zeros will be displayed.

6 Type **(619) 505-1234** as the phone number.

The entry for the Breakfast field will be Yes or No. The daily charge
for each patron, which you will enter later, will be based upon whether
breakfast is included. The room number will be entered as a number.

To enter data for the Breakfast and Room Number fields:

1 Type **Yes** as the Breakfast field entry and then press ⊙

2 Type **2** as the Room Number entry and then press ⊙

The format day/month/year is used to enter dates as field entries. For
example, you will enter May 10, 1996, as 5/10/96.

To enter the check-in and check-out dates:

1 Type **5/10/96** as the check-in date.

2 Type **5/14/96** as the check-out date.

A field entry is not limited to one word, number, or date. In the Comments field for each patron, you will enter one or more sentences.

To enter a comment:

1 Press → until the cell selector is in the Comments field.
You will enter the number of days, daily charge, and amount due later.

2 In the Comments field, type **Suffers from allergies. Prefers a room with adequate ventilation.** and then press (ENTER)
Remember, if you enter a long string of text, Works will display only the text that fits within the current field. The rest of the text is stored and can be displayed if you widen the field. Notice in Figure 1.8 that the entire comment is visible in the formula bar.

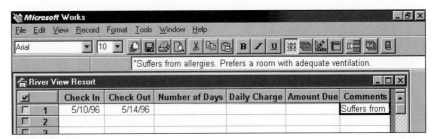

Figure 1.8

Entering a Calculated Field

The contents of the Number of Days and Amount Due fields are entered using formulas; the contents of the Daily Charge field are entered using a function. All these entries must begin with an equal sign, which will cause Works to evaluate the field and repeat the calculation throughout every record in the database.

To find the number of days the patron is staying:

1 Place the active cell in the Number of Days field.

2 Type **=Check Out-Check In** and then press (ENTER)
The screen should look like Figure 1.9. Because you started the cell entry with an equal sign, the entry will be used automatically in the Number of Days field of each record in the database.

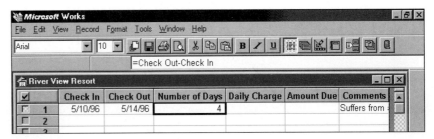

Figure 1.9

The daily charge is determined by whether the patron attends breakfast each day. The charge for a room and breakfast is $75 per night. The charge for a room only is $65 per night. You will use the IF function to determine the daily charge.

To determine the daily charge, the IF function evaluates and provides an answer based on the contents of the Breakfast field. If the Breakfast field contains *Yes*, the daily charge is $75; if the Breakfast field does not contain *Yes*, the daily charge is $65. The IF function is not case-sensitive. The Breakfast field can contain *Yes, YES*, or *yes* and the daily charge will still be $75.

To determine the daily charge:

1 Place the active cell in the Daily Charge field.

2 Type =IF(Breakfast="Yes",75,65) and then press (ENTER)
The screen should look like Figure 1.10.

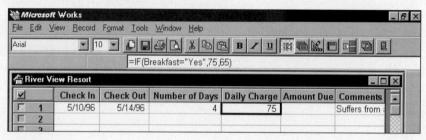

Figure 1.10

The next step is to determine the amount due by multiplying the number of days by the daily charge.

To determine the amount due:

1 Select the Amount Due field.

2 Type =Number of Days*Daily Charge and then press (ENTER)
You should see 300 as the amount due.

USING A FORM

A *form* in Works is similar to a printed form or an index card. Each record is displayed as a single screen of information within Form view. You can select the Form View button on the Toolbar to switch to Form view, as shown later in Figure 1.11.

Before the owner of the River View Resort purchased a computer, the bed-and-breakfast staff kept all customer data on index cards. The owner of the resort would like to have employees enter information into the database by using Form view, not List view. Form view looks a lot like the index cards that the employees are used to.

To move around in Form view, you can use the keyboard or the mouse. Table 1.2 describes how to use the keyboard to move the insertion point. With a mouse, you can move the insertion point by clicking the desired

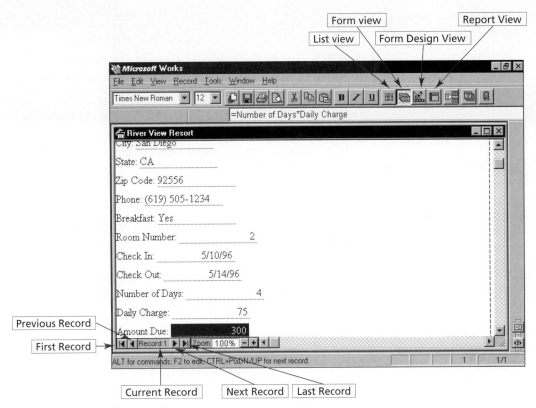

Figure 1.11

location, or you can move among records by clicking the buttons in the lower-left corner of the screen, as shown in Figure 1.11.

Table 1.2

Key(s)	Action
$\downarrow$, $\uparrow$, $\rightarrow$, $\leftarrow$	Moves one position in the direction of the arrow.
TAB	Moves to the next field.
SHIFT + TAB	Moves to the previous field.
PGDN	Moves down one screen.
PGUP	Moves up one screen.
CTRL + PGDN	Moves to the next record.
CTRL + PGUP	Moves to the previous record.
CTRL + HOME	Moves to the first record in the database.
CTRL + END	Moves to a blank form at the end of the database.
F5	Moves to a specified field or record (F5 is called the GoTo key).

Note that the result of pressing PGDN is different from that of pressing CTRL + PGDN. You can use PGDN if the current record does not fit on one screen. Pressing PGDN will move the insertion point one screen down, but the insertion point will remain within the same record. Pressing CTRL + PGDN will move to the next record.

To display a blank record in Form view:

1 Select the Form View button on the Toolbar.
You should see Figure 1.11. Notice that all field names end with a colon and that all field contents are underlined.

2 Select the Next Record button to move to Record 2.
You should see a blank record.

3 Press (↑) to move to the Last Name field.

To enter data into the blank record:

1 For the last name, type **Spring** and then press (TAB)

2 For the first name, type **Nicole** and then press (TAB)

3 Use Table 1.3 to enter the rest of the record. Remember to place a double quotation mark before the zip code. The number of days, daily rate, and amount due will appear automatically.

Table 1.3

Field	Contents
Address	123 Longview Court
City	Brookline
State	MA
Zip Code	02134
Phone	(617) 344-2345
Breakfast	No
Room Number	6
Check In	5/29/96
Check Out	6/2/96
Comments	Visited this time last year. Requests the Patio Room.

EDITING FIELD CONTENTS IN FORM VIEW

To edit field entries you can select the field and then press (F2), the Edit key. Or, you can click the formula bar. Table 1.4 shows the keys you can use to edit data in the formula bar.

Table 1.4

Key	Action
(←)	Moves one character left.
(→)	Moves one character right.
(HOME)	Moves to the beginning of the formula bar.
(END)	Moves to the end of the formula bar.
(BKSP)	Deletes the character to the left of the insertion point.
(DEL)	Deletes the character to the right of the insertion point.

Assume that the phone number for Danielle Fobrant is incorrect.

To change the phone number:

1 Move the insertion point to Record 1.

2 Move the insertion point to Danielle's phone number.

3 Press (F2) to activate the formula bar.

4 Use the arrow keys and the (DEL) or (BKSP) keys to change the phone number to 504-1234.

5 Press (ENTER) to complete the change.

Suppose that the check-in date is also incorrect. When you change the check-in date to 5/12/96, you will note how all cells with dependent formulas, such as the Number of Days, change automatically.

To change the check-in date:

1 Select Danielle's check-in date.

2 Press (F2) and then change the date to 5/12/95.
The Number of Days entry should change to 2, as shown in Figure 1.12.

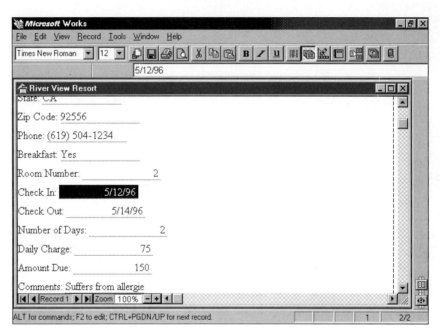

Figure 1.12

ENHANCING THE FORM DESIGN

You can enhance a form in several ways to improve its organization and to ease data entry. An enhanced form is especially important to someone who is unfamiliar with the database and is uncertain about what data to enter in each field.

To enhance the form design you must switch to the Form Design view. Any changes you make in Form Design view will affect the form design for every record in the database.

Modifying Field Names and Sizes

Suppose you decide that the name for the Daily Charge field should be more descriptive.

To change the field name Daily Charge to Daily Rate:

1 Select the Form Design button on the Toolbar.
Check Figure 1.11 if you have forgotten where the Form Design button is on the Toolbar.

2 Select *Daily Charge:*

3 Press (F2) to activate the formula bar.

4 Delete *Charge:*

5 Type **Rate:** and press (ENTER)

Caution   Make sure you add a colon at the end of each field name. The colon indicates to Works that the text is a field name and not plain text.

Your next move is to make the Comments field a little wider and at least two rows high.

To change the size of the Comments field:

1 Select the box to the right of the Comments field.
The box should be selected, as shown in Figure 1.13.

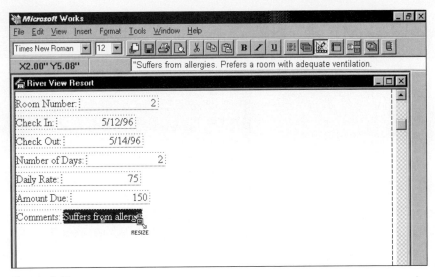

Figure 1.13

2 Place the pointer in the bottom-right corner of the box.
The pointer should change shape and have the word *RESIZE* below it, as
shown in Figure 1.13.

3 Slowly drag the bottom-right corner of the box until it is as large
as the one in Figure 1.14.

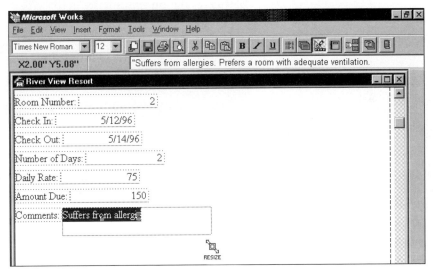

Figure 1.14

4 Release the mouse button.
Notice that the text has wrapped around in the field, as shown in Figure 1.15.

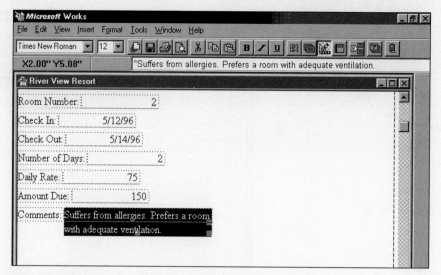

Figure 1.15

You can make fields narrower as well as wider. Many of the fields will look better and conserve space if they are made narrower.

To decrease the width of several fields:

1 Change the widths of the Breakfast, Room Number, Check In, Check Out, Number of Days, Daily Rate, and Amount Due fields so they appear as wide as the ones in Figure 1.16.

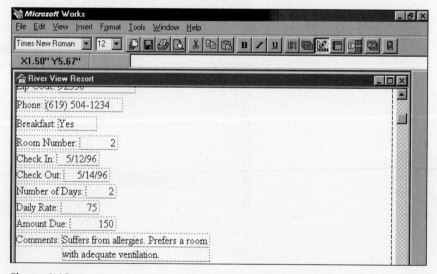

Figure 1.16

You need to change one more field. The street address for Danielle does not fit in the Address field.

To widen the Address field:

1 Make the Address field wider so the entire street address fits. You should see *57 South Mercado Drive.*

If necessary, you can save your file as *River View Resort,* exit Works now, and continue this project later.

Moving Fields

The index cards that the staff at the bed-and-breakfast used to record data did not list all fields in a single column. Fields were grouped and spread apart to improve their organization. For example, the guest's name, address, and phone number were grouped so they were easier to locate. You will move the on-screen fields so the form looks like the cards. The completed form will look like Figure 1.21 (shown later).

Fields can be moved easily by using the Works drag-and-drop feature. Once something is selected, it can be dragged with the mouse to a new location.

To move the street address, city, state, and zip code:

1 Select the Address field name.
The pointer should say *DRAG* underneath it, as shown in Figure 1.17.

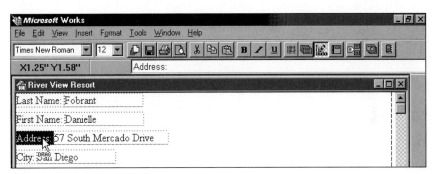

Figure 1.17

2 Drag the field just past the center of the screen and then release the mouse button.
The Address field should have moved as shown in Figure 1.18.

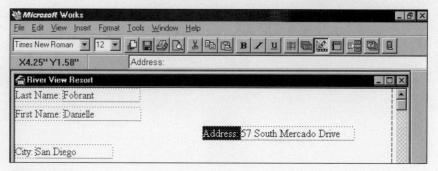

Figure 1.18

3 Move the City, State, and Zip Code fields underneath the Address field, as shown in Figure 1.19.

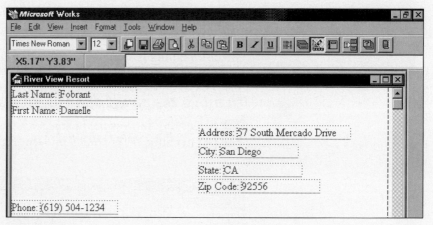

Figure 1.19

The Last Name and First Name fields should be moved to the left of the address.

To move the First Name and Last Name fields:

1 Select the First Name field and drag it straight down next to the Address field.

2 Select the Last Name field and drag it just below the First Name field.

The screen should look like Figure 1.20.

To type the rest of the field names:

1 Type all the field names shown in Table 1.1. Be sure to press **ENTER** after typing each name.

2 After typing the last field name, select Done.
The screen should look like Figure 1.5.

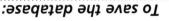

Figure 1.5

Because you have finished entering all the field names, this is a good time to save the database. The database is currently called Unsaved Database 1. You will give it a more descriptive name.

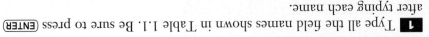

To save the database:

1 Choose Save from the File menu.

2 Within the Save In box, select drive A:.

3 For the file name, type **River View Resort** and then press **ENTER**

ENTERING DATA

After typing all the field names, you will be ready to type the field contents. Danielle Fobrant will be the first visitor at the resort.

Entering Text, Numbers, and Dates

To enter data, you will place the active cell in the desired location and then type the data.

To enter a guest's name:

1 Press **CTRL**+**HOME** to move the active cell to Record 1 under the Last Name field.

2 Type **Fobrant** and press ←
The cell selector should have moved to the First Name field.

3 Type **Danielle** and then press **ENTER**
The screen should look like Figure 1.6. Notice in the formula bar that Works has inserted a double quotation mark ('') to indicate that the field entry is text. Entering text in List view is just like entering text in a spreadsheet.

Figure 1.6

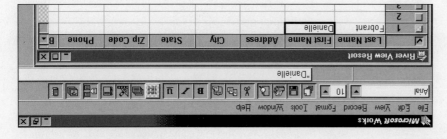

To enter Danielle's address and phone number:

1 Press → to move one cell to the right.

2 In the Address field, type **57 South Mercado Drive** and then press →. Notice that this entry is so long that it spills over into the adjacent column.

3 Type **San Diego** as the city and then press ENTER. *San Diego* should cover most of the street address, as shown in Figure 1.7. This is okay for now.

Figure 1.7

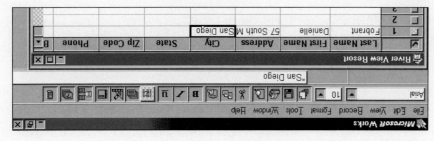

4 Press → to move to the next field.

5 Type **CA** as the state and **"92556** as the zip code. A quotation mark precedes the Zip Code entry so the entry will be treated as text and any leading zeros will be displayed.

6 Type **(619) 505-1234** as the phone number.

The entry for the Breakfast field will be Yes or No. The daily charge for each patron, which you will enter later, will be based upon whether breakfast is included. The room number will be entered as a number.

To enter data for the Breakfast and Room Number fields:

1 Type **Yes** as the Breakfast field entry and then press →.

2 Type **2** as the Room Number entry and then press →.

The format day/month/year is used to enter dates as field entries. For example, you will enter May 10, 1996, as 5/10/96.

To enter the check-in and check-out dates:

1 Type **5/10/96** as the check-in date.

2 Type **5/14/96** as the check-out date.

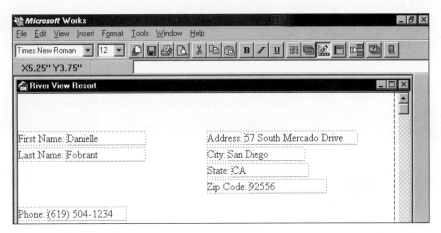

Figure 1.20

Several fields still need to be moved. You can use Figure 1.21 as a guide to structuring the rest of the form.

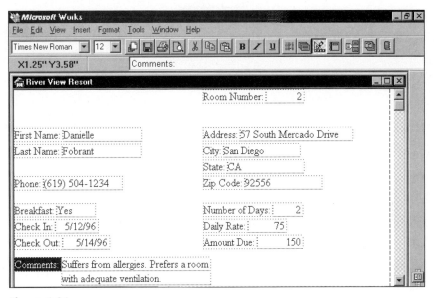

Figure 1.21

 To complete the restructuring of the form:

1 Rearrange the rest of the fields so the form resembles Figure 1.21. Notice that the Room Number field is at the top of the form.

2 Save the file again. Make sure you keep the name as *River View Resort*.

Adding Descriptive Labels

Text labels are text that you use to add descriptions to the form. Works treats text labels as text and not as field names because they do not end with a colon (remember that field names always end with a colon in Form view). In addition, Works automatically inserts a quotation mark before each text label—the quotation mark appears in the formula bar—but does not insert quotation marks before field names.

You need to enter two labels at the top of the form: *The River View Resort* and your name.

To enter two labels at the top of the form:

1 Place the insertion point in the upper-left corner of the form.

2 Type **The River View Resort** and press ⒺⓃⓉⒺⓇ

3 Below the label *The River View Resort,* type your name.

The screen should look like Figure 1.22. Of course, you will see your name rather than Ricky Paloverde's.

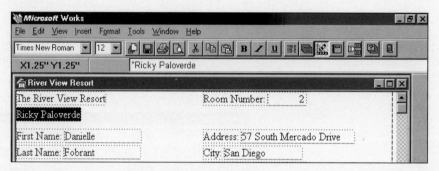

Figure 1.22

Descriptive labels next to field entries help the user know what kind of data to enter. For example, the Breakfast field requires the text *Yes* or *No.* To help prevent data-entry errors in the Breakfast field, you will enter the label *(Yes or No)* next to the field.

To add a descriptive label:

1 Move the insertion point next to the Breakfast field.

2 Type **(Yes or No)** and then press ⒺⓃⓉⒺⓇ

The screen should look like Figure 1.23. Now the user of this form knows that he or she should enter *Yes* or *No.*

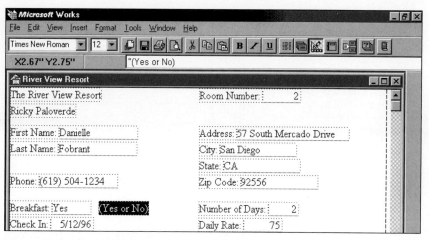

Figure 1.23

Applying Text Styles and Formatting Numbers

Within the Database tool, four character styles are available: bold, underline, italic, and strikethrough. Because the labels at the top of the form serve as titles, you will apply an italic character style to distinguish them from the rest of the text.

To apply an italic character style:

1 Select *The River View Resort* at the top of the form.

2 Select the Italic button on the Toolbar.
The text for the title should be in italics.

3 Apply an italic character style to your name.
The screen should look like Figure 1.24.

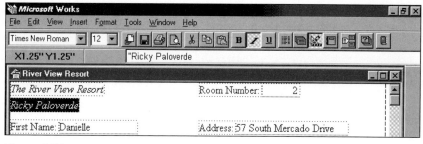

Figure 1.24

Numbers that represent dollar amounts usually stand out more when preceded by a dollar sign ($) and formatted with two decimal places.

To apply the Currency format to the Daily Rate field:

1 Select the box next to the Daily Rate field name.

2 Choose Field from the Format menu.

3 Select Number under Format and the currency option under Appearance, as shown in the dialog box in Figure 1.25.

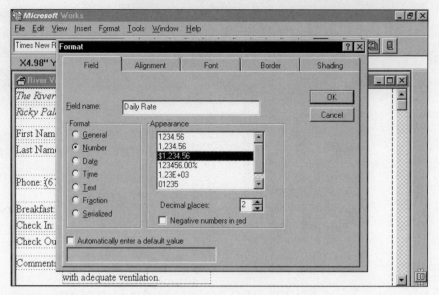

Figure 1.25

4 Select OK to complete the command.

You should see $75.00. If the field is filled with a series of pound (#) signs, drag the field to make it wider.

To apply the currency format to the Amount Due field:

1 Apply a currency format to the Amount Due field.

2 Save the database file, keeping the name *River View Resort*.

You have now finished enhancing the form design. It is wise to save your work often, especially after making changes.

ADDING A RECORD TO A CUSTOMIZED FORM

After you modify the design of a form, you can switch from the Form Design view to the Form view to add more records.

This database needs one more record, as shown in Figure 1.26.

To move to a blank record at the end of the database and type new data:

1 Select the Form View button on the Toolbar.

2 Select the Last Record button to move to a blank record at the end of the database.

If you forget where this button is located, refer to Figure 1.11.

3 Type the record shown in Figure 1.26.

Remember from Table 1.2 that you can move from one field to the next by pressing (TAB). Pressing (SHIFT) + (TAB) will move the insertion point to previous fields. You should not type calculated fields, because they will appear automatically.

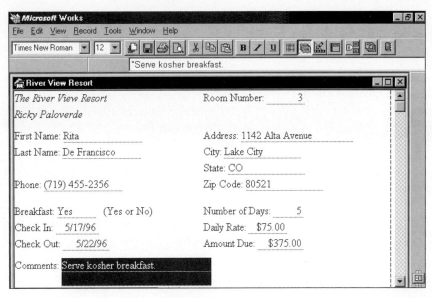

Figure 1.26

PRINTING IN FORM VIEW

Form view is good for printing one record at a time, especially as an invoice or a receipt.

To print the first record:

1 Choose Print from the File menu.

The dialog box shown in Figure 1.27 appears. Because the All Records option is selected in the figure, all records will be printed. When you want to print only the current record, select Current Record Only. You'll print all the records this time.

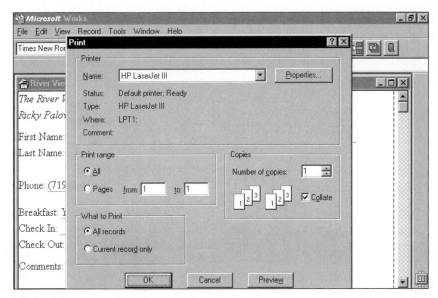

Figure 1.27

2 Select OK to print the records.

3 Save your database file again.

THE NEXT STEP

In this project you created a database that contains text, date, and numeric data. The Breakfast field contains either a yes or no entry that is used to determine the daily rate, and calculated fields determine the length of stay and the amount due.

Think of similar databases you could design. For instance, a video store database could include a field indicating whether a videotape has been rented. It also could have a calculated field that determines how many days a video has been rented.

This concludes Project 1 with the Database tool. You can either exit Works or go on to work the Study Questions, Review Exercises, and Assignments.

SUMMARY AND EXERCISES

Summary

- A program that manages a database is called a database management system (DBMS).
- A database is an organized collection of data that contains a key that uniquely identifies each record.
- A form design in Works can be similar to the design of a printed form or an index card.
- To edit labels, field names, or field entries, you can press $F2$, the Edit key, and then make the desired changes.
- You can enhance a form by adding descriptive labels and moving fields.
- Works will apply the form you design for the first record to each succeeding record in the database.
- In Form view, field names end with a colon.

Key Terms and Operations

Key Terms
calculated field
database management
  system (DBMS)
database structure
field
field contents
field name
form
Form Design view
Form view

key
List view
record
Report view
text label

Operations
Add records
Change database
  views
Create a database
  structure

Create calculated
  fields
Design a form
Edit a form
Edit fields and
  records
Enter fields and
  records
Modify a database
  structure

Study Questions

Multiple Choice

1. In List view, a row of related information is called a:
   a. directory.   c. record.
   b. report.   d. query.

2. Before data can be entered into a database, which of the following must be created?
   a. directory   c. query
   b. structure   d. report

3. A field containing =*Number of Days & Daily Charge* is what type of field?
   a. logical   c. label
   b. calculated   d. comment

4. If *175* appears in the formula bar, the contents of which of the following field types is displayed?
   a. logical   c. numeric
   b. calculated   d. comment

5. In Form view, field names must end with a:
   a. colon (:).   c. hyphen (-).
   b. semicolon (;).   d. caret (^).

6. A field that uniquely identifies each record in a database is called a:
   a. field name.   c. record.
   b. key.   d. label.

7. Which of the following database components contains descriptive text that makes the database form easier to use?
   a. a field   c. a logical expression
   b. a record   d. a label

8. Which function key is the Edit key?
   a. F2   c. F5
   b. F3   d. F10

9. A program that manages a database is called:
   a. integrated software.
   b. an operating system.
   c. a database management system (DBMS).
   d. a record server.

10. A form in Works is most like which of the following?
    a. a spreadsheet with multiple rows
    b. a table in a word processing document
    c. a printed report
    d. a pre-printed form

Short Answer

1. When creating a new database, your first task is to name the _____ that will contain your data.

2. The first new database file is automatically given the name _____.

3. All data related to one person or thing is called a _____.

4. In _____ view, you can change the look of your database form.

5. The _____ key will allow you to move to a specified field or record.

6. A program that manages databases is called a(n) _____.

7. In _____ view, you can only display one record at a time.

8. The current record number appears on the _____ of the status bar.

9. Works' default view is _____ view.

10. When your screen displays many records, one record per row, you are in _____ view.

For Discussion

1. Give three examples of databases. Do not list any databases mentioned in this project.

2. Is a catalog an example of a database? Explain.

3. Is a history book an example of a database? Explain.

4. What is the difference between a field and a record?

5. How can you enhance the design of a form?

Review Exercises

Creating a Used Car Database

You own a used car lot. In this exercise, you will create a database that contains the following data.

Make	Model	Color	Year	Cost	Price	Profit
Honda	Civic	Red	1993	$7,500	$10,000	
Ford	Tempo	Beige	1990	$3,900	$4,500	
Honda	Prelude	Black	1986	$3,100	$3,900	

1. Create the table above. When creating the Profit field, leave it blank.

2. Switch to Form Design view and then create a professional-looking form. Set proper field widths, and format any numbers that need it. The form should have the title *Ricky Paloverde's Used Cars* (set in italics), except that you will type your name instead of Ricky Paloverde's. Organize the form neatly.

3. Add an equation to the Profit field to subtract the cost from the price to find the profit on the sale of each car.

4. Add two more records. Use any cars of your own choosing.

5. Save the database, assigning it the name *Used Cars*.

6. Print the first record of the database.

Creating a Database of Your Collection

Create a database to help manage a collection of items. For example, you might create a database that keeps track of stamps, pottery, sports cards, dolls, etc. It can include a number for each item, the description, cost, where found, age, estimated value, comments, and so on. The type of item is unimportant, but you must observe the guidelines cited in the following steps.

1. Place your name and the name of the collection at the top of the form. Both should be displayed in a bold character style.

2. Create at least six fields of appropriate length. One should be called *Comments* and be wide enough to contain remarks about each item.

3. Enter at least five records.

4. Save the file and use the item type (such as *Stamps*) as the file name.

5. Print the first record.

Assignments

Creating a Company Address Database

You have decided to create a database of the companies you send bills to each week. Once a database is defined, you can create a mailing list report. In this assignment, you will create the database structure and add three records. In a later assignment, you will create a report.

Create the database. Include at least three fictitious records. Save the database as *Bills*.

Creating a Bibliographic Database

As a student, you are constantly compiling references at the school library. You know that a database gives you the ability to easily manage large amounts of information.

Create a bibliographic database of the works you consult for your research papers. Consider including the following fields:

The author's first and last name

The title of the work

The type of publication (book, journal article, chapter in an edited book, etc.)

The date of publication

The publisher

The ISBN

The call number

A field to store annotated comments or a brief abstract

Add three references. Save the database as *Bibliography*.

Creating a Customer Database

As the president of First Savings and Loan, you want to send a quarterly newsletter to all the bank's customers. Create a database of customers. When the database structure is defined, add five records. Save the database as *Bank Customers*. Print the first record.

PROJECT 2: VIEWING A DATABASE

Objectives

After completing this project, you should be able to:

▶ Edit field contents in List view

▶ Change field widths

▶ Sort records

▶ Insert and delete fields

▶ Set a default value

▶ Search for data and use filters

▶ Print in List view

▶ Hide fields

CASE STUDY: USING A DATABASE

You have a customer database for the River View Resort that consists of a few fields and records. You've used the Form view to view the database one record at a time, and so far this has worked well because the database is relatively small. For example, if you want to find a customer named Jackson, you only need to press (CTRL) + (PGDN) a few times in Form view to find the customer's record. When the database becomes larger and contains hundreds or thousands of records instead of just a handful, it becomes more difficult to find data. To find Jackson's record in a large database you might have to press (CTRL) + (PGDN) hundreds of times. You could even accidentally jump right past the record.

Form view works well when you want to display one record at a time. What if you wanted to list everyone who was having breakfast on a particular morning? Browsing through a large database in Form view could be a nightmare.

Designing the Solution

The real power of a database management system is its ability to quickly access desired data and present it in an appropriate manner. In this project you will use List view to list simultaneously all records that meet certain criteria. For example, the resort needs to know approximately how many breakfasts to prepare every morning. You will place all records that meet this criterion into a list. If the list does not fit well on the screen, you can adjust field widths in List view to view the information better.

A database management system also lets you sort out records in alphabetical and numerical order. You typically enter records into a database in no particular order or, as in this case, in the order in which the data was acquired. If you need an alphabetical list of all customer names, you can tell Works to sort the database from A to Z.

OPENING AN EXISTING DATABASE

To view the database, you first need to retrieve it from the data disk.

To open the River View Resort database file:

1 If you haven't done so already, load Works.

2 Open the existing database file called *River View Resort*.

USING LIST VIEW

The River View Resort database you created in the previous project can be viewed in a variety of ways. Form view enables you to design descriptive forms for entering data, but it displays only one record at a time. Figure 2.1 shows the first record from the *River View Resort* database, in the Form view with which you are familiar.

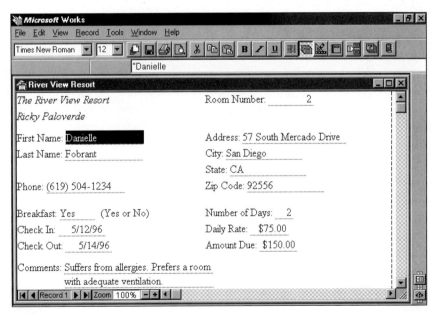

Figure 2.1

List view typically displays up to 16 records at a time in a grid of rows and columns similar to those of a spreadsheet. You cannot enter or edit descriptive labels in List view, but you can easily perform operations that affect the data entered in multiple records. For example, you can delete, copy, or move fields and records as a group. In addition, when you search for data, multiple records are displayed on the screen as a list.

To switch between Form and List views, you can choose Form or List from the View menu, or you can select the buttons on the Toolbar.

To display the database in List view:

1 Start Works if you haven't done so already.

2 Open the database file *River View Resort*.

3 Choose the View menu.
The menu shown in Figure 2.2 appears. The checkmark before Form indicates that the database is currently in Form view.

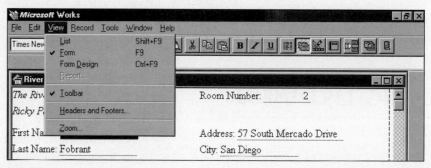

Figure 2.2

4 Choose List to switch to List view.
The screen should look like Figure 2.3. If you do not see the entire database, press (CTRL) + (HOME) to jump to the top of the file.

Figure 2.3

List view displays each record as a row and each field as a column. Field names no longer end with a colon and are centered as column headings. Record numbers are listed on the left of the database window. You can enter and edit field names and field contents, change the size of any field, and format any data. In databases with many fields (like the one in Figure 2.3), you will not be able to see all the fields on-screen at once.

All field widths in List view are automatically set to 10 characters or long enough to accommodate wide field names. Even though different widths may have been set in Form view, they do not carry over to List view. Long field contents, such as the last name De Francisco, may be cut off.

EDITING FIELD CONTENTS IN LIST VIEW

Because List view displays multiple records on the same screen, you can easily move from one record to another to edit data. To edit data in List view, you would select the data and then press (F2). Table 2.1 shows the keys that move the insertion point in List view.

Table 2.1

Key(s)	Action
⬅, ➡	Moves one field left or one field right.
⬆, ⬇	Moves one record up or one record down.
(HOME)	Moves to beginning of record.
(END)	Moves to end of record.
(PGUP)	Moves one screen up.
(PGDN)	Moves one screen down.
(CTRL) + (HOME)	Moves to beginning of file.
(CTRL) + (END)	Moves to end of file.
(TAB)	Moves one field right.
(SHIFT) + (TAB)	Moves one field left.
(F5)	Moves to a specified record or field within a record.

> **Tip**   You can use the horizontal scroll bar and the mouse to move between fields while in List view.

To see the fields that are currently off the screen:

1 Move to the Comments field.

2 Browse through the fields until you get back to the Last Name field. You can use the GoTo key, (F5), to jump quickly to a particular record, or a field within a record, to edit data.

To change Nicole Spring's entry for breakfast:

1 Press (F5)

You enter a record number or field name in the dialog box that appears, as shown in Figure 2.4.

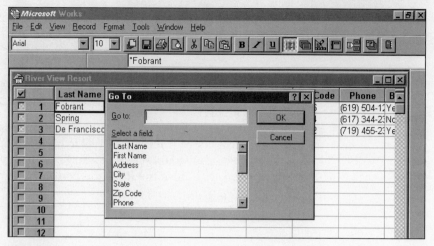

Figure 2.4

2 Type **2** and then press (ENTER)
You should be at record number 2.

3 Press (F5) again.

4 Select Breakfast in the list box and then select OK.
The Breakfast field should be selected.

5 Press (F2) to edit the field.

6 Change *No* to *Yes*.

Danielle's Comments field also needs editing. It should state that she prefers a room with a window that opens instead of a room with adequate ventilation. Although you could easily use the arrow keys to locate the proper field, you will use (F5).

To change Danielle's Comments field:

1 Use (F5) to move to Danielle's Comments field.

2 Use (F2) to change *Prefers a room with adequate ventilation* to *Prefers a room with a window that opens.*

CHANGING FIELD WIDTHS

The display of De Francisco does not fit within the Last Name field. To display the entire field contents, you need to widen the field.

To widen the Last Name field:

1 Select the Last Name field.

2 Choose Field Width from the Format menu.
You should see the dialog box shown in Figure 2.5.

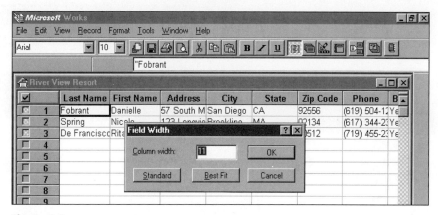

Figure 2.5

3 Type **15** as the new field width and then press (ENTER)

Notice in Figure 2.5 that you could have selected the Best Fit option. The Best Fit option will automatically adjust the column width to fit the field contents.

Fields in List view can be narrowed as well as widened. Some fields in this database are wider than necessary. The Room Number field can be reduced to take up less space.

To reduce the size of two fields:

1 Select the Room Number field.

2 Choose Field Width from the Format menu.

3 Change the width to 6 characters.

4 Select the State field.

5 Choose Field Width from the Format menu.

6 Type **6** and press (ENTER)
The screen should look like Figure 2.6. Notice that the State and Room Number fields are narrower.

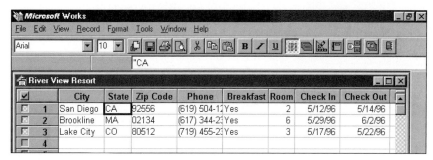

Figure 2.6

Changes made to field contents in List view are reflected in Form view, but changes made to field widths do not affect the corresponding field widths in Form view.

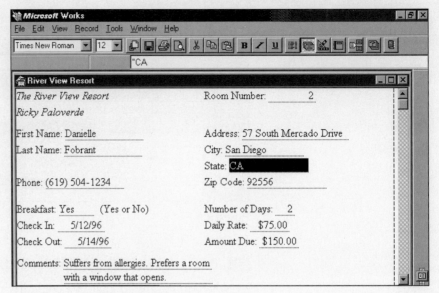

Figure 2.7

To switch to Form view:

1 Select the Form View button on the Toolbar.
The screen should look like Figure 2.7.

Notice that changes to field widths made in List view have not affected the field widths in Form view. For example, the State field was changed to six characters in List view, but it remains a lot wider in Form view.

ADDING RECORDS

So far, data about each guest was entered on the date each person checked in. Danielle checked in on 5/12/96, Nicole on 5/29/96, and Rita on 5/17/96. You realize, however, that the bed-and-breakfast staff neglected to enter records for several guests. Jason Argos checked in on 5/13/96, Laura Sabonis on 5/9/96, and Robert Jackson on 5/31/96. You must add these records to the database. The records do not need to be entered in chronological order. You can add the data to the end of the database and then sort the records by the Check In field.

To add records at the end of the database:

1 Switch to List view.

2 Move the cursor to the first blank line below the last record in the database.

3 Use the following list as a guide for entering data for the three new records. Because they contain formulas, the Number of Days, Daily Rate, and Amount Due fields will be automatically displayed.

Field	Field Contents
Last Name	Argos
First Name	Jason
Address	455 Sioux Circle
City	Custer
State	SD
Zip Code	60712
Phone	(605) 444-9878
Breakfast	Yes
Room Number	1
Check In	5/13/95
Check Out	5/18/95
Comments	Requests information about the annual buffalo festival.

Field	Field Contents
Last Name	Sabonis
First Name	Laura
Address	321 Archer Blvd.
City	Toledo
State	OH
Zip Code	32167
Phone	(419) 556-7789
Breakfast	No
Room Number	4
Check In	5/9/95
Check Out	5/12/95
Comments	Plans to bring her dog, Buster.

Field	Field Contents
Last Name	Jackson
First Name	Robert
Address	2541 Ginkgo Drive
City	Nashville
State	TN
Zip Code	45578
Phone	(615) 898-2321
Breakfast	No
Room Number	5
Check In	5/31/95
Check Out	6/1/95
Comments	Requests a nonsmoking room.

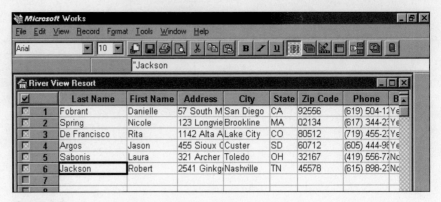

Figure 2.8

When all entries have been made, the screen in List view should look like Figure 2.8.

 EXIT If necessary, you can save your file as *River View Resort,* exit Works now, and continue this project later.

SORTING RECORDS

Sorting improves the usefulness of a database by rearranging records in alphabetical, numerical, or chronological order. For example, a telephone directory lists names in alphabetical order. A database of tennis players would probably list players by their ranking. Astronomical charts list information chronologically.

The field by which a database is sorted is called the *sort field.* In Works you can have up to three sort fields at one time. In a telephone directory, the first sort field is the last name, the second is the first name, and the third is the middle name or initial. Telephone directories list everyone in alphabetical order by last name. If two or more people have the same last name, then they are listed in alphabetical order by first name. If two or more people have the same last name and first name, then they are sorted by their middle name or initial.

Sort fields can be defined in ascending or descending order. The default, ascending order, is from A to Z, 0 to 9, and the oldest date to the most recent date. Descending order is the reverse of ascending order.

To sort the records by the Check In field:

1 Place the insertion point anywhere in the Check In field.
Placing the insertion point in the sort field is not necessary. In this case, however, doing so makes seeing the effect of the sort easier.

2 Choose Sort Records from the Records menu.
If you are asked whether you want First-time Help, select OK to bypass the dialog box. You should see the Sort Records dialog box shown in Figure 2.9, in which you can specify up to three sort fields.

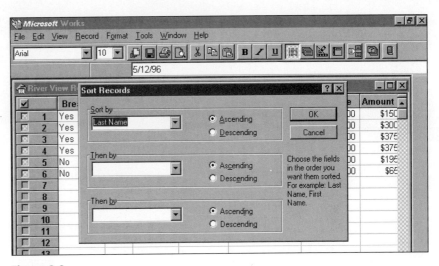

Figure 2.9

3 Select Check In in the list box under Sort By.
Notice that the sort order is preset to ascending order. You can specify descending order by selecting the appropriate option button.

4 Select OK to perform the sort in ascending order.
The screen should look like Figure 2.10. All records are now sorted by the check-in date.

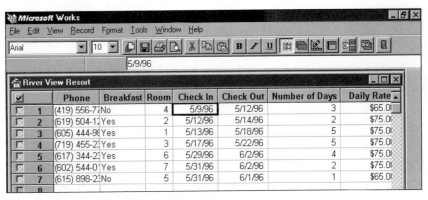

Figure 2.10

CREATING A MULTILEVEL SORT

Sorting by two or more fields is referred to as a ***multilevel sort.*** Multilevel sorts are useful for databases such as large phone or address lists, in which multiple records share common characteristics. In a phone book, for example, all persons with the last name *Smith* are listed in alphabetical order by first name and sometimes even by middle name or initial.

Before creating a multilevel sort, you need to add the following information to the database as the seventh record.

Field	Field Contents
Last Name	Jackson
First Name	Beth
Address	3511 W. 1st Avenue
City	Mesa
State	AZ
Zip Code	86280
Phone	(602) 544-0121
Room Number	7
Breakfast	Yes
Check In	5/31/95
Check Out	6/2/95
Comments	Beth is an artist. Wants a room with a view of the river.

Reminder Remember to enter a quotation mark (") before entering a zip code, to indicate that the entry is text and not a numeric value.

To perform a multilevel sort:

1 Press (CTRL) + (HOME) to move the insertion point to the top of the database.
This step makes it easier to see the effect of the sort.

2 Choose Sort Records from the Records menu.
Notice that Works has kept the name of the Check In field in the 1st Field list box. The field name specified in the most recent sort always appears in the Sort Records dialog box.

3 Select Last Name in the Sort By list box.

4 In the first Then By list box, select First Name.

5 Select OK to perform the sort.
The records should be sorted by last name and then first name, as shown in Figure 2.11. Notice that Beth Jackson comes before Robert Jackson.

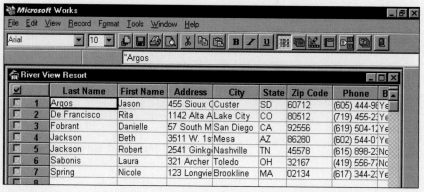

Figure 2.11

INSERTING AND DELETING FIELDS

The database needs a field to keep track of whether each guest has paid for his or her stay at the bed-and-breakfast. To insert a new field called Paid, you will insert a blank field and then create the new field name.

To insert a new field:

1 Select the First Name field.

2 Choose Insert Field from the Record menu.

3 Select Before to insert the new field before the First Name field. You should see the Insert Field dialog box.

4 Type **Paid** and then select Add to add this field.

5 Select Done to complete the process. You should see a blank field called Paid, as shown in Figure 2.12.

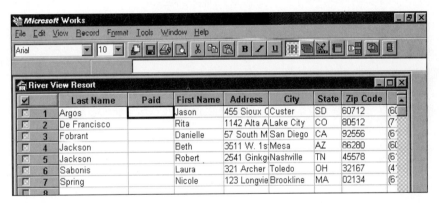

Figure 2.12

The new Paid field should not separate the last and first names, so you will delete the field you just created and then insert the field in a better location. The Paid field is empty, but a field does not need to be empty before you delete it. Also, if you accidentally delete a field, you can undelete it if you choose Undo from the Edit menu.

To delete the field you just created:

1 Place the insertion point anywhere in the Paid field.

2 Choose Delete Field from the Record menu.

3 Select OK to permanently delete the field.

The Paid field would look better between the Phone and Breakfast fields.

To insert a field between Phone and Breakfast:

1 Place the insertion point in the Phone field.

2 Choose Insert Field from the Record menu.

3 Select After for the insertion placement.

4 Type **Paid** and then select Add.

5 Select Done to add the field.
You should see the new Paid field between the Phone and Breakfast fields.

You can see the new Paid field in the Form Design view, but it won't be located where you'd expect.

To move the Paid field to a new location in the Form Design view:

1 Select the Form Design View button on the Toolbar.
Notice where the new Paid field appears. (Your Paid field may be in a slightly different position than the one in Figure 2.13.)

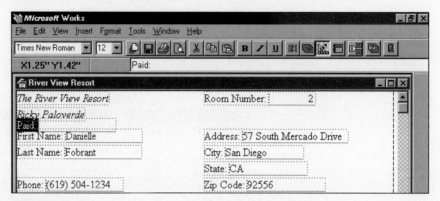

Figure 2.13

2 Drag the Paid field name just under the Room Number field, as shown in Figure 2.14.

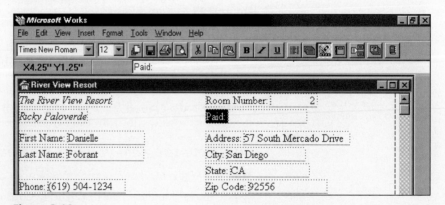

Figure 2.14

SETTING A DEFAULT VALUE

Because most bed-and-breakfast guests pay their bill when they check out, the Paid field will initially contain the text entry *No.* After the bill has been paid, the Paid field should be changed to read *Yes.* Rather than having to first enter *No* into the Paid field in every record and then later change it to

Yes, you can set a ***default value*** for the Paid field. The default value will automatically appear in every record.

To set a default value for a field, you would move to the first record of the database, start the entry with an equal sign, and then enter the value. Default text must be surrounded by quotation marks. For example, to specify *No* as the default value for the Paid field, you would type = "No". Default numbers do not require quotation marks, so the number 10 would be entered as = 10.

To set the default value for the Paid field:

1 Select the List View button on the Toolbar.

2 Move to the top of the database.

3 Select the Paid field of the first record of the database.

4 Type **="No"** as the field's default value and then press (ENTER)
The screen should look like Figure 2.15.

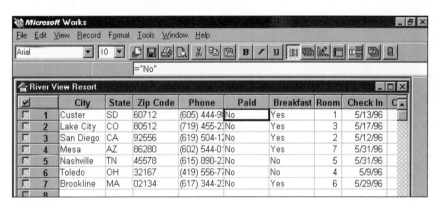

Figure 2.15

Assume that Danielle Fobrant and Laura Sabonis have checked out of the resort and paid their bill. To show this, you need to enter *Yes* into their Paid fields.

To change Danielle Fobrant's and Laura Sabonis's Paid fields:

1 Place the insertion point in the Paid field in Danielle's record.

2 Type **Yes** and then press (ENTER)

3 Place the insertion point in the Paid field in Laura Sabonis's record.

4 Type **Yes** and then press (ENTER)

SEARCHING FOR DATA

Works lets you look for data in two ways: You can find a specific item by initiating a *find* for matching data or you can create a *filter*. To find records in a database, you would use the Find command in the Edit menu. When you ***find*** records you look for data that meets one condition. To filter the database, you would use the Filters command in the Tools menu. When you *filter* a database, you find records that meet multiple conditions. Both methods display records that match certain conditions you have specified. For example, you could find all guests in the database who are from California. Or, you could create a filter to list all guests who will be served breakfast each day and who will be staying more than three days.

> **Tip** In general, a filter is more flexible than a find, because a find merely allows you to search for a word or a phrase one record at a time. Use a filter when you want to display multiple records meeting specific criteria.

Assume that you want data about all guests from Colorado who are currently listed in the database. You would choose Find from the Edit menu and then type the phrase *CO.* After finding the first occurrence of the phrase, you can find the next occurrence by pressing (CTRL)+**F** and then pressing (ENTER). If you continue pressing (CTRL)+**F** after Works has reached the bottom of the database, Works will jump to the top of the database and start the search again.

To find the text string Jackson:

1 Make sure you are in List view and then press (CTRL)+(HOME) to move to the top of the database.
Works always searches forward through the document starting from the current location.

2 Choose Find from the Edit menu.
The dialog box shown in Figure 2.16 appears.

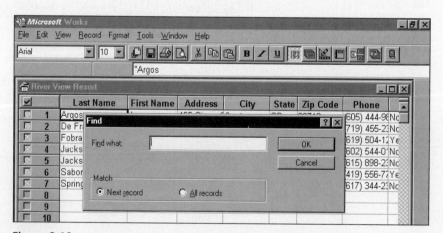

Figure 2.16

3 Type **CO** and press (ENTER)
Works finds the first occurrence of the string *CO.* Because searches are not case-sensitive, Works finds any field in any record containing either *CO* or *co,* such as *Francisco.* It also finds the string *co* embedded in names such as *Nicole* or the word *Court.*

4 Press (CTRL)+**F** and then (ENTER) until you find *CO* as in the state abbreviation CO.
Works finds the state CO, as shown in Figure 2.17.

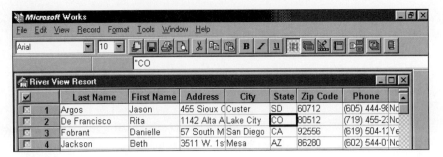

Figure 2.17

Works has found *CO* in the State field. If you continue to press (CTRL)+ **F**, Works will find instances of the string *CO* in any field. To narrow the scope of the search, you will select one or more fields before performing the next search.

To search for CO *in the State field only:*

1 Move to the top of the database.

2 Place the insertion point in the State field.

3 Choose Select Field from the Edit menu.
Notice that the State field is selected, as shown in Figure 2.18.

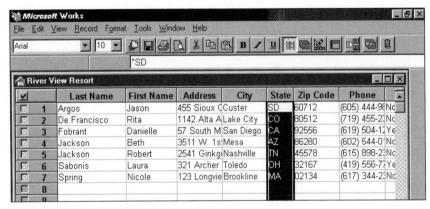

Figure 2.18

4 Choose Find from the Edit menu.
The phrase *CO* should already appear in the dialog box.

5 Select OK to perform the search.
The search remains within the State field.

HIDING AND DISPLAYING RECORDS USING FIND

At times you will want to concentrate on a certain group of records. In these cases, you will use the All Records option in the Find dialog box to tell Works to display only records meeting certain criteria—in this case, records that contain the word *Jackson* in the Last Name field. You will tell Works to hide all other records.

To display only specific records:

1 Select the Last Name field.

2 Choose Find from the Edit menu.
The string *CO* should already appear in the dialog box.

3 Press (DEL) once to clear the entry.

4 Type **Jackson** in the text box.

5 Select All Records to display only those records that contain the string.

6 Select OK to complete the command.
Now the screen should show only the two records that contain the name *Jackson* in the Last Name field, as in Figure 2.19.

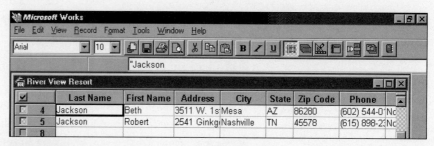

Figure 2.19

All other records are hidden. The numbers *2/7* on the left side of the status bar indicate that there are currently two visible records from a total of seven. Those two records are the ones that satisfied the search criterion.

This type of search works well if you want to limit the number of records with which you are currently working. When you are finished, you can redisplay all the records. To redisplay all records in the database, you can choose Show All Records from the Record menu.

To redisplay all records:

1 Choose Show from the Record menu.

2 Select All Records to redisplay the entire database.

FILTERING A DATABASE

Data searches are quick and easy, but they allow you to find records that match only one condition. Filters take longer to develop, but they enable you to find records that match multiple conditions. With sophisticated filters, you also can specify conditions to find text, numbers, or dates that fall within a range.

To specify conditions for a filter, you would choose Filters from the Tools menu. You will design a filter that lists all records that meet two conditions. It will look for all guests who attend breakfast and are staying at the resort for two or more days.

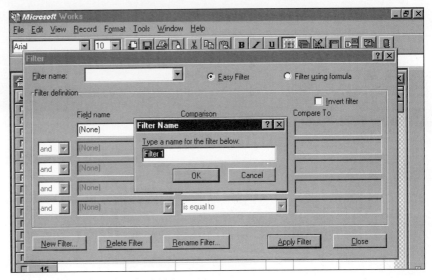

Figure 2.20

 To define the filter:

1 Choose Filters from the Tools menu.
Overlapping dialog boxes appear, like the ones in Figure 2.20. Works is waiting for you to enter a name for the filter.

2 Type **Meals** as the first filter name and then press (ENTER)

3 Under Field Name, select Breakfast from the list box.
Notice that under Comparison, it states *is equal to*. You do not need to change this because you are looking for everyone whose Breakfast field is equal to Yes.

4 Under Compare To, type **Yes**

5 In the second list box under Field Name, select Number of Days, as shown in Figure 2.21.

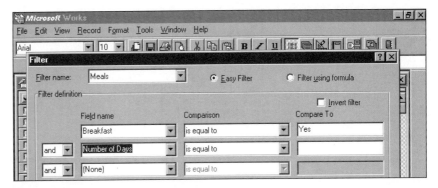

Figure 2.21

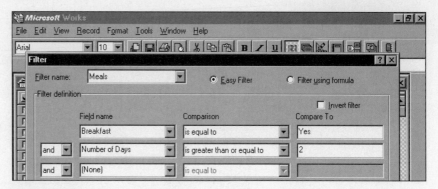

Figure 2.22

6 In the second Comparison list box, select *is greater than or equal to.*

7 In the second Compare To text box, type **2**
The screen should look like Figure 2.22.

8 Select Apply Filter to apply the filter.

9 Press ⊙ until you are in the Number of Days field.
The screen should look like Figure 2.23. Only guests who have breakfast and who are staying two or more days are listed.

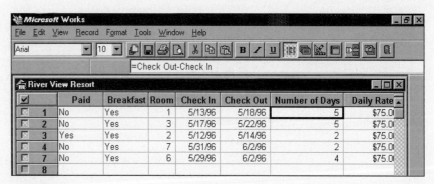

Figure 2.23

10 To view all records again, choose Show All Records from the Record menu.

11 Choose Save from the File menu.

There is no special command for saving a filter; a filter is saved as part of the database. Whenever you save the file *River View Resort,* the filter Meals is automatically saved with the database.

PRINTING IN LIST VIEW

Most databases are too wide to fit on one sheet of 8.5-by-11-inch paper. To create a narrower database to print in List view, you can hide fields that are not needed in the printout.

To preview the entire database:

1 Choose Print Preview from the File menu.

2 Select Zoom In.
The screen should look like Figure 2.24. The database is too wide to fit on one page.

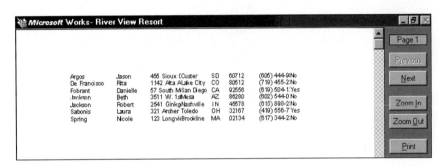

Figure 2.24

3 Select Next to see the second page of the printout.

4 Select Next to see the last page of the printout.

5 Select the Cancel button to exit the preview.

You can hide fields to create a narrower database by setting their field widths to 0. For example, assume that you want a printout of only Last Name, First Name, Breakfast, Amount Due, and Room Number.

To hide fields:

1 Place the insertion point in the Paid field of any record.

2 Choose Field Width from the Format menu.

3 Type **0** and then press (ENTER)
Setting the field width to 0 hides the display of the field entries until you reset the field width. Because it is currently in the Paid field, which now has a width of 0, the insertion point has disappeared.

4 Press ⊖ to move the insertion point from a hidden to a displayed field.

5 Use the same method to hide all fields except for Last Name, First Name, Breakfast, Room Number, and Amount Due.
The screen should look like Figure 2.25.

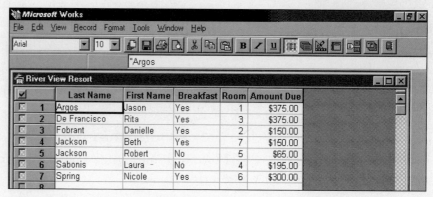

Figure 2.25

Tip   While in List view, you can set the field width to 0 by dragging the right margin of the field name to the left.

To print the database:

1 Choose Print from the File menu.

2 Print the database.
The database should fit on one printed page.

To redisplay hidden fields, you can use (F5) or the Go To command in the Edit menu to go to each of the fields that you hid and then reset each field to its original width.

To redisplay the hidden fields:

1 Press (F5)
You should see the Go To dialog box shown in Figure 2.26.

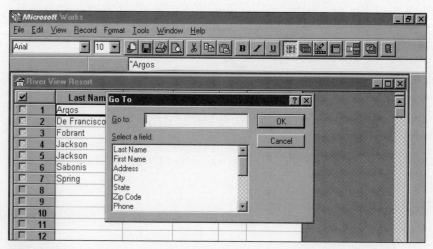

Figure 2.26

2 Select Paid in the Select a Field list box, and then press (ENTER)
The insertion point in the database window should disappear, because it is currently in the Paid field, which has a width of 0.

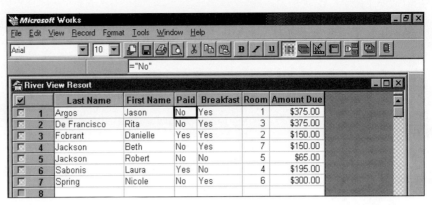

Figure 2.27

3 Choose Field Width from the Format menu.

4 Select Best Fit.
The screen should look like Figure 2.27. Notice that the Paid field entries have reappeared.

5 Redisplay all the remaining hidden fields by using the method in the previous steps. Set the field widths to Best Fit or, if needed, to something wider. You do not have to save the file again because you saved it recently.

THE NEXT STEP

In addition to knowing how to create a database structure and input records, you now know how to manipulate the data that a database contains. The ability to sort a database and create filters greatly increases the usefulness of a DBMS.

Think of a bibliographic database that you might create while conducting research for a term paper. There may be times when you need to list the records in alphabetical order by author, whereas at other times you may need to view records that have a copyright date later than 1990.

This concludes Project 2 with the Works Database tool. You can either exit Works or go on to work the Study Questions, Review Exercises, and Assignments.

SUMMARY AND EXERCISES

Summary

- List view lists multiple records in a grid of rows and columns similar to those in a spreadsheet.
- Editing field contents in List view changes corresponding field contents in Form view.
- Changing field widths in List view does not change corresponding field widths in Form view.

- You can add records to the end of a database.
- You can sort records using as many as three sort fields.
- You can insert and delete fields in List view.
- To create a default value that appears in every record of the database, you would place an equal sign before a cell entry.
- You can use the Find command to perform a data search according to one condition.
- You can create a filter to perform a data search satisfying multiple conditions.
- To hide a field in List view, you can set the field width to 0.
- To retrieve a hidden field, you can go to the hidden field and reset the field width.

Key Terms and Operations

Key Terms	**Operations**
default value	Delete a field
filter	Design a filter
find	Display hidden fields
multilevel sort	Display hidden records
sort field	Find records
sorting	Hide fields
	Insert a field
	Sort a database

Study Questions

Multiple Choice

1. The edit key is:
   a. (F2).
   b. (F3).
   c. (F5).
   d. (F9).

2. To change the view of a database so only individuals who live in New York are listed, you would:
   a. Create a multilevel sort.
   b. Change the database that displays all records from List view to Form view.
   c. Design a filter.
   d. Sort on only the state field.

3. To organize a database so all individuals are listed in alphabetical order by last name, you would:
   a. Find everyone by last name.
   b. Change the database from List view to Form view.
   c. Design a filter.
   d. Sort the database by one field.

4. You need to view a list of customers who have a credit limit of at least $500. Which expression would you use?
   a. greater than 500
   b. not equal to 500
   c. greater than or equal to 500
   d. less than or equal to 500

5. You need to quickly locate a record in a large database that contains the phrase *Hardy Reel* somewhere in the record. The fastest way to locate this record would be to:
   a. Design a filter with *Hardy Reel* in the expression.
   b. Switch to List view and then press F5 until the record is located.
   c. Switch to Form view and then press F5 until the record is located.
   d. Use the Find option from the Edit menu.

6. In a filter, which expression would locate all dates between 5/7/95 and 6/20/96, not including those dates?
   a. greater than 5/7/95 AND less than 6/20/96
   b. less than 6/20/96
   c. not equal to 5/7/95 OR 6/20/96
   d. greater than or equal to 5/7/95 AND less than or equal to 6/20/96

7. You want to print a database that currently appears in List view, but with three fields excluded from the printout. What should you do?
   a. Remove those three fields from the database.
   b. Design a filter to exclude certain records from view.
   c. Set the field width of those three fields to 0.
   d. Create a multilevel sort on those three fields.

8. If you search for the word *the,* which of the following would *not* be located by the search?
   a. There   c. heart
   b. THE   d. mother

9. In List view, field names are _____ at the top of the field.
   a. centered   c. left-aligned
   b. right-aligned   d. justified

10. Which of the following sets the default value of a field to Yes?
    a. =Yes   c. ="Yes
    b. ="Yes"   d. "Yes

Short Answer

1. In List view, pressing → or _____ moves the insertion point one field to the right.

2. In List view, pressing ← or _____ moves the insertion point one field to the left.

3. Pressing _____ in List view moves the insertion point to the end of the database.

4. Pressing _____ moves the insertion point to the end of a record.

5. Default values must be preceded by a(n) _____.

6. To search for data, use the _____ command from the Edit menu.

7. A _____ allows you to display records that meet specific multiple criteria.

8. To view the records that were hidden by a filter, use the _____ command in the Record menu.

9. After a filter has hidden one or more records, you can use the _____ command to redisplay all records.

10. If you use text as a default cell entry, you must surround the text with _____.

For Discussion

1. When is it more appropriate to use Form view to do data entry? When is List view more appropriate for this task?

2. If your List view is too wide to print on one page, and you want to hide some of the fields, what steps must you take?

3. How can you redisplay the hidden fields?

4. After entering data in Form view, you switch to List view and find that some of the records are blank. How can you remove the extra records?

5. Assume that the resort database has a new field called Number of Guests. Write a condition for a filter that finds all records that have more than 2 guests and are staying in rooms numbered 20 or higher.

Review Exercises

Using the Used Cars Database

Use List view to manipulate data in the *Used Cars* database file, which you created in a Review Exercise in Project 1. Change the currency formats to 0 decimal places if necessary.

1. Open the database file *Used Cars*.

2. Display the database in List view.

3. Add a field called Sold at the end of all the fields.

4. Set the default value to No for the Sold field.

5. In List view, change the width of the Sold field to 5.

6. Add two more records. You should have ten cars.

7. Search for and list only cars made by Honda.

8. Create a filter that lists all black cars whose price is less than $5,000.

9. Delete the previous filter and then create a new filter that lists all cars whose year is between 1989 and the current year.

10. Show all records.

11. Save the database, assigning it the name *More Used Cars*.

12. Print the database in List view.

Creating a Music Inventory Database

Create a list of your CDs, cassettes, or record albums. If you don't have any, invent some.

1. Create a form that has at least six fields. Name one of the fields Category and another Comments. In the Category field you will enter categories such as rock, classical, jazz, and so on.

2. In List view, enter the names of at least five recordings. Include at least one classical CD, cassette, or album.

3. Add a field called Condition. The Condition field will contain the current condition of the CD, tape, or album.

4. Set the default value of the Condition field to 1. The best condition is 1 and the worst is 5.

5. Create a filter that lists all records whose category is classical and whose condition is 1, 2, or 3.

6. Hide the Comments field.

7. Save the file. Use any file name that is appropriate.

8. Print the database.

Assignments

Sorting a Company Database

Retrieve the file *Bills* that you created at the end of Project 1. Display the database in List view. Add three records to the database. Sort the database for all the companies listed, by company name. Print the sorted list. Save the updated file as *Second Bills*.

Designing a Filter

Retrieve the file *Bibliography*. Add three references to the database. Design a filter that locates any references published between 1990 and 1994. Display the filter in List view, and print a copy of the list. Save the updated file as *Second Bibliography*.

Sorting a Database and Hiding Fields from View

You need to prepare a list of customers who will receive the bank's quarterly newsletter by bulk mail. Retrieve the file *Bank Customers*. Create a multilevel sort, first by zip code and then by last name. Hide all fields except the name and zip code fields. Display the database in List view, and print the list. Because no records were added and no filters were defined, you will not need to update the file.

PROJECT 3: CREATING A REPORT

Objectives

After completing this project, you should be able to:

▶ Create a new report

▶ Use Report view

▶ Sort databases to create groups of related records

▶ Create group summaries and report summaries

▶ Insert and delete columns and rows in reports

▶ Modify report titles and column headings

▶ Save, preview, and print reports

CASE STUDY: DESIGNING A CUSTOM DATABASE REPORT

In addition to sorting records in a database or filtering records that meet specific conditions, most DBMSs allow users to create custom **reports**. A custom report presents records in a database with more detail than in List view. A custom report can contain explanatory labels, grouped records, and summary data.

As manager of the River View Resort, you need to design a report that summarizes the amount due for each guest. The report will group guests according to whether or not they have paid for the room. It will also display a summary of the total amount due for each group, as well as the total amount due for all guests. You will enhance the report by adding a centered title at the top of the page.

Designing the Solution

A report is created using the ReportCreator, which is found in the Tools menu. The ReportCreator enables you to design a report, which displays data in a more detailed manner than the list of records in List view. In creating a report, you will place a title at the top of the page, sum certain numeric fields, create groups of related records, and specify the formatting of other aspects of the database layout. The summarizing and layout features of reports are ideally suited for designing descriptive output for presentations.

CREATING A NEW REPORT

Figure 3.1 shows a completed report of all guests of the resort who have paid or have not yet paid their bill.

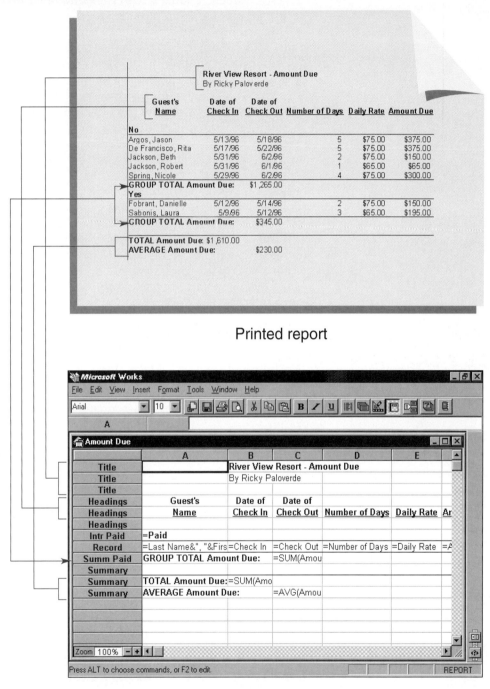

Printed report

Report view

Figure 3.1

Figure 3.1 shows both a printed report and a Report view similar to the one that generated the report. You can refer to the report and Report view as often as you like when completing this project.

You'll notice a few things immediately in the report. At the top are the titles "River View Resort—Amount Due" and the name Ricky Paloverde. The Last Name and First Name column headings have been reduced to "Guest's Name." The Paid field is used to organize records into groups. People who have paid are grouped together and people who have not paid are grouped together. In addition, summaries have been created for the Amount Due column. This type of report could be used to see how much money customers owe (or have already paid).

When a new report is generated in Report view, four *row labels* appear automatically: *Title, Headings, Record,* and *Summary.* The row types determine where Works will print different kinds of information. The data placed in the ***Title*** will appear once at the beginning of each report and generally contains the report title, such as "River View Resort–Amount Due." The contents of the ***Headings*** will appear at the top of each page and usually are used for column headings. The ***Record*** row describes how the records of the database will be displayed in the report. The row automatically allocated for ***Summary*** contains fields that summarize the entire report, such as "TOTAL Amount Due:" (shown later in Figure 3.2).

If you want to group records, you can use ***Intr* Field Name** (*Intr* followed by a field name). For example *Intr Paid* groups records based on whether or not a person has paid. ***Summ* Field Name** (*Summ* followed by a field name), such as *Summ Paid,* enables you to create summaries of groups of records. You'll see options for sorting and grouping records when you run the ReportCreator.

Table 3.1 summarizes report row labels.

Table 3.1

Row Label	Description
Title	Used for report titles or headings.
Headings	Appear at the top of each page and are typically used for column headings.
Intr *Field Name*	*Intr* is short for *introductory.* Used to place introductory text before groups of records.
Record	Prints once for each record until there are no more records or the page is full. Prints as many times in the report as there are records.
Summ *Field Name*	Summarizes records that have been grouped according to a particular field. In Figure 3.2 (shown later), records are grouped by the Breakfast field. The amount due for each group also has been calculated.
Summary	Calculates totals, averages, or other values for all the records in the database.

The Title, Headings, Record, and Summary row labels automatically appear when you create a report. The ***Intr* Field Name** and ***Summ* Field Name** row labels appear only when you group related records. In the following numbered steps, you will create a quick report that uses Works' default row labels and Intr and Summ. First, you will type a title and specify which fields from the database will appear in the report.

In this project, you will use the *River View Resort* database file you developed in Project 2.

To open River View Resort:

1 Start Works if you haven't done so already.

2 Open the *River View Resort* database file.

3 Display the database in List view, as shown in Figure 3.2.

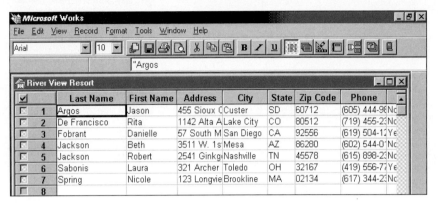

Figure 3.2

To create a quick report:

1 Choose ReportCreator from the Tools menu.
You should see the Report Name dialog box shown in Figure 3.3. Works is waiting for you to enter the report title.

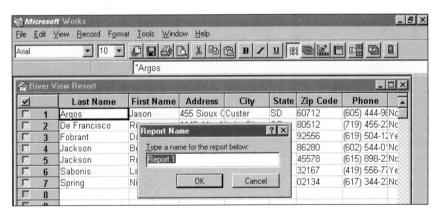

Figure 3.3

2 Type **Amount Due** as the title and then press (ENTER)
You should see the ReportCreator dialog box.

3 Select Landscape for the report orientation and then select Next.
Works is waiting for you to specify which fields you want in the report.

4 Select Add All to add all the fields.
The screen should look like Figure 3.4.

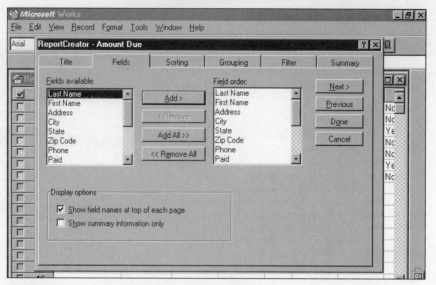

Figure 3.4

5 Select Next to move to the next dialog box.
Works is now asking whether you want to sort the records.

6 Select Paid in the Sort By list box to sort on the Paid field.
The screen should look like Figure 3.5.

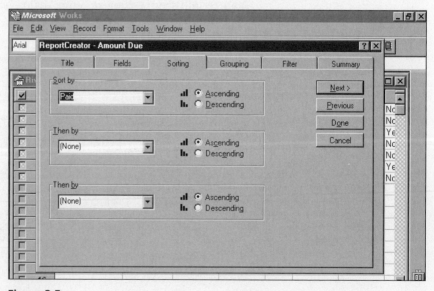

Figure 3.5

7 Select Next to move to the next dialog box.
Works now wants to know details on how you are grouping records.

8 Select When Contents Change, and then select Show Group Heading.
The screen should look like Figure 3.6. When the contents of records
change, the records will automatically be regrouped (if necessary). Also,
group headings will appear at the top of each group.

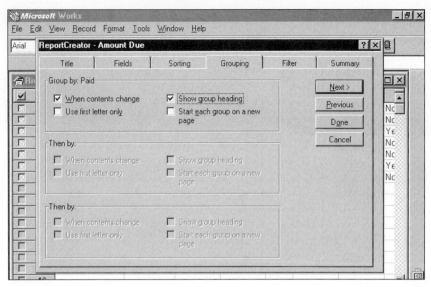

Figure 3.6

9 Select Next to move to the next dialog box.
You should see a dialog box that asks how you will filter the records. Because this is a basic report, you will not use a filter.

10 Select Next to move to the next dialog box.
Works now wants to know how you will summarize the data.

11 In the list box, select Amount Due, and under Summaries, select Sum. This will sum the Amount Due field for all the records.

12 Select At End of Each Group.
Notice in Figure 3.7 that summaries will appear at the end of each group and at the end of the report.

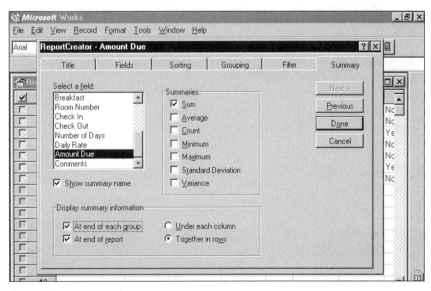

Figure 3.7

13 Select Done to complete the report definition.

You should see a dialog box that asks whether you want to preview the report.

14 Select Preview to see the report on-screen.

You should see a preview of the report.

15 Select Cancel to close the preview.

You should now be in Report view. The screen in Figure 3.8 displays the underlying structure of the report. This is the result of the ReportCreator.

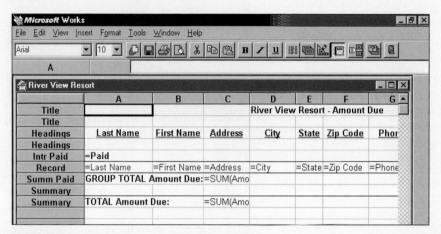

Figure 3.8

When Works generates a default report, it creates two Title rows. Works places the report title in the first row and leaves the second row blank to provide a blank line between the report title and the column headings.

In the first Headings row, Works automatically uses the field names that you specify from the database to create column headings for each page. For example, Last Name, First Name, Address, and so on are field names that are being used as column headings. The second Headings line places a blank line between the column headings and the first record on the page.

The Intr Paid row contains the field name *Paid* preceded by an equal sign. This appears because you grouped all the records by the Paid field. The Paid field contains either Yes or No. Everyone whose Paid field is "Yes" will be grouped, as will everyone whose Paid field is "No."

The Record row contains field names preceded by an equal sign. The equal sign indicates that the entry is a formula that will print the contents of the field. If the equal sign were omitted, Works would treat these entries as labels. For example, when Works prints the first record, the formula =*Last Name* prints the contents of the first field, Argos. Then, =*First Name* prints the contents of the second field, Jason. Printing continues in this way until all the specified fields in all the records have been printed.

In the Summ Paid row you should see *GROUP TOTAL Amount Due:*. Each group of records will have a summary that will state the amount due for the entire group.

The Summary row in the report in Figure 3.8 contains *TOTAL Amount Due:*. This places the total amount due at the bottom of the report.

PREVIEWING THE REPORT

You will now preview the report again. You will try to determine how each line in the report was generated by the screen in Figure 3.8.

To preview the report:

1 Choose Print Preview from the File menu.
A preview appears, but the text is too small for you to see the individual field contents in the report.

2 Select the Zoom In button two times.
The screen should look like Figure 3.9. Notice that the columns of the report are too narrow to display the entire field contents of fields such as Address, so the data is *truncated,* or cut off at the right side of the column.

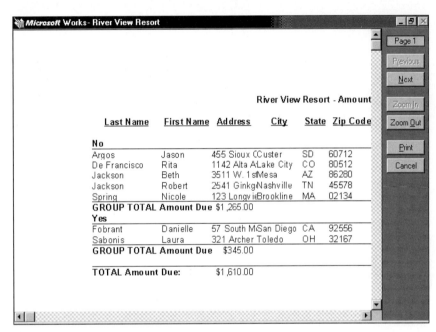

Figure 3.9

The report requires two pages to display all field data for all records.

3 Select the Next button to see the next page.

4 Select Cancel to exit the preview.

DELETING COLUMNS

Earlier you told Works to include all fields from the database in the report. To fit the report on one printed page, the completed report will have only seven columns: Last Name, First Name, Check In, Check Out, Number of Days, Daily Rate, and Amount Due. Fields not needed in the report can be deleted. If you delete fields in the Report view, they are deleted from the report only and not from the original database. You will delete the

Address, City, State, Zip Code, Phone, Paid, Breakfast, Room Number, and Comments fields. Before deleting these fields, you will move a couple of SUM functions. You need to move this function; otherwise, it will be deleted when you delete unnecessary columns.

To copy two SUM functions:

1 Place the active cell in column C in the Summ Paid row.

2 Choose Cut from the Edit menu.

3 Place the active cell in column L in the Summ Paid row.

4 Choose Paste from the Edit menu.

5 Place the active cell in column C in the second Summary row.

6 Choose Cut from the Edit menu.

7 Place the active cell in column K in the second Summary row.

8 Choose Paste from the Edit menu.

The screen should look like Figure 3.10.

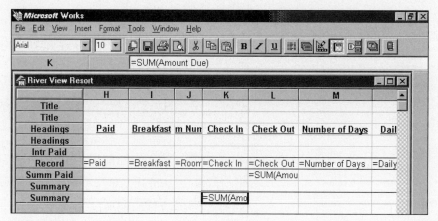

Figure 3.10

You are now ready to delete the unneeded columns.

To delete columns:

1 Place the insertion point anywhere in column C.

2 Select from column C to column J.

The screen should look like Figure 3.11.

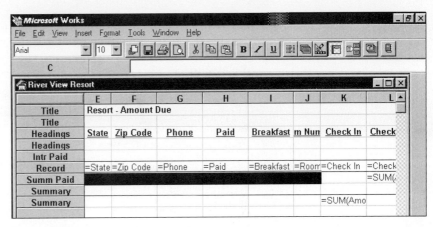

Figure 3.11

3 Choose Delete Column from the Insert menu.

4 Press ← to deselect the range.
The screen should look like Figure 3.12.

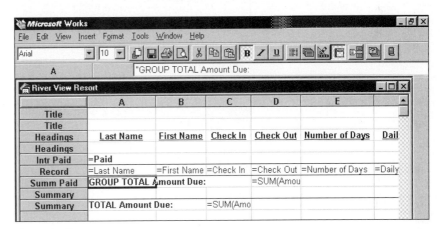

Figure 3.12

To delete the last column:

1 Place the insertion point anywhere in column H.

2 Choose Delete Column from the Insert menu.

Quick Fix If you accidentally delete a row instead of a column, you can choose Undo from the Edit menu.

Notice that the report title is missing in Figure 3.12. When you deleted a range of columns, the title was also deleted. You can reenter the title in the first row of the report.

To reenter the title:

1 Select the first Title row in column C.

2 Type **River View Resort–Amount Due** and press (ENTER)

3 Apply the bold character style to the title.
Now you can preview the modified report.

To preview the report:

1 Choose Print Preview from the File menu.
When the preview appears, it is still difficult to discern the field entries.

2 Select the Zoom In button.
The screen should look like Figure 3.13.

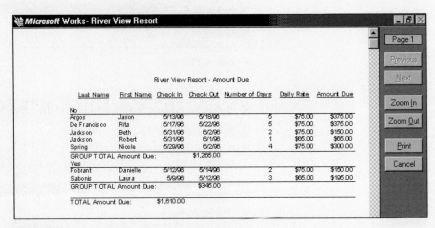

Figure 3.13

3 Select Cancel to close the preview.
Deleting columns in Report view has no effect on the original database.
You can verify this by changing to List view.

To view the database in List view:

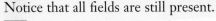

1 Select the List View button on the Toolbar.
Notice that all fields are still present.

2 Select the Report View button on the Toolbar to return to the report.

If necessary, you can save your file as *Amount Due,* exit Works now, and continue this project later.

INSERTING ROWS

The title in the completed report will consist of two lines: *River View Resort—Amount Due* and your name. Below these lines you will have a blank line. Because you will need a total of three Title rows, you will begin by inserting a blank row.

To insert a Title row:

1 Place the active cell anywhere in the second Title row.

2 Choose Insert Row from the Insert menu.

3 Select Title and then Insert.
You now have three Title rows.

The next step is to insert a Headings row so you can add a line of text to the column headings.

To insert a Headings row:

1 Select *Last Name* in the first Headings row.

2 Choose Insert Row from the Insert menu.

3 Select Headings and then Insert.

4 Press ⏎ to deselect the row.
The screen should look like Figure 3.14. You now have three Headings rows.

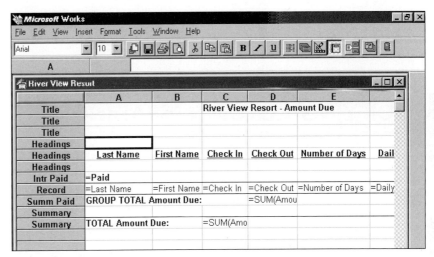

Figure 3.14

MODIFYING REPORT TITLES

The title of the report should consist of *River View Resort—Amount Due* and your name. You will now place your name in the title.

To add your name to the title of the report:

1 Place the insertion point in column C of the second Title row.

2 Type **By** followed by your name and then press (ENTER)

To view the report:

1 Choose Print Preview from the File menu.

2 When the preview appears, select the Zoom In button.
The preview should look like Figure 3.15.

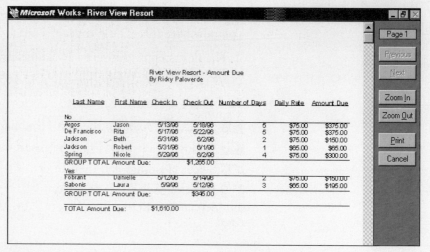

Figure 3.15

3 Select Cancel to return to Report view.

MODIFYING COLUMN HEADINGS

You can make several column headings more descriptive. For example, instead of *First Name* and *Last Name,* you can have *Guest's Name* in column A; instead of *Check In* and *Check Out,* you can have *Date of Check In* and *Date of Check Out.*

To add text to column headings:

1 Place the insertion point in the first Headings row in column A.

2 Type **Guest's** and then press (ENTER)
Guest's should still be selected.

3 Apply the bold character style to the heading *Guest's.*

4 Choose Alignment from the Format menu.

5 In the dialog box, select Center for the horizontal alignment.

6 Place the insertion point in the second Headings row of column A.

7 Press (F2) to activate the formula bar.

8 Delete *Last* so only *Name* appears.

9 Place the insertion point in the second Headings row of column B.

10 Delete *First Name.*
The Headings rows should now look like the ones in Figure 3.16.

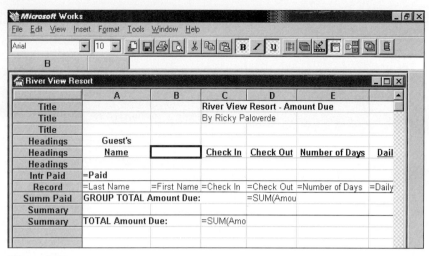

Figure 3.16

 To modify the* Check In *and* Check Out *headings:

1 Select the first Headings row of column C.

2 Type **Date of** and then press (ENTER)

3 Apply the bold character style to the heading *Date of.*

4 Center *Date of.*

5 Select the first Headings row of column D.

6 Type **Date of** and then press (ENTER)

7 Apply the bold character style to the heading *Date of.*

8 Center *Date of.*

The Headings rows should now look like those in Figure 3.17.

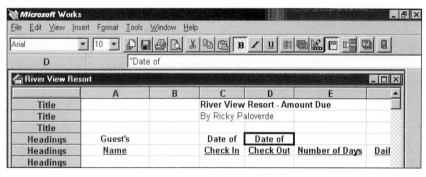

Figure 3.17

COMBINING THE CONTENTS OF TWO FIELDS INTO ONE

When you preview your report, the Last Name and First Name fields currently appear in separate columns as shown below:

```
Fobrant    Danielle
```

These two fields would look better if you could combine them into one field, separated by a comma and a space:

```
Fobrant, Danielle
```

You can combine text fields by using the Works concatenation character called an ampersand (&). The ampersand indicates to Works that you want to combine the preceding text with the following text. You could, for example, enter =*Last Name&First Name,* which would appear in the printed report as:

```
FobrantDanielle
```

For a comma and space to appear, you would need to surround these characters with double quotation marks and then place them between the two field names. The entry =*Last Name&"," &First Name* would print as:

```
Fobrant, Danielle
```

Two ampersands are needed in the preceding example. The first ampersand combines Last Name with the comma and space; the second ampersand combines the comma and space with First Name.

To combine the Last Name and First Name fields into one field:

1 Place the active cell in column A in the Record row.

2 Press (F2) to activate the formula bar.

3 Type **&", "&First Name** and press (ENTER)
Your entry should look like the one in the formula bar of Figure 3.18.

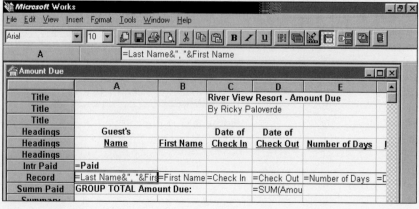

Figure 3.18

Because you now have the First Name field combined with the Last Name field in column A, you can delete the original First Name field in column B. Otherwise, the first name would appear twice in the report.

To delete the First Name field:

1 Place the active cell anywhere in column B.

2 Choose Delete Column from the Insert menu.
The First Name field should be gone.

When you preview the report you'll see the concatenated Last Name and First Name fields.

To preview the report:

1 Choose Print Preview from the File menu.

2 Zoom in to see the first field.
The screen should look like Figure 3.19. Notice that the Guest's Name column is too narrow to accommodate both the first and last names of all guests.

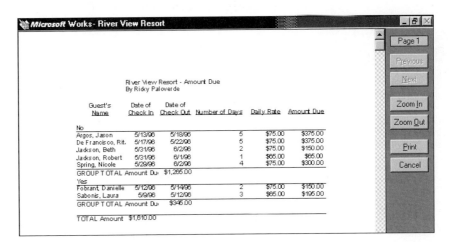

Figure 3.19

3 Select Cancel to close the preview.

CHANGING COLUMN WIDTHS IN REPORT VIEW

You need another modification to the River View Resort—Amount Due report. The Guest's Name column is too narrow to accommodate long names.

To change the Guest's Name column width:

1 Place the insertion point in column A.

2 Choose Column Width from the Format menu.

3 Type **20** and then select OK.

4 Preview the report and then zoom in.

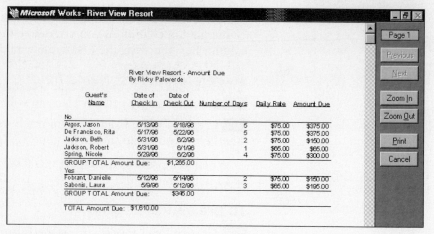

Figure 3.20

Notice that Rita De Francisco's entire name is now visible, as shown in Figure 3.20.

5 Select Cancel to close the preview.

ADDING A FUNCTION TO THE REPORT SUMMARY

In the report Summary row, you have the function SUM(Amount Due). The SUM function, which was added to the report when you ran the ReportCreator, adds all the numbers from the Amount Due column. Assume that in addition to knowing the total amount due, you want to know the average amount due for all customers. You can do this by placing another function in a Summary row. The following table lists the functions available in Report view.

Table 3.2

Function	Description
SUM	Finds the sum of a field from multiple records.
AVG	Finds the average of a field from multiple records.
COUNT	Counts the number of nonblank field entries from multiple records.
MAX	Finds the maximum value in a field from multiple records.
MIN	Finds the minimum value in a field from multiple records.
STD	Finds the standard deviation of a field from multiple records.
VAR	Finds the variance of a field from multiple records.

You need to add a Summary row at the end of the report and then place a description and AVG function in the row. All functions are available by choosing the Field Summary command in the Insert menu.

To add a Summary row:

1 Place the active cell below the last Summary row.

2 Choose Insert Row from the Insert menu.
You should see the Insert Row dialog box.

3 Select Summary (it should already be selected) and then Insert. You should see a new Summary row.

To add text and an AVG function in the new Summary row:

1 In column A in the new Summary row, type **AVERAGE Amount Due:** and then press (ENTER)

2 Apply a bold character style.

3 Place the active cell in column C in the new Summary row.

4 Choose Field Summary from the Insert menu.

5 Under Select a Field, select Amount Due.

6 Under Statistic, select AVG.
The screen should look like Figure 3.21.

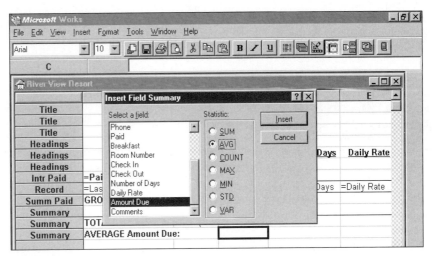

Figure 3.21

7 Select Insert to insert the function.
You should see the new function =*AVG(Amount Due)* in the formula bar.

8 Select Number from the Format menu.

9 Select Currency and then select OK to apply a currency format to the average amount due.

You can now preview the modifications.

To preview the report:

1 Select Print Preview from the File menu.

2 Zoom in.
The screen should look like Figure 3.22.

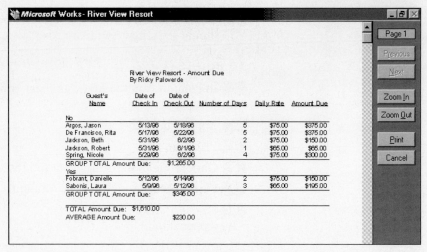

Figure 3.22

3 Select Cancel to close the preview.

SAVING REPORTS

Like filters, reports are not saved as files separate from the database. To save a report, you would save the database file in which the report was created. Every time you open the file, the report will be listed in the View menu. You will save the report along with the database file, using the name *Amount Due*. Because you are using a new file name, you should use the Save As command to save the file. By using the name *Amount Due*, you can keep the file *River View Resort* in its original form, without any modifications.

To save the database and report:

1 Choose Save As from the File menu.

2 Type **Amount Due** as the new file name.
The report will be saved with the database.

PRINTING REPORTS

Printing a report is similar to previewing and printing a database in List view. If the report is too wide to fit on one printed page, anything that does not fit on the first page will print on subsequent pages. This report should fit on one page.

To print the report:

1 Choose Print Preview from the File menu.

2 Select Zoom In twice to get a closer look.
The report should look like the one in Figure 3.23.

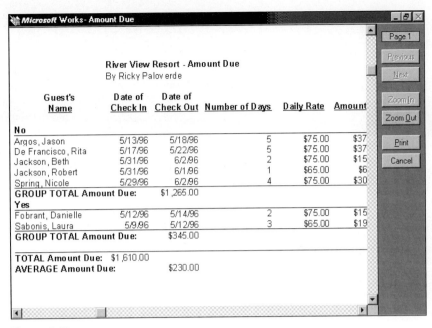

Figure 3.23

3 Select Print to print a copy of the report.

THE NEXT STEP

Reporting is a powerful feature of the Works Database tool. As you have seen, the user has a great deal of flexibility in formatting a database report.

Often, the appearance of a report can influence how printed information is received. Careful attention to titles, headings, and the overall layout of a report makes information easier to comprehend. Think of the various bank statements you have seen. Data from a banking account is kept in a database. Some statements are easier to read than others, and the difference is often due to how the database report is defined.

This concludes Project 3 with the Works Database tool. You can either exit Works or go on to work the Study Questions, Review Exercises, and Assignments and the Additional Assignments and Term Paper Project.

SUMMARY AND EXERCISES

Summary

- The ReportCreator enables you to generate a report.
- The four default row labels are Title, Headings, Record, and Summary.
- Intr *Field Name* and Summ *Field Name* enable you to define groups and summaries of groups of related records.
- You can insert rows and columns in a report.
- You can modify report titles and column headings.
- Reports are saved when you save the database.

Key Terms and Operations

Key Terms
Heading
Intr *Field Name*
Record
report
row label
Summ *Field Name*
Summary
Title
truncated

Operations
Create a report
Create group summaries
Delete a column/row
Insert a column/row
Use functions in a report
Use Report view

Study Questions

Multiple Choice

1. The _____ view enables you to summarize groups of records.
   a. Report
   b. Filter
   c. Form
   d. List

2. The field names indicating the information to be included in a report are preceded by which of the following in Report view?
   a. .
   b. ,
   c. +
   d. =

3. Which of the following is not a default row label?
   a. Title
   b. Headings
   c. Record
   d. Summ

4. In Report view the text "River View Resort—Amount Due" appears. This represents:
   a. a title.
   b. a summary.
   c. a record.
   d. a field.

5. Which menu contains a command to preview a report?
   a. Edit
   b. File
   c. Tools
   d. Insert

6. Which menu contains a command to design a new report?
   a. Edit
   b. File
   c. Tools
   d. Insert

7. Which menu is used to access information explaining the procedures?
   a. Help
   b. Edit
   c. File
   d. Insert

8. You can accomplish all of the following from Report view except:
   a. adding records to a database.
   b. adding a title to a report.
   c. grouping fields in a report.
   d. adding a heading to a report.

9. Which row of Report view contains a code to print group summaries?
   a. Title
   b. Record
   c. Summ *Field Name*
   d. Summary

10. In Works, a report is saved to disk when:
    a. the report is printed.
    b. the database file is updated using the Save or Save As command.
    c. you choose Save Report from the File menu.
    d. you choose Report from the Save menu.

Short Answer

1. The report generator is called _____.

2. The default name for reports is _____.

3. There are _____ default row types created by the report generator.

4. If you have 30 active records in your database, the record row will be printed _____ times.

5. Column headings appear at the top of _____ page(s).

6. To group related records, you must _____ the database.

7. After displaying a report, you can press _____ to return to report view.

8. The _____ and _____ row types contain functions for summarizing fields.

9. The _____ option in the Sort dialog box places a row between groups.

10. The _____ function counts the number of records in groups.

For Discussion

1. Describe how to add Intro *field name* and Summ *field name* rows to your report.

2. Describe the purpose of the Intro *field name* row.

3. What is the difference between typing `Last Name` and `=Last Name` in the record row?

4. Describe the differences among Form, List, and Report Views.

5. What functions can be used in formulas in Report View?

Review Exercises

Creating a Report from the *Used Car* Database

In the numbered steps that follow, you will create a report that finds the average price of all the used cars.

1. Open the database file *Used Cars*.

2. Choose ReportCreator from the Tools menu.

3. Type `Cars` for the name of the report.

4. Type `Ricky Paloverde's Used Cars` to serve as the report title, but use your name instead of Ricky Paloverde's.

5. Select all fields for the report except Sold, Cost, and Profit.

6. Group the report by the Make field.

7. Create a function that averages the Price field for records in each group and for all records in the database.

8. Preview the report.

9. Save the database, assigning it the name *Used Cars Report*.

10. Print the report.

Designing a Report for a Company Database

Retrieve the file *Second Bills* from the data disk. Create a report of all the companies to whom you pay bills each month. The report title should be two lines: "Monthly Bills" and your name. Sort the database by state. Print a copy of the report. Save the updated database (with the report file) as *Third Bills*.

Assignments

Creating a Personal Address Book

Microsoft Works has many built-in TaskWizards that provide step-by-step instructions for automating many tasks. One TaskWizard creates the database structure of a personal address book and, optionally, a report of the addresses. You will use this TaskWizard to create your own personal address book and report.

1. Select TaskWizards from the Works Task Launcher.

2. Select Address Book under Common Tasks, as shown in Figure 3.24.

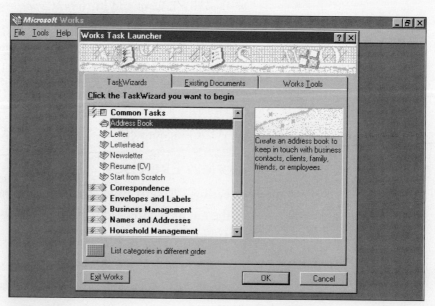

Figure 3.24

3. Select OK.

4. Select Yes to run the TaskWizard.

5. Select Personal and then Next.

You should see a dialog box with a list of all the fields that Works will use.

6. Select Next.

The screen should look like Figure 3.25. Works is giving you the chance to modify the database before creating it. Also, Works is giving you the opportunity to generate a report.

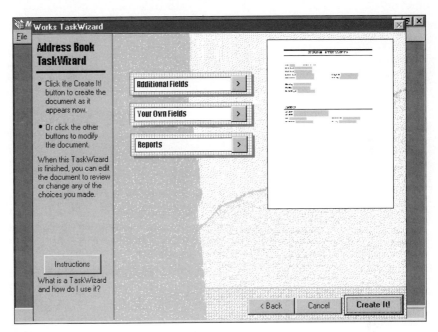

Figure 3.25

7. Select Reports.

8. Select Alphabetized Directory and then select OK.

9. Select Create It! and then Create Document.

Works will take a minute to create the database and report structures. Afterward, the screen will look like Figure 3.26

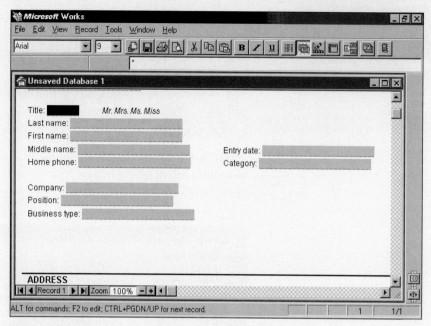

Figure 3.26

10. Enter the first record.

   The category refers to what kind of relationship you have with the person (business, personal, etc.), and the business type refers to what type of business the person is involved in. Note that after entering the business type you will have to press (TAB) to finish entering the rest of the record.

11. Enter at least four more records.

12. Print the first record in Form view and then print the report. You should have two printouts.

13. Save your work.

Listing Bibliographic Data by Type

Open the database file *Second Bibliography*. Create a report that sorts all records by publication type and by date. Use a report title of your choice. After the report is defined, save the file as *Third Bibliography*. Print the report.

Printing a Mailing List

A manager at First Savings and Loan needs a list of all customers currently in the database. Open the file *Bank Customers*. Create a report that lists all customers. Sort the list by city and by last name. Group the report by city. Save the updated database as *Second Bank Customers*. Print the report.

ADDITIONAL ASSIGNMENTS

CREATING A DATABASE AND REPORT FOR A DAY-CARE CENTER

You are the manager of the Valley Day-Care Center and you want to computerize operations. Currently, all data about the children is recorded on index cards. Figure 3.27 provides an example of a typical index card. All field contents are in italics.

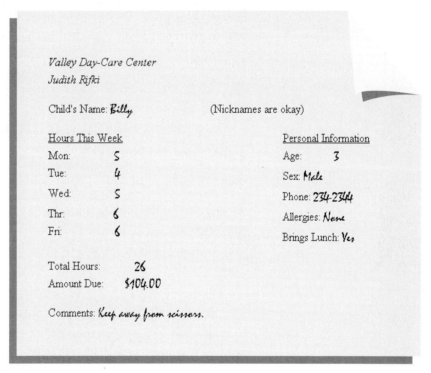

Figure 3.27

Creating a Form

1 Use Figure 3.27 as your guide in creating a database. You should:

- Create all fields.
- Determine the total hours with a formula that adds the hours from each day of the week.
- Calculate the amount due with a formula that multiplies the total hours by $4.00.
- Enter the default value, *Yes*, in the Brings Lunch field.

2 Enter at least six records. The Brings Lunch field should contain *No* for at least three children.

3 Create a form like Figure 3.27. Be sure to:

- Place the name of the day-care center and your name in the heading.
- Set the proper field widths.
- Include all descriptive labels.
- Apply the proper format to the Amount Due field.
- Make the Comments field two rows high.

4 Save the file, assigning it the name *Valley Day-Care*.

5 Print the first record in Form view.

Finding All Three-Year-Olds

You will now find which children are three years old.

1 Display the database in List view.

2 Hide the days of the week, the phone number, allergies, and comments.

3 Make the Age and Sex fields narrower.

4 Search the database and list on the screen only children who are three years old.
Hint: Use a filter.

5 Select Print from the File menu to print the list of three-year-olds.

Finding All Lunchless Children Who Stayed Five Hours or More on Monday

1 Unhide the Mon field.

2 Hide the Age and Sex fields.

3 Create a filter that lists all children who stayed five hours or more on Monday and did not bring a lunch.

4 Print the database.

5 Show all records in the database.

Creating a Report

Now you need to create a report that groups children's records according to their age.

1 Create a report with the ReportCreator.

2 Include all fields except the days of the week in the report.

3 Group records by the Age field.

4 Use the COUNT function to count how many children's names are present.
This essentially counts the number of children in the day-care center. The result should be in the Summary row.

5 Save the database.

6 Print the report.

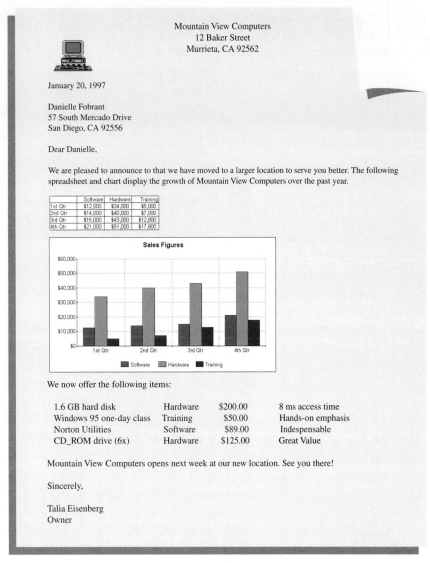

Figure 1.1

Designing the Solution

Your first task will be to design the word processing, spreadsheet, and database documents that will be integrated into the form letter. Then you will modify the letter so it can be merged with a list of names and addresses. Such a letter is not addressed to anyone in particular; it contains *placeholders,* which are replaced by names and addresses from a separate database. This merge feature enables you to create one letter and then print it many times, each time with a different name and address.

CREATING A NEW DOCUMENT

You will begin by creating the letter that will later be modified as a form letter. Figure 1.2 contains the initial text for the form letter.

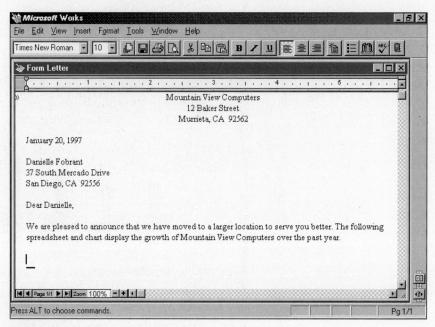

Figure 1.2

To begin creating the form letter:

1 Launch Works' Word Processing tool.

2 Choose Normal from the View menu to set the display format.

3 Enter the text from Figure 1.2 as a new word processing document. Use the current date. Or, if you have the student data files, open the file *Form Letter*.

4 Make sure you have two blank lines at the end of the document, because you will be adding more information to the letter.

5 Save the file as *Form Letter*.

USING MULTIPLE DOCUMENTS IN WORKS

To complete the form letter, you will need to create a spreadsheet and a chart in the Spreadsheet tool and a database in the Database tool. You will have three files open in three separate windows: a word processing window, a spreadsheet window, and a database window. You can switch between the documents either by using the Window menu or by manipulating individual document windows.

Reminder Working with windows is discussed in the *Introduction to Windows* and the *Overview* of this module.

To open a new spreadsheet window:

1 Choose New from the File menu.
The Works Task Launcher dialog box shown in Figure 1.3 should appear. If the screen looks different, select the Works Tools tab.

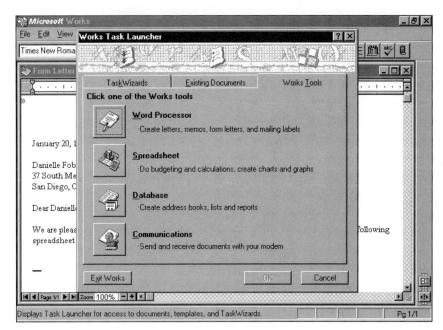

Figure 1.3

2 Select the Spreadsheet button in the dialog box.
You should see a new spreadsheet window.

To switch from one window to another, select the name of the desired window from the Window menu, which lists all open files. The current window is called the ***active window***. In Figure 1.4, the spreadsheet window is active, as indicated by the checkmark in front of the default file name, Unsaved Spreadsheet 1.

Figure 1.4

You also may change the active window by selecting the title bar of the desired window.

To display all open files:

1 Choose Window.
The screen should look like Figure 1.4.

2 Choose Tile from the Window menu.
The screen should look like Figure 1.5.

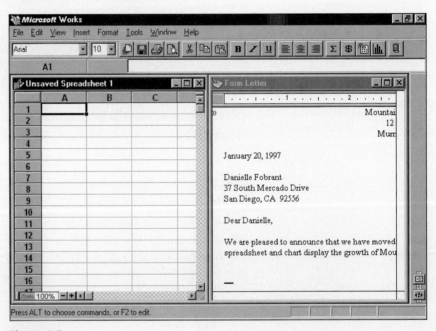

Figure 1.5

3 Choose Cascade from the Window menu.
The screen should look like Figure 1.6.

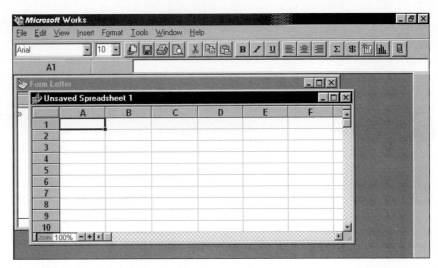

Figure 1.6

You can make a window active by clicking it, by choosing its name from the Window menu, or by pressing (CTRL) + (TAB). When you press (CTRL) + (TAB) the cursor jumps from one window to the next, making each successive window active.

CREATING A SPREADSHEET AND A CHART OF QUARTERLY SALES

Within the form letter, you will include a spreadsheet that describes how sales figures have increased over the past year.

To create and save a spreadsheet of sales figures:

1 Make sure you are in the spreadsheet window.

2 Maximize the spreadsheet window.

3 Make sure the point size is set to 10. If it isn't, choose Select All from the Edit menu and then select 10 on the Toolbar under Font Size.

4 Create the spreadsheet shown in Figure 1.7.
Important: Be sure to format numbers with no decimal places and align all column headings.

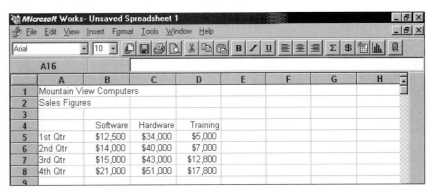

Figure 1.7

5 Save the spreadsheet as *Sales Figures*.

The form letter will also contain a bar chart of the spreadsheet data.

To create and name a bar chart of the spreadsheet data:

1 Select the range of data shown in Figure 1.8.

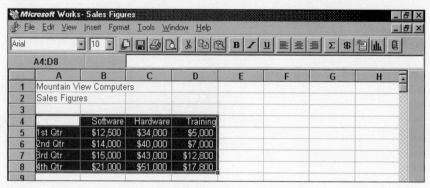

Figure 1.8

2 Choose Create New Chart from the Tools menu.
The New Chart dialog box appears. Change the settings to match those in Figure 1.9.

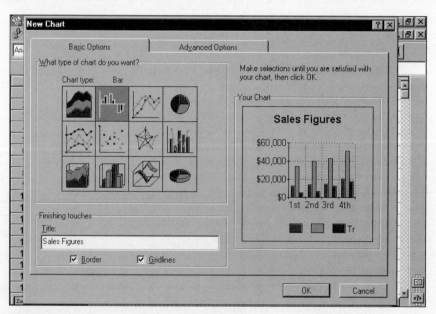

Figure 1.9

3 When finished, select OK to complete the command.
The chart shown in Figure 1.10 should appear.

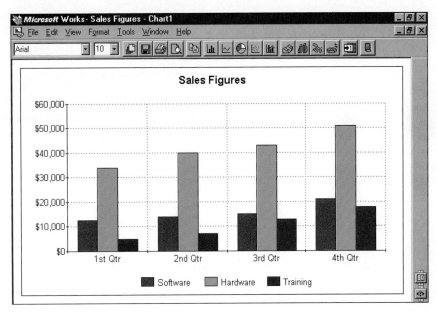

Figure 1.10

4 Choose Rename Chart from the Tools menu.

5 Type **Sales** for the chart name.

6 Select the Rename button, and then select OK.

7 Return to the Spreadsheet view by choosing Spreadsheet from the View menu.

8 Save the spreadsheet.

Reminder A chart will not be saved unless updates to the spreadsheet are saved to disk.

CREATING A DATABASE OF NEW PRODUCTS

The form letter should include a list of new products.

To open a new database window:

1 Choose New from the File menu.

2 Select the Database button in the dialog box.
You should see a new database window.

3 Create the database shown in Figure 1.11. Remember to format the Price field to Currency, with two decimal places.

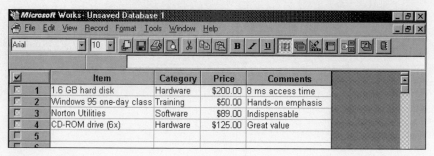

Figure 1.11

4 Save the file, assigning it the name *New Products*.

COPYING A SPREADSHEET INTO A WORD PROCESSING DOCUMENT

Now you will place a copy of the spreadsheet into the form letter. When you copy information, it is placed into a temporary storage location in memory called the *clipboard*. It is as though you were temporarily clipping a copy of the spreadsheet there to store it for later use.

To copy a spreadsheet to a word processing document:

1 Choose Sales Figures from the Window menu.

2 Make sure you are in the Spreadsheet view and then select the range A4:D8, as shown in Figure 1.12.

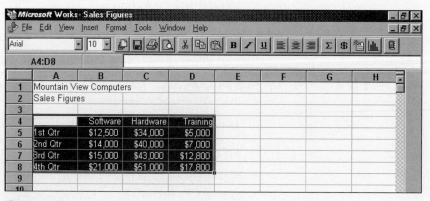

Figure 1.12

3 Choose Copy from the Edit menu.
A copy of the information is now on the clipboard.

4 Choose Form Letter from the Window menu.

5 Move the insertion point to the bottom of the document.

6 Choose Paste from the Edit menu.
The screen should look like Figure 1.13.

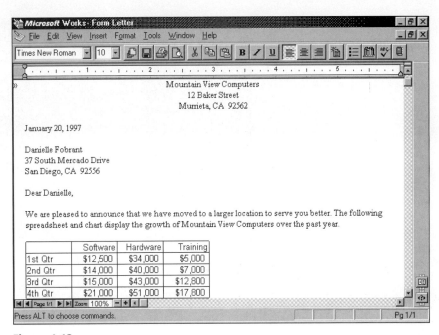

Figure 1.13

INSERTING A CHART INTO A WORD PROCESSING DOCUMENT

To place a chart into a word processing document, you will not copy the chart, as you would a spreadsheet; instead, you will insert the chart by using the Chart command in the Insert menu.

To insert a chart into a word processing document:

1 Move to the end of the document (you should already be there).

2 Press (ENTER) twice to insert two blank lines.

3 Choose Chart from the Insert menu.
You should see the Insert Chart dialog box.

4 Select the spreadsheet *Sales Figures.*

5 Select the chart named *Sales.*
The screen should look like Figure 1.14.

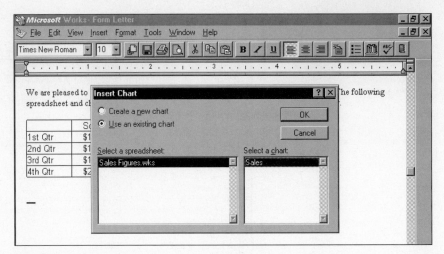

Figure 1.14

6 Select OK to insert the chart.

The chart appears in the word processing document.

7 Preview the document.

You should see the word processing document, including the spreadsheet and chart, as shown in Figure 1.15.

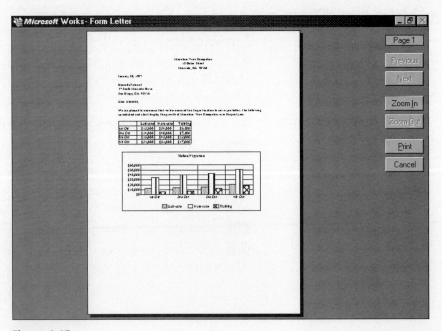

Figure 1.15

8 Select Cancel to exit the preview.

After inserting the chart, you can change its size and orientation. The chart is an object that can be resized using the mouse. The chart is currently proportionally spaced, so you do not need to resize it.

COPYING A DATABASE INTO A WORD PROCESSING DOCUMENT

To insert database information into a word processing document, you will display the database in List view and then copy the information. The copying procedure is the same as the one you used to copy the spreadsheet.

To copy a database into a word processing document:

1 Press (CTRL)+(END) to move to the end of the word processing document.

2 Press (ENTER) twice to add two blank lines.

3 Choose New Products from the Window menu to go to the database window.

4 Select the database.

5 Choose Copy from the Edit menu.

6 Choose Form Letter from the Window menu to return to the word processing document.

7 Choose Paste from the Edit menu.
The screen should look like Figure 1.16.

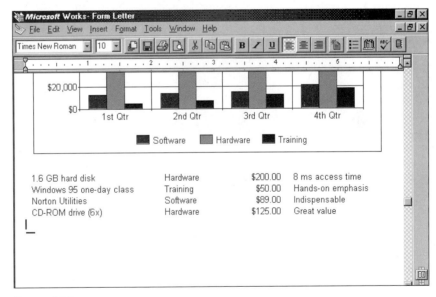

Figure 1.16

The letter is almost complete. You need to add some descriptive text above the database and some closing remarks.

To add text to the letter:

1 Add all the text that appears above and below the database in Figure 1.17. At the end of the letter enter your name, not Talia Eisenberg's.

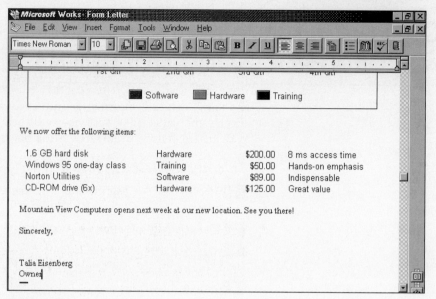

Figure 1.17

2 Preview the document.

The document should look like Figure 1.18. The entire document should fit on one page.

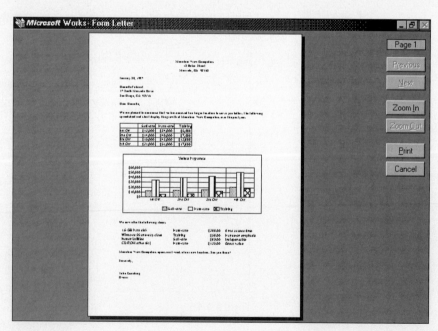

Figure 1.18

3 Select Cancel to exit the preview.

EXIT If necessary, you can save all files, exit Works now, and continue this project later.

ADDING CLIP ART

In Works you can add *clip art* or other drawn images to a document. The form letter will look better if some art is added to the right of the store address.

To insert a clip-art image:

1 Place the insertion point to the left of the first line of the store address, as shown in Figure 1.19. Don't put the insertion point in the header or footer.

Figure 1.19

2 Choose ClipArt from the Insert menu.
The clip-art dialog box appears.

> **Tip** If no clip art is visible or if an error message appears when you choose ClipArt from the Insert menu, the ClipArt Gallery may not be available on the computer you are using. If that is the case, save the file as *Form Letter* and skip these numbered steps.

3 Select Business.

4 Select the clip-art image of a computer. When selected, the image is surrounded with a border, as shown in Figure 1.20.

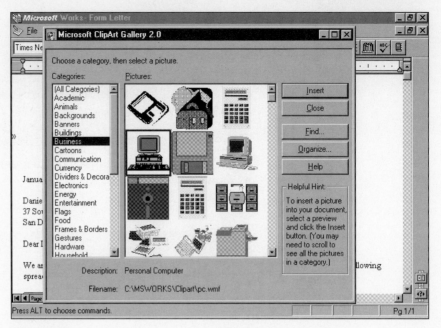

Figure 1.20

5 Select Insert to add the image to the word processing document. The clip art is inserted into the form letter.

The art is currently too large and needs to be reduced in size.

To change the size of the clip art:

1 Click anywhere inside the clip-art image.
When selected, the image is surrounded with a light-colored border, as shown in Figure 1.21.

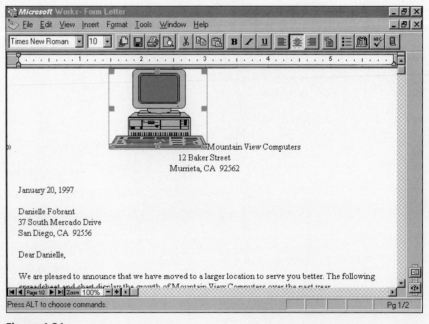

Figure 1.21

2 Drag the small square in the lower-right corner of the border around the image. Move the square up and to the left until the image is about 1 inch wide. Use the ruler to measure the clip art.
The screen should look like Figure 1.22.

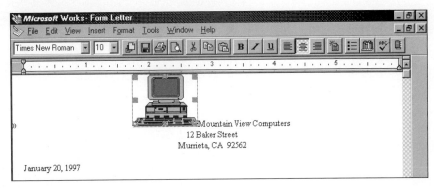

Figure 1.22

You can make the top of the document look really professional if you wrap the text on the side of the clip art. To do this, you should be in Page Layout view. Page Layout view is similar to Normal view, but it shows you a truer representation of what the printed document will look like. It is almost as though you are working with the document in Print Preview mode.

 To switch to Page Layout view and then wrap text:

1 Choose Page Layout from the View menu.
The screen should look like Figure 1.23.

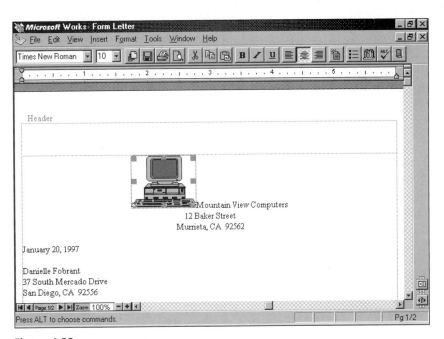

Figure 1.23

2 Choose Text Wrap from the Format menu.
You should see the dialog box in Figure 1.24.

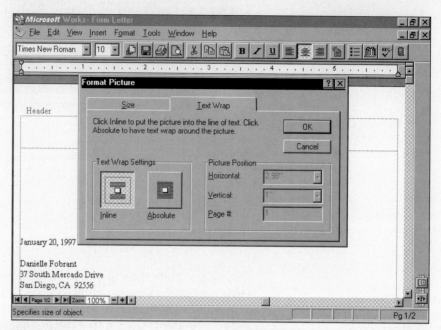

Figure 1.24

3 Select Absolute and then select OK to complete the command.
The document should look like Figure 1.25.

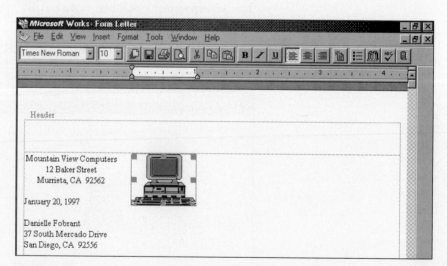

Figure 1.25

4 Drag the image of the computer to the left side of the page, as shown
in Figure 1.26.

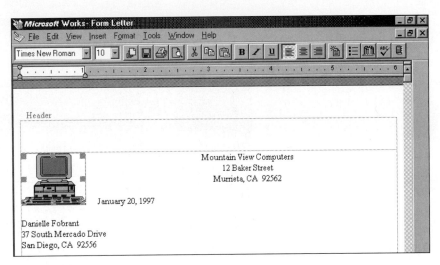

Figure 1.26

5 Place the insertion point between the clip art and the date and press (ENTER) twice.
The screen should look like Figure 1.27.

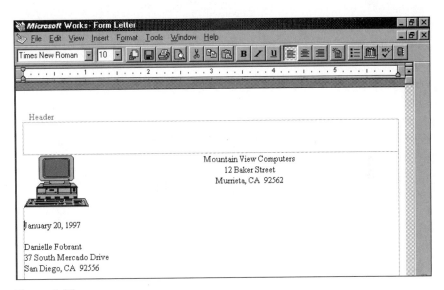

Figure 1.27

6 Preview the document.
The screen should look like Figure 1.28.

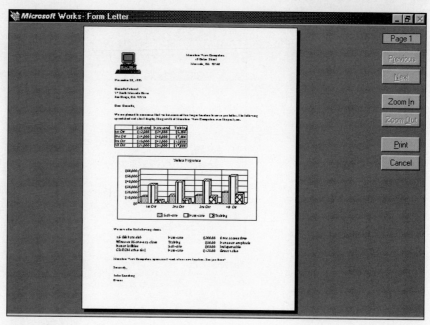

Figure 1.28

7 Select Cancel to exit the preview.

8 Save the file as *Form Letter*.

MERGING A FORM LETTER AND A LIST OF NAMES AND ADDRESSES

One of the most powerful features of Works is its ability to merge a database and a word processing document. This ability goes beyond simply copying data from one tool to another. By merging data, you can take a form letter and print it many times, each time with a different name and address from a list in the Database tool.

Merging a form letter with a list of names and addresses requires three basic steps:

- Create a database of names and addresses in which each record contains address data for a different person.
- Create a form letter that contains placeholders that tell Works where to place the names and addresses from the database.
- Choose Form Letters from the Tools menu to print the merged letter and database. One letter will be printed for each record in the database.

You will start by creating a database of names and addresses. Next, you will modify the form letter so it contains the placeholders. Finally, you will merge the files. Figure 1.29 provides a graphical overview of the merging process, which you will complete in this project.

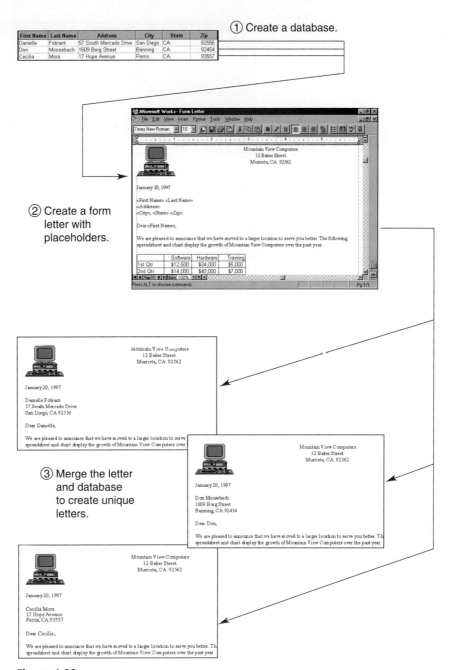

① Create a database.

② Create a form letter with placeholders.

③ Merge the letter and database to create unique letters.

Figure 1.29

Creating a List of Names and Addresses

A letter announcing the grand opening of a new retail store would most likely go out to hundreds of people. Your mailing will be limited to three computer-store customers: Danielle Fobrant, Don Moosebach, and Cecilia Mora. You will enter their names and addresses into a database that looks like Figure 1.30.

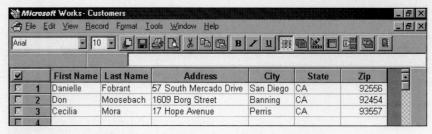

Figure 1.30

To create a database of names and addresses:

1 Choose the command to create a new database file.

2 Enter the field names as shown in Figure 1.30.

3 Enter the data shown in Figure 1.30 as the first three records in the database.

4 Save the file, assigning it the name *Customers*.

Designing a Form Letter

The form letter currently contains Danielle Fobrant's name. You need to delete her name and address and insert placeholders that correspond to field names in the database. You will delete the words *Danielle* and *Fobrant* and insert placeholders for the First Name and Last Name fields. When you print the letter, Works will take the data in the First Name and Last Name fields in the first record of the database and place the data into the form letter in the positions labeled *First Name* and *Last Name*. Of course, the letter also will have positions for the street address, city, state, and zip code.

The form letter will print as many times as there are records. The first time it will use Danielle Fobrant's record; the second time, Don Moosebach's record; and the third time, Cecilia Mora's record.

In the following numbered steps, you will modify the document *Form Letter* by adding placeholders for the address data from the file *Customers*.

To insert placeholders into the form letter:

1 Choose Form Letter from the Window menu.

2 Place the insertion point just to the left of the name *Danielle,* as shown in Figure 1.31.

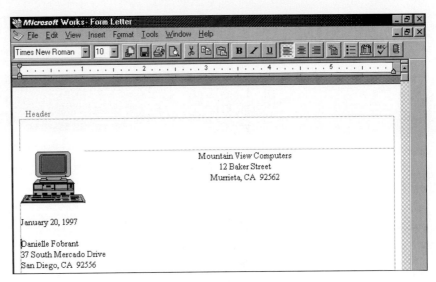

Figure 1.31

3 Choose Database Field from the Insert menu.

4 Select Use a Different Database.
You should see the dialog box shown in Figure 1.32. The file names might be different.

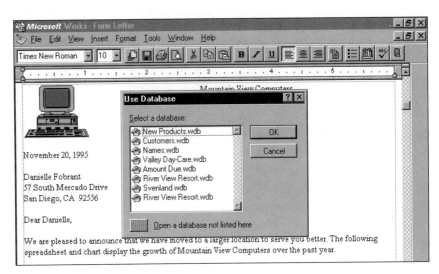

Figure 1.32

5 Select Customers.wdb.
The three letters *wdb* stand for Works database. Almost all files in Windows 95 have three-letter extensions that identify the file type. When working with Windows 95, you seldom see extensions. By the way, *wps* is the extension for Works word processing files and *wks* is the extension for spreadsheets.

6 Select OK.
The First Name field should be selected in the dialog box.

7 Select Insert.

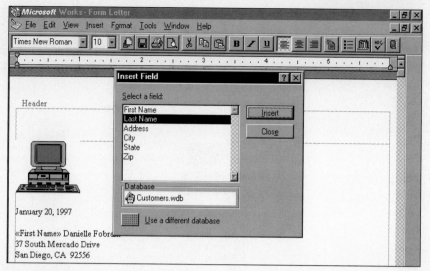

Figure 1.33

Notice in the form letter that the *<<First Name>>* placeholder has appeared next to Danielle, as shown in Figure 1.33.

8 Select Insert.

The *<<Last Name>>* placeholder should now be in the form letter.

9 Select Close to return to the form letter.

When you print the form letter, wherever <<First Name>> and <<Last Name>> appear, the first name and last name from a record in the database will appear in the printout. Soon you will delete the words *Danielle Fobrant* because they are no longer needed.

To insert the remaining fields:

1 Place the insertion point to the left of the address *57 South Mercado Drive*.

2 Choose Database Field from the Insert menu.

3 Select Address and then select Insert.

4 Select Close.

5 Place the insertion point to the left of *San Diego*.

6 Choose Database Field from the Insert menu.

7 Select City and then select Insert.

8 Select State and then select Insert.

9 Select Zip and then select Insert.

10 Select Close to return to the form letter.

The screen should look like Figure 1.34.

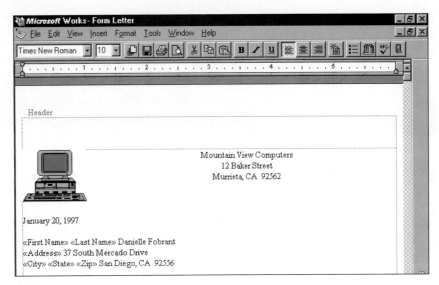

Figure 1.34

Because you no longer need Danielle Fobrant's name and address, you can delete them.

To delete Danielle Fobrant's name and address:

1 Delete Danielle Fobrant's name.

2 Delete Danielle's street address, city, state, and zip code.

3 Between the fields <<City>> and <<State>> type ,
You need a comma (,) between the city and state because this makes your printout look better. The screen should look like Figure 1.35.

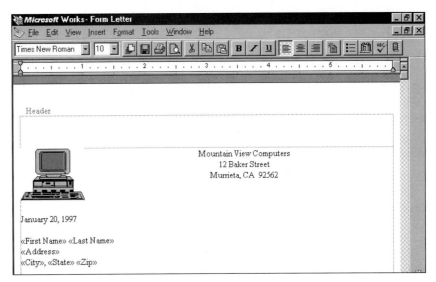

Figure 1.35

One more placeholder must be added. The letter starts out "Dear Danielle:". Instead of *Danielle* you should insert the <<First Name>> placeholder.

To delete Danielle *and insert the* <<*First Name*>> *placeholder:*

1 Place the insertion point right after the word *Dear* and right before the name *Danielle*. The insertion point should have a space before it.

2 Choose Database Field from the Insert menu.

3 Select First Name.

4 Select Insert and then Close.

5 Delete the name *Danielle*.

The screen should look like Figure 1.36.

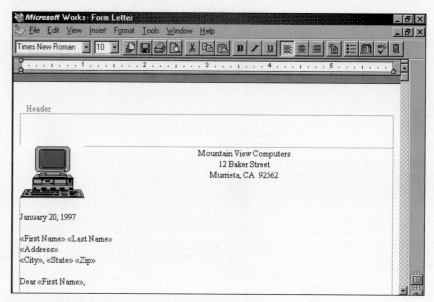

Figure 1.36

Merging the Names and Addresses with the Form Letter

You are now ready for Works to merge the names and addresses with the form letter and make three printouts for you. Each printout will have a different name and address taken from the *Customer* database.

To merge and print the files:

1 Choose Form Letters from the Tools menu.

2 Select the Printing tab.

You should see the dialog box shown in Figure 1.37.

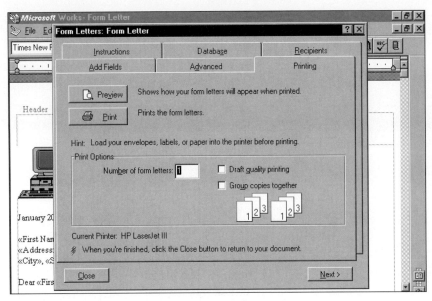

Figure 1.37

3 Select Preview.

4 Select OK to preview all records.

5 Select Zoom In twice.

Notice that the first form letter has Danielle Fobrant's name and address, as shown in Figure 1.38.

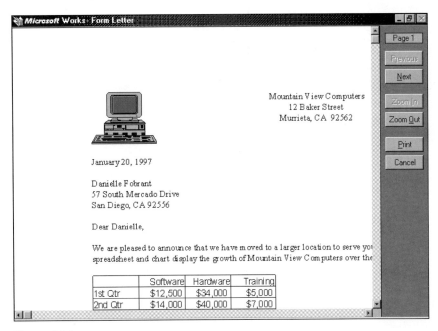

Figure 1.38

6 Select Next to see the next letter.

The second page of the printout has Don Moosebach's name and address.

7 Select Next to see the next letter.

The third page of the printout has Cecilia Mora's name and address.

8 Select Cancel to exit the preview.

9 Select Print to print the three form letters.

10 Select OK to complete the command.

THE NEXT STEP

You have successfully integrated data from the three Works tools. The form letter you created is typical of form letters sent by various organizations.

Businesses send form letters to potential customers. Colleges and universities may send grade reports or registration information by creating a form letter that includes data specific to each student. Think of other ways in which word processing, spreadsheet, and database files can be integrated.

This concludes Project 1 using the Works Word Processing, Spreadsheet, and Database tools together. You can either exit Works or go on to work the Study Questions, Review Exercises, and Assignments and the Additional Assignment and Term Paper Project.

SUMMARY AND EXERCISES

Summary

- You can copy data from one Works tool to another.
- To create a mass mailing, you can merge a form letter from the Word Processing tool with a list of names and addresses from the Database tool.
- You can display multiple windows on-screen at one time.
- Spreadsheets and databases can be copied into a word processing document.
- Charts can be inserted into a word processing document.
- Graphics, such as clip art or drawings, can be inserted into a word processing document.

Key Terms and Operations

Key Terms	Operations
active window	Add clip art
clip art	Create a form letter
clipboard	Insert a chart
mail merge	Insert a database
placeholder	Insert a spreadsheet
	Insert placeholders
	Manage multiple windows
	Print merged form letters

Study Questions

Multiple Choice

1. Which menu is used to switch between documents that are open?
   a. File
   b. Edit
   c. Window
   d. Help

2. A form letter that will print for all individuals in a database file contains which of the following to indicate where data appears in the letter?
   a. a footnote
   b. a placeholder
   c. a spreadsheet cell
   d. a database file

3. Which menu is used to add clip art to a document?
   a. File
   b. View
   c. Edit
   d. Insert

4. If a database has the field name First Name, which of the following is a valid placeholder?
   a. <<First Name>>
   b. {First Name}
   c. [First Name]
   d. #First Name#

5. To print a form letter, all of the following are true except:
   a. Placeholders specifying the fields from the database file must be in the form letter.
   b. You choose Form Letters from the Tools menu to print the form letter.
   c. You must have a database file containing the names and addresses for the form letter.
   d. You must have a spreadsheet file containing the names and addresses for the form letter.

6. To switch between documents in Works, which key sequence is used?
   a. CTRL + ESC
   b. SHIFT + SPACE
   c. COMMAND + SELECT
   d. CTRL + TAB

7. To display all open documents so they overlap on the screen, you would choose:
   a. Open from the File menu.
   b. Select All from the Edit menu.
   c. Cascade from the Window menu.
   d. Tile from the Window menu.

8. Placeholders are used to indicate:
   a. where field data will appear in a form letter.
   b. where a spreadsheet chart is inserted into a word processing document.
   c. the location of a chart pasted into a database form.
   d. a clip-art image that is too large to display on the screen.

9. Printing a letter for all records in a database is called:
   a. mail copying.
   b. data printing.
   c. letter formatting.
   d. mail merging.

10. In the Word Processing tool, _____ view displays are a truer representation of your printed document than Normal view.
    a. Printed Page
    b. Printout
    c. Page Layout
    d. True Type

Short Answer

1. To create a mass mailing, you can merge a _____ with a database of names and addresses.

2. If multiple windows are open, the window in which you are currently working is called the _____ window.

3. To insert a spreadsheet range into a word processing document, you must first copy the range to a temporary memory location called the _____.

4. The three letter extension for a Works database is _____.

5. To place a chart into a word processing document, choose Chart from the _____ menu.

6. To merge a word processing document with a database, choose _____ from the Tools menu.

7. If you merge a 20-record database with a form letter, _____ letters will print.

8. To wrap text around clip art, you choose _____ from the Format menu.

9. The _____ gallery consists of a collection of graphical images that can be inserted into your document.

10. To insert a placeholder for a database field into a word processing document, choose _____ from the Insert menu.

For Discussion

1. What are the steps required for a mail merge?

2. How do you change the size of a clip-art image in the Word Processing tool?

3. Describe some of the different categories of clip art available in Works.

4. In the project, you worked with a form letter for a computer store. Give an example of how a student could use merged form letters.

Review Exercises

Creating a Report for a Wildlife Preserve

You work at a wildlife preserve that contains elk, zebras, giraffes, elephants, and camels. To describe the preserve, you will create a one-page report in the Word Processing tool and include in the report a chart and a database.

1. Write a short paragraph that describes the preserve. At the top of the report, be sure to include a title and your name.

2. Create a pie chart that displays, as percentages, how many animals there are in each animal group. Each slice of the pie should represent one group. Use the following data in the spreadsheet.

Group	Number
Elk	27
Zebra	32
Giraffe	19
Elephant	12
Camel	8

3. Insert the chart into the word processing document.

4. Create the following database. The gestation period is in days, the life span is in years, and the speed is in miles per hour.

Animal	Gestation	Life Span	Speed
Elk	250	15	45
Zebra	365	15	40
Giraffe	425	10	32
Elephant	645	40	25
Camel	365	20	2.5

5. Sort the database alphabetically by animal name.

6. Copy the database into the word processing document.

7. Add any text that is necessary to describe the chart and database.

8. Save all three files. Choose appropriate file names.

9. Print the word processing document.

Merging a Memo with a List of Employee Names

You are the president of a large firm. Using the mail merge feature, print a memo that describes the end-of-year bonus for each employee.

1. Create the following database. Save it, assigning it an appropriate file name.

Fname	Lname	Job Title	Bonus
Rex	Lavlond	Pilot	550
Donna	Ramos	Technician	480
Jacob	Ariel	VP of Sales	250

2. Type the memo that follows, inserting field names where necessary. Type the current date and your name, not John Shnimpstly's. Save the memo, assigning it an appropriate file name. Reformat the document so it looks more professional.

```
Interoffice Memo
To:<<Fname>> <<Lname>>
From:John Shnimpstly, President
Date:November 23, 1996
Subject:Bonus of <<Bonus>> dollars

    Hi, <<Fname>>. Your generous end-of-year bonus is <<Bonus>>
dollars. You are a terrific <<Job Title>>!
```

3. Merge the memo and the list of names. You should get three printouts.

Assignments

Creating a Flyer for a Nursery

Create a one-page flyer describing upcoming events at a plant nursery. Include at least two clip-art images. Your flyer should include the database shown in Figure 1.39, copied from the Database tool.

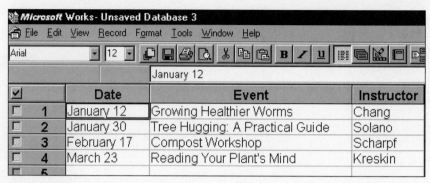

Figure 1.39

Creating a Document about Napa Valley Grapes

Assume that the Napa Valley Wine Growers Association has asked you to create an integrated document describing the amount of acreage dedicated to different grape varieties. They tell you that in 1971 there were six main varieties of grapes for red wine: Cabernet Sauvignon (planted on 2,127 acres), Pinot Noir (1,025), Merlot (203), Zinfandel (535), Cabernet Franc (25), Petite Sirah (577), and all the others (1,364). In 1991 the figures had changed: Cabernet Sauvignon (planted on 9,768 acres), Pinot Noir (2,636), Merlot (2,563), Zinfandel (2,179), Cabernet Franc (646), Petite Sirah (412), and all the others (889).

Use the preceding data to create two spreadsheets in Works, one for 1971 and one for 1991. Each should list wine varieties and how much acreage was dedicated to each one. Create a pie chart for each spreadsheet and put the date, either 1971 or 1991, as a title at the top of each chart. Insert both charts (but not the spreadsheets) into a word processing document. Write some text to introduce each chart. For example, you can mention that Cabernet Sauvignon has become very popular because of its strong, rich, voluptuous fruit flavor.

Save the document as *Napa Valley* and then print it.

ADDITIONAL ASSIGNMENT

CREATING A COVER LETTER TO ACCOMPANY A RÉSUMÉ

Cover letters, which accompany résumés, serve to introduce you and elicit an interview from a prospective employer. You are applying for a job, and you need a cover letter to accompany a résumé (you created a résumé in an Additional Assignment in the word processing section). You are applying for a similar position at three different companies, so you need three cover letters—one for each company. Create one cover letter and then merge it with a list of names and addresses of three prospective employers. Here are some guidelines for creating the cover letter:

- Use a business-letter format.
- State the purpose of the letter in the opening sentence.
- Indicate how you heard about the job opening.
- Describe how your experiences can contribute to the job and company.
- Mention, if possible, your familiarity with the company.
- Indicate that a résumé is enclosed and that you are available for a personal interview.

Creating a List of Prospective Employers

1 Create a database of employers to whom you will send the cover letter. You should have eight fields: Title, First Name, Last Name, Company, Street Address, City, State, and Zip. The Title field refers to a person's courtesy title—that is, Mr., Mrs., Miss, or Ms. Invent the names, companies, and addresses.

2 Save the database. Use a suitable file name.

Creating the Cover Letter

1 Using the preceding guidelines, create a cover letter. Invent the position for which you are applying. Insert the field names from the database file. Add any text that you feel is pertinent.

2 Save the cover letter. Use a suitable file name.

Merging the Cover Letter and the Database

1 Choose the command to merge the files. You should have three printouts.

2 Print the cover letter, without merging.

TERM PAPER PROJECT

COMBINING THE PARTS OF THE TERM PAPER

In this project, you will combine all the descriptions you have created of the island of Svenland. Into the main body of text of the file *Svenland,* you need to copy a spreadsheet, *Svenland;* insert a chart, Chart1 from *Svenland;* and copy a database, also *Svenland.* As you can see, all the files have the same file name but different extensions.

1 Open the word processing file Svenland, the spreadsheet file *Svenland,* and the database file *Svenland.*

2 Copy the spreadsheet into the appropriate location in the term paper. Add any descriptive text that you feel is appropriate.

3 Insert Chart1 from *Svenland* into the term paper just below the spreadsheet. Resize the chart if necessary. Add any descriptive text that you feel is appropriate.

4 Copy the database *Svenland* into the proper location in the term paper. Add any descriptive text that you feel is appropriate.

5 Where the document talks about the location of Svenland, insert a ClipArt image of the map of the world.

6 Preview the term paper.

7 Print the term paper.

PART VI

Communications

With the right tools, a computer can cease being an island and can join the world of ***telecommunications,*** the merger of telephone communications and computers. Telecommunications enables you to make airline reservations, get current weather reports, keep track of stocks, and access encyclopedias, to name only a few possibilities. You can also tie into your bank's electronic banking services or become a ***telecommuter,*** an employee who uses a personal computer to work away from his or her office. The telecommuter's computer is connected via modem and telephone lines to the employer's computer.

Before becoming a part of this exciting world, you must overcome one minor obstacle. Telecommunications standards are not like the standards of television and radio; you can't just flip a switch to receive information. For you to telecommunicate, an array of settings for the computer you are using must correspond precisely to those of the computer with which you want to communicate. Once you clear this small hurdle, telecommunicating across the country will become as easy as making a phone call.

PROJECT 1: COMMUNICATING WITH ANOTHER COMPUTER

Objectives

After completing this project, you should be able to:

▶ Create a communications file

▶ Define communications settings

▶ Connect with a remote computer

▶ Receive a file

▶ Send a file

▶ Disconnect from a remote computer

CASE STUDY: TELECOMMUNICATING WITH A COMPUTER

Assume that you need to access international databases and communicate with individuals from around the world. For example, what if a new species of tree were discovered and an image of it was placed on a computer so that anyone with the right communications tools could connect to the computer and look at the tree? You could look at it if you had communications hardware and software.

Designing the Solution

This project will simulate how the Communications tool in Works can be used to connect the computer with other computers by using the phone lines to transfer data. First, a communications file is opened or created. Then, the communications settings are checked. Finally, the modem is used to connect the computer you are using to a remote computer.

USING TELECOMMUNICATIONS

Before data can be transmitted over phone lines, it must be converted from a *digital signal,* the signal with which computers work, to an *analog signal,* the signal that phone lines carry. Digital signals consist of electrical pulses that represent **bits,** 1s and 0s. A pulse indicates a 1; the absence of a pulse indicates a 0. Bits are usually placed together in groups of eight to create **bytes,** each of which can be thought of as being roughly equivalent to a character. For example, in many computers, 01000001 represents the letter *A*. The digital signal for 01000001 has a time sequence in which there is an absence of a pulse (0), a pulse (1), five time sequences in which pulses are absent (00000), and then one pulse (1).

Most phone lines are designed to carry analog signals, not digital signals. Your voice is a good example of an analog signal. When you speak, you do not blurt out pulses at intermittent intervals. Your words flow in a continuous stream of sound. To be transmitted over phone lines, digital pulses are converted into two sounds, one that represents a 1 and one that represents a 0. A **modem,** or MOdulator/DEModulator, is found at each end of a two-computer telecommunications system. The modem of the source computer **modulates,** or translates, the digital signal into an analog signal; the modem at the target computer **demodulates,** or translates, the analog signal back into digital form. This process is shown in Figure 1.1.

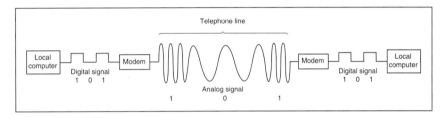

Figure 1.1

Modems can be either internal (located inside the computer) or external (placed outside the computer). Both types of modems have cables that connect them to an analog telephone line.

A large number of computer systems offer their services and resources to the public. You must pay to use many of them, but some are free. For example, if you want to look up late-breaking news stories, you need to sign up with an information service such as CompuServe, America Online, the Microsoft Network, or Prodigy, all of which charge a monthly fee. If you want to exchange information with computer users who have similar interests, you can dial into one of thousands of electronic bulletin boards set up to disseminate information, usually for free. As with all information services, you will always pay the phone company for the phone call.

Later in this project you will see how to connect to the CompuServe information service.

Creating a Communications File

In this project, you will define all the settings required to set up a communications link between two computers. After establishing the settings, you will see a communications session with CompuServe. If you have access to CompuServe, you can actually connect to the service as described in the numbered steps. If you don't have access to CompuServe, read through the text to get a feel for how it works. By the way, you typically don't use

Works to dial into CompuServe. CompuServe has a graphical interface called WinCIM that is even easier to use than the numbered steps described here. Most of the concepts that you learn here will carry over to WinCIM or any other service that you use.

To communicate with another computer, you need to create a communications file in which you specify the settings.

To create a communications file:

1 Select the Communications icon in the Works Task Launcher dialog box.

The screen should look like Figure 1.2. When you start a new communications session, Works provides the Easy Connect dialog box. If you have already established settings for a communications session and given them a name, such as USC, you can select that name from this dialog box.

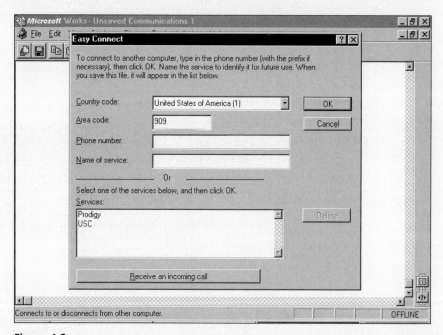

Figure 1.2

Notice that the default file name is Unsaved Communication 1. The word *OFFLINE* on the right side of the status bar indicates that you are not currently connected to another computer.

2 Select Cancel to close the dialog box.

DEFINING THE SETTINGS

Communications settings are defined in three dialog boxes: Communications, Terminal, and Phone. Another dialog box called Transfer enables you to establish settings for transferring files between computers. You will see the Transfer dialog box in the Transferring Files section, later in this module.

To establish a communications session, you often only need to enter a phone number in the Easy Connect dialog box, because the default settings in the rest of the boxes are compatible with a wide variety of remote computers. If the default settings do not allow communication, you must change the settings to correspond to those used by the remote computer. The easiest way to determine the needed settings is usually to call the remote system's help line, which can provide technical information about the other machine, or the *sysop* (system operator), a person who manages an information service.

Assume that the default settings aren't set correctly for CompuServe. Let's see how to set them.

Specifying Communication Settings

Within the Communication dialog box are options for defining how the computer will "talk" to a remote computer.

To define communication settings:

1 Choose Communication from the Settings menu.
The Settings dialog box appears, as shown in Figure 1.3. Notice that the Communication tab is active.

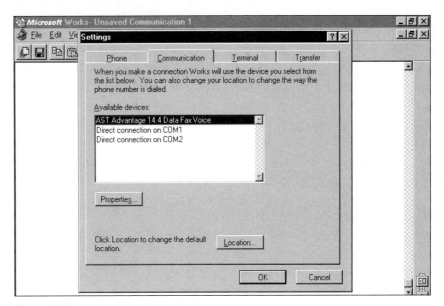

Figure 1.3

2 Select the name of your modem, as shown in Figure 1.3.
In this dialog box you will choose the name of your modem. In Figure 1.3 the modem is an AST 14.4 Data Fax Voice. Other popular modems are made by Hayes, Motorola, U.S. Robotics, Supra, and Practical Peripherals. Once you select the modem, you can enter a detailed description of its settings by selecting Properties.

To set the properties of your modem:

1 Select Properties.

You should see the dialog box in Figure 1.4. Notice that the General tab is selected.

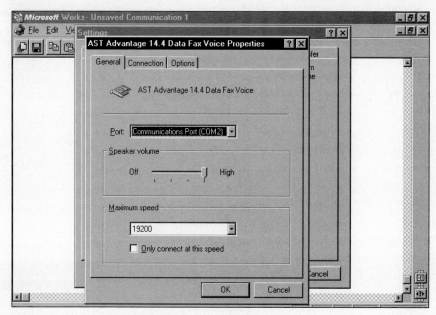

Figure 1.4

The three main options are Port, Speaker Volume, and Maximum Speed. Computers often have more than one communications *port,* or passage in and out of the computer. COM1 and COM2 stand for serial communications ports 1 and 2, respectively. To set the port, you must know how the modem was configured. You can check the manual or talk to your service representative to select the right option. By the way, modems are usually connected to COM2.

When your modem dials a phone number, you can actually hear the modem dialing a number. The speaker volume option controls how loud this is.

The last option lets you adjust how quickly your modem will send data back and forth with the remote computer. This is measured in ***bits per second (bps).*** The higher the bps, the faster the data travels. The modems on each end of a communications session must be set to the same bps. Modems typically work at 14,400 or 28,800 bps. You may also find 2,400, 4,800, and 9,600 bps. When you buy a modem, the packaging will indicate the bps.

You can set several more properties for the modem by selecting the Connection tab.

To choose the Connection tab to set more properties:

1 Select the Connection tab.

You should see Figure 1.5.

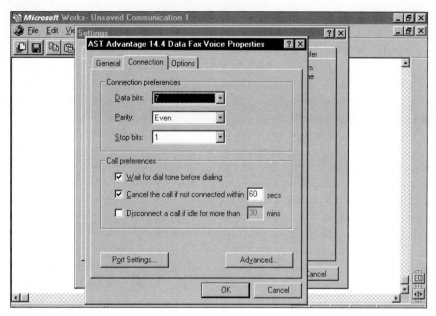

Figure 1.5

In general "computerese," 8 bits always makes a byte. In communications, however, either 7 or 8 *data bits* can be used to represent a character. For the communicating computers to distinguish one character from another, either 1 or 2 *stop bits* are inserted at the end of each character, to keep track of where one character ends and the next one begins. Figure 1.6 illustrates the standard data and stop-bit combinations.

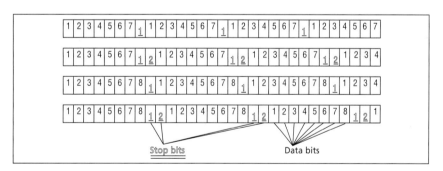

Figure 1.6

To set *parity* is to determine the method that a sending and receiving computer will use to check for data transmission errors. You must be sure to match the computer's parity settings with those of the remote computers. Five settings are common: None, Odd, Even, Mark, and Space.

To adjust the connection properties:

1 Change all settings in the dialog box to match Figure 1.5.

2 Select OK.

3 Select OK to exit from the Settings dialog box.

EXIT If necessary, you can exit Works now and continue this project later.

Specifying Terminal Settings

A *terminal* is a keyboard and monitor not directly attached to a local computer, but attached to some distant computer. When you connect to a remote computer by means of a modem and telephone lines, the local computer is like a terminal that signs in and behaves like a guest of the remote computer. Bank tellers use terminals, airline ticket agents use terminals, even cashiers use terminals (their cash registers can be sophisticated terminals connected to a remote computer). Because the computer you are using will act like a terminal, you will use the Terminal dialog box to define how the keyboard and screen will operate when connected to a remote computer.

 ### To view the terminal settings:

1 Choose Terminal from the Settings menu.

The Settings dialog box again appears, except this time the Terminal tab is active, as shown in Figure 1.7.

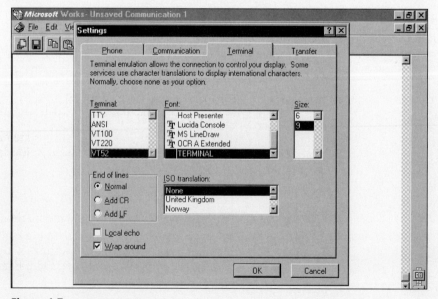

Figure 1.7

A PC can *emulate,* or imitate, several standard terminal types. Two of the most common are the VT100 and the ANSI. If you are unsure about which terminal to emulate, use VT100.

The font and point size of your text also can be adjusted. Terminal is a sans serif typeface that many people like using during communications sessions. A point size of 9 should work well also.

The End of Lines options enable you to adjust the carriage-return and line-feed characters of incoming data. When a computer encounters the end of a line, it usually inserts a carriage return to send the insertion point back to the left side of the screen and a line feed to move the insertion point to the next line. Suppose the computer has received data from a remote computer, but the new lines of the data received don't begin on the left side of the screen. You need to insert carriage returns by selecting the Add CR option. If one line overwrites another, there probably are no line feeds; you need to select the Add LF option. Typically, these options are chosen after you are connected with the remote computer.

If you connect to an international information service that doesn't use the English language, you may need to change the ISO Translation setting in order to receive international characters. In the Terminal Settings dialog box shown in Figure 1.7, an ISO Translation list box is seen. The ISO options are listed by country. If you are connecting to a service using English, None should be selected.

If incoming lines of text are more than 80 characters wide (the width of most screens), Wrap Around causes the extra characters to automatically wrap down to the next line. In certain situations you will choose Local Echo, which lets you see what you're typing on-screen while you are typing it. Typically you see on the screen what you are typing, but on some rare occasions, you won't see what you're typing unless you choose Local Echo.

To adjust the terminal settings:

1 Change your settings so they match the ones in Figure 1.7.

2 Select OK to apply the new settings.

Specifying Phone Settings

Within the Phone dialog box, you can specify how a modem makes or answers calls. To define the phone settings, you can choose Phone from the Settings menu.

To define the phone settings:

1 Choose Phone from the Settings menu.
The Settings dialog box will appear, with the Phone folder active, as shown in Figure 1.8.

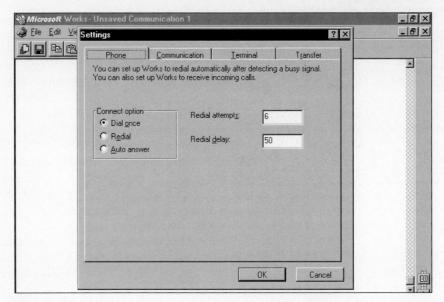

Figure 1.8

In the Connect Option box, you can specify that you want to dial the number once or multiple times. You can also have the modem automatically answer incoming calls from other computers by selecting the Auto Answer option.

Other options you can set are the number of redial attempts and the redial delay. These options usually are not changed from the default (6 and 50).

To adjust the phone settings:

1 Change your settings so they match the ones in Figure 1.8.

2 Select OK to apply the new settings.

MAKING THE CONNECTION

Once you are sure all the settings are correct, you are ready to make the connection with another computer. The following steps take you through the connection process with CompuServe, a major information retrieval service. Of course, you need to have a CompuServe account, which consists of a user ID number and a password. As with most information services, CompuServe requires that you identify yourself with an ID number and a password to *login,* or formally connect your computer with the remote computer. The ID number is supplied by CompuServe; you invent your own password.

The following numbered steps show you how to dial into CompuServe's 800 number. Typically, you would dial into a local CompuServe number, not an 800 number. If you don't have a CompuServe account, just read the following numbered steps.

To connect with CompuServe:

1 Choose Easy Connect from the Phone menu.

2 Type the area code, phone number, and name of service, as shown in Figure 1.9.

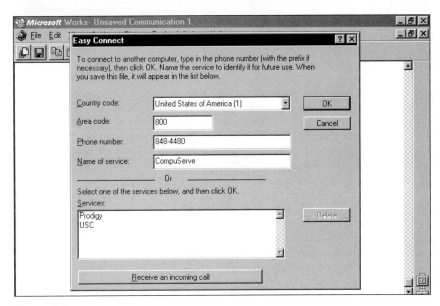

Figure 1.9

3 Select OK.

You should see the dialog box in Figure 1.10. Works is giving you a second chance to specify the phone number and other options.

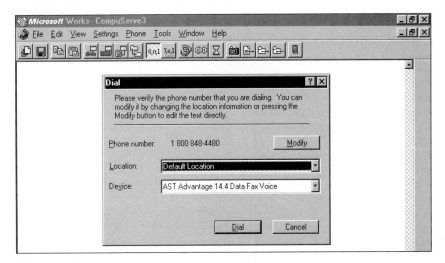

Figure 1.10

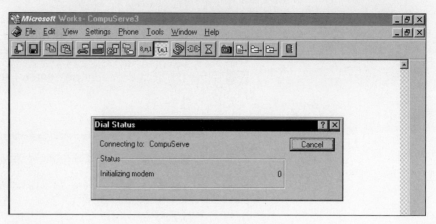

Figure 1.11

4 Select OK.

Now you should see the Dial Status dialog box shown in Figure 1.11. This box will disappear in about 15 seconds when the actual connection is made. After the connection is made to CompuServe, you will see a prompt that says *Host:*.

5 At the Host: prompt, type **CIS** and press (ENTER)

CIS stands for CompuServe Information Service.

6 At the user number prompt, type your user number and press (ENTER)

The number is assigned to you when you sign up with CompuServe.

7 At the password prompt, type your password and press (ENTER)

You should see CompuServe's opening menu, which basically lists what's new at CompuServe.

8 Press (ENTER) a couple of times until you reach the main menu shown in Figure 1.12.

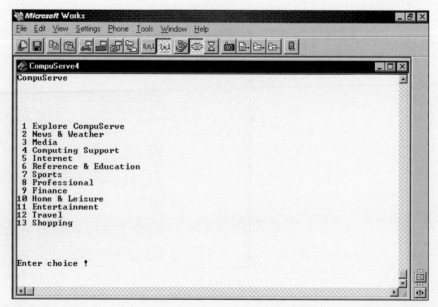

Figure 1.12

Now that you are into CompuServe, where do you go first? There are computer fanatics who spend hours a day online—we'll spend just a few minutes. Let's start by going to a forum. *Forums* are locations where you can exchange information with other CompuServe members who share your particular interests. Every forum has a message board, data libraries, and conference rooms.

To go to the gardening forum:

1 Type **10** and then press (ENTER)

Option number 10 corresponds to Home & Leisure. You should see a new menu that lists several new options related to Home & Leisure.

2 Type **8** and then press (ENTER)

Option 8 corresponds to Hobbies.

3 Type **8** and then press (ENTER)

In this menu, option 8 corresponds to Gardening.

You should see several options related to the Gardening forum, or interest group, as shown in Figure 1.13. If you choose option 2 (Messages), you can leave messages for or examine messages from other members of the forum. Notice the other options. Which one would you choose?

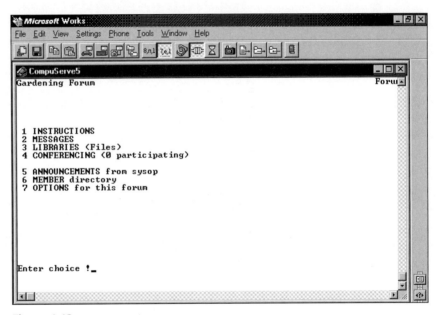

Figure 1.13

TRANSFERRING FILES

You can transfer data from a remote computer to a local computer, a process called *downloading,* or you can transfer files from a local computer to a remote computer, a process called *uploading.* You can download and upload text, programs, or graphical data.

Receiving a File

When you download data, you must specify a ***protocol,*** or set of rules that Works will follow to check for and correct errors while transmitting data. The remote computer will most likely have several protocols from which to choose. Works has four: Kermit, Xmodem/CRC, Ymodem, and Zmodem. You will use Xmodem/CRC. During an Xmodem/CRC file transfer, data is transferred in blocks of 128 bytes. If the receiving computer detects an error, the entire block is retransmitted. Although Xmodem's block size is rather small for high speed modems, its simplicity and ease of use have made it one of the most widely implemented microcomputer protocols. You will set the protocol in the Settings dialog box under the Transfer tab.

To set the protocol to Xmodem/CRC:

1 Choose Transfer from the Settings menu.
You should see the dialog box in Figure 1.14.

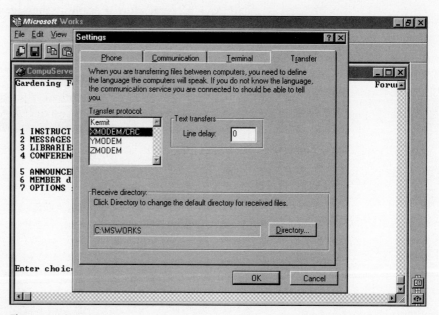

Figure 1.14

2 Select XMODEM/CRC as the protocol to use.

Downloading a file requires two steps. First, you must instruct the remote computer to send the file. Second, you must choose Receive File from the Works Tools menu and then enter a file name for the file that is being transferred.

In Figure 1.13, option 3 (Library) offers a library of files that can be downloaded. You will download a graphical image of a myrtle tree.

To download a graphical image:

1 Type **3** and then press (ENTER)
You should see the Gardening Forum menu shown in Figure 1.15. Notice that option 10 corresponds to Trees/Bonsai.

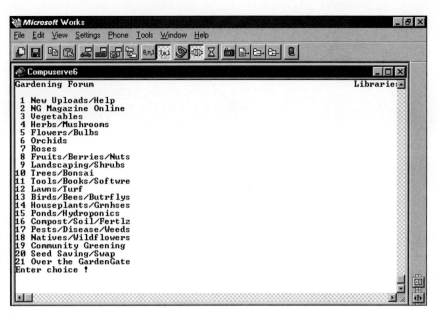

Figure 1.15

2 Type **10** and press (ENTER)
Now you have several more options. Option 4 is for downloading files. In this case, you'll be downloading a file related to trees.
3 Type **4** and press (ENTER)
CompuServe is asking you to type the name of the file. Typically, you would first browse the available files before choosing option 4. Assume that you browsed the files earlier, and now you know the exact name of the file that you want.
4 Type **myrtle.jpg** and press (ENTER)
CompuServe now asks what type of protocol you would like to use, as shown in Figure 1.16. Locally, you set the protocol to Xmodem, so you should tell CompuServe to use the same protocol.

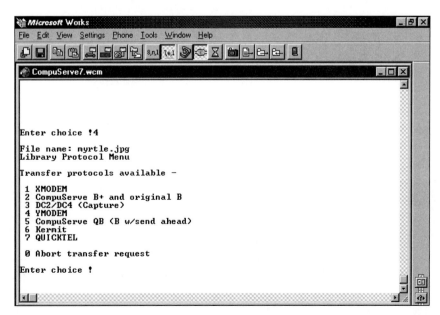

Figure 1.16

5 Type **1** and press (ENTER)

6 Choose Receive File from the Tools menu.

You should see the dialog box in which CompuServe is asking for a file name to use to save the file on the hard disk. The file name you type does not have to be the same as the CompuServe file name.

7 Type **myrtle.jpg**

The screen should look like Figure 1.17. The downloaded file will be named *myrtle.jpg*.

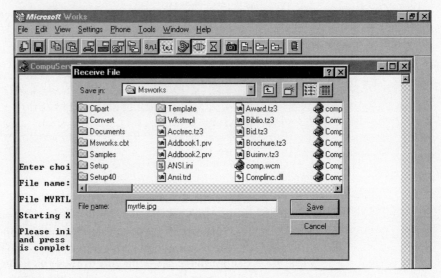

Figure 1.17

8 Press (ENTER)

You now should see a dialog box reporting the status of the download, including an update on the number of bytes transferred, as shown in Figure 1.18.

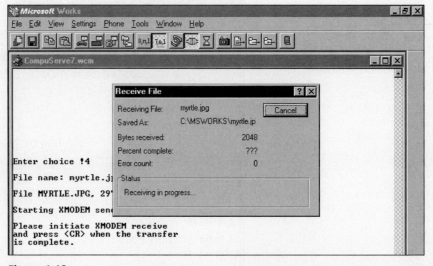

Figure 1.18

After the file has finished downloading, you will get a message that the transfer was successful and then you will get the CompuServe prompt again. You can view the downloaded graphical image by loading it into a graphical viewing program like Apple's QuickTime Picture Viewer, Collage Complete, or Hijaak.

9 Type **T** and press (ENTER)

Typing the letter *T* takes you back to CompuServe's opening menu.

Sending a File

If you have a file that you think would be of interest to others, you can upload the file to the information service. Typically, uploaded files are programs, articles, or graphical images that the sender has created.

Uploading files is very similar to downloading files. First, you would choose the appropriate command to indicate to the information service that you want to upload a file. Next, within Works, you would choose Send File from the Tools menu. Works prompts you to specify a file name. After that, you would choose OK. Because the procedure is so similar to downloading files, step-by-step instructions are not included in this module.

DISCONNECTING

To disconnect from an information service is to *logout,* or terminate the communications session. To logout, you would typically choose the appropriate menu option or type a word such as *Bye.* Works doesn't realize that you have logged out, however, so you must explicitly tell it so by choosing Hang Up from the Phone menu. After you have disconnected, the word *OFFLINE* appears on the status bar.

To logout and disconnect from CompuServe:

1 Type **bye** at the CompuServe prompt.

CompuServe will ask whether you're sure.

2 Select OK to continue the logout.

3 Choose Hang Up from the Phone menu.

Now you have disconnected.

You have just successfully downloaded a graphical image or picture. Typically, files that have the extensions JPG, GIF, or TIF are graphical images. If you have a graphics viewer such as Apple's QuickTime Picture Viewer you can view certain graphics files and even place them into Works. To insert graphical images into Works you would choose Object from the Insert menu.

To view the downloaded file:

1 Choose New from the File menu.

2 Select Word Processor from the Works Task Launcher.

3 Choose Object from the Insert menu.

4 Select QuickTime Picture from within the dialog box.

The screen should look like Figure 1.19. If you don't see QuickTime Picture, you don't have this program loaded on the computer.

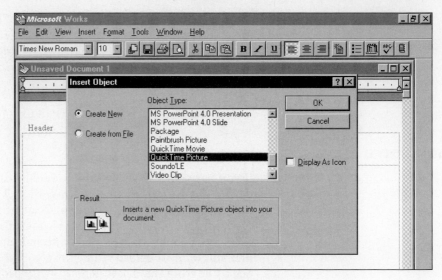

Figure 1.19

5 Select OK.

You should see a dialog box with a list of graphical images.

6 Select the file *myrtle.jpg* and then select OK.

You should see the QuickTime Picture Viewer with a myrtle tree, as shown in Figure 1.20.

Figure 1.20

7 Select Exit & Return to Unsaved Document 1 from the File menu.

You should see a dialog box that asks whether you want to update the image within the current Works document.

8 Select Yes to update the image.

The image of the myrtle tree is now within Works.

9 Size the image so it looks like Figure 1.21.

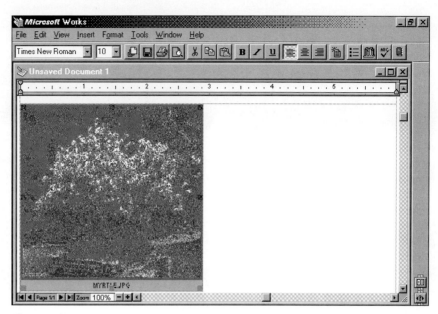

Figure 1.21

10 Select Text Wrap from the Format menu and then select Absolute and OK.

This step lets you enter text and have it wrap to the right of the image.

11 Click to the right of the image and then type **The myrtle tree shown in the figure was downloaded from CompuServe.**

The screen should look like Figure 1.22. This image will print in color if you are using a color printer.

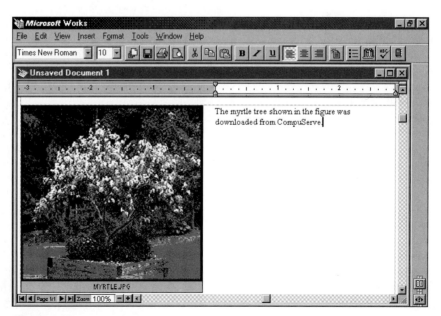

Figure 1.22

12 Save and print your work.

The Next Step

You now know how computers communicate with one another. Spend some time researching the telecommunications opportunities at your school or place of employment. Many businesses and educational institutions are connected to the Internet, which provides access to services around the world.

This concludes Project 1 with the Works Communication tool. You can either exit Works or go on to work the Study Questions, Review Exercises, and Assignments.

Summary and Exercises

Summary

- Telecommunications is the merger of telephone communications and computers.
- For a computer to communicate over phone lines, the computer must have a modem.
- With the options in the Communication Settings dialog box, you can define how a computer "talks" with a remote computer.
- With the options in the Terminal Settings dialog box, you can define how the keyboard and screen operate when connected to a remote computer.
- With the options in the Phone Settings dialog box, you can specify how the modem makes and answers calls.
- Information services, such as CompuServe, typically require an ID number and password.
- To receive (download) a file, you must instruct the remote computer to send the file and the local computer to receive the file.
- To send (upload) a file, you must instruct the remote computer to receive the file and the local computer to send the file.
- To disconnect from an information service, you would logout from the service and then disconnect Works.

Key Terms and Operations

Key Terms

analog signal
bit
bits per second·(bps)
byte
data bit
demodulate
digital signal
download
emulate
forum
login
logout
modem
modulate
parity

port
protocol
stop bit
sysop
telecommunications
telecommuter
terminal
upload

Operations

Connect to a remote computer
Create a communications file
Disconnect from a remote computer
Receive a file
Send a file

Study Questions

Multiple Choice

1. Which hardware component is required in order to telecommunicate?
   a. a high-capacity hard disk
   b. a color monitor
   c. a modem
   d. a sound card

2. Transferring a file to a remote location is called:
   a. receiving.
   b. uploading.
   c. downloading.
   d. handshaking.

3. Which of the following refers to the speed at which data is transferred through the phone lines?
   a. bps
   b. stop bit
   c. modulator
   d. protocol

4. Which of the following extensions is used for graphical image files?
   a. JPG
   b. GIF
   c. TIF
   d. All of the above.

5. The type of signal with which computers work is called:
   a. digital signal.
   b. parity.
   c. sysop.
   d. analog signal.

6. Which of the following specifies where one character ends in a data transfer signal?
   a. modem
   b. digital signal
   c. data bit
   d. stop bit

7. The method for detecting data transmission errors is referred to as the:
   a. stop bit.
   b. parity.
   c. analog signal.
   d. demodulation.

8. Which of the following is a popular protocol?
   a. Xmodem
   b. sysop
   c. 9600 baud
   d. COM4

9. The process of converting analog signals to digital signals and vice versa is called:
   a. downloading.
   c. modulation/demodulation.
   b. uploading.
   d. handshaking.

10. A person who works at home using a modem is called a:
   a. sysop.
   c. telecommuter.
   b. information provider.
   d. service provider.

Short Answer

1. COM1 and COM2 are examples of communications _____.

2. To set the terminal type to VT100, you use the _____ command in the Settings menu.

3. To choose a modem, you use the _____ command in the Settings.

4. In this project, you used the _____ information service.

5. Hayes, Motorola, Practical Peripherals, and Supra are examples of companies that make _____.

6. In this project you used the _____ protocol.

7. To exit CompuServe you type _____.

8. *Sysop* is short for _____.

9. A(n) _____ modem is located outside a computer.

10. The number of _____, either 7 or 8, specifies the number of bits used to represent one character.

For Discussion

1. Describe downloading.

2. Describe uploading.

3. Describe a job that lends itself to telecommuting.

4. Describe how to formally login to an information service.

5. Describe what kind of information is available on an information service.

Review Exercise

Selecting Communications Hardware

You need to buy a new modem for a microcomputer. Go to a computer store or get a computer magazine and pick out the modem that best suits your needs. Using the Works word processor, write a short report that answers the following questions.

1. What is the brand name and model number of the modem?

2. Is the modem internal or external?

3. What is the bps rate? Can the bps rate be adjusted?

4. Can the modem be used with both tone and pulse telephones?

5. Does the modem come with communications software?

6. Does the modem come with a subscription to an information service, such as CompuServe or Prodigy? If not, how much is a subscription?

7. When the modem accesses a number, do you get audible feedback as the modem dials the number and as the remote computer's "phone" rings?

8. Why did you select this particular modem?

Assignment

Using a Modem

Find a computer that has telecommunications capabilities, and connect to an information service of some type. Create a Works communications file to save the modem, terminal, and phone settings.

Additional Assignment

Exploring the World Wide Web

Most colleges, universities, and information service companies such as America Online and CompuServe offer access to the *Internet,* a massive, worldwide, interconnected collection of computers. Although the infrastructure for the Internet was first laid more than 20 years ago, only in the past few years has its resources become easily available to the average computer user.

Originally known as the ARPAnet, the Internet was created to link computers at military sites. Later, university professors and computer-savvy students used it to exchange ideas, data, and programs. Other users jumped on the Internet bandwagon, but the growth was slow because accessing the Internet required a substantial degree of computer skills. Then, in the early 1990s a system for navigating the Internet called the *World Wide Web* was developed at the CERN particle physics research lab in Switzerland.

The World Wide Web consists of pages (known as *Web pages*) of information that contain links (called *hyperlinks*) to other pages of information. You can jump from one Web page to another by clicking points on the screen. Web pages, which can contain text, pictures, sound clips, and video clips, can reside on a local computer or on any one of thousands of computers across the globe. A collection of related pages at one particular place is called a *Web site.*

To explore the World Wide Web you need Internet access and a *Web browser,* a program that lets you view Web pages. Typical Web browsers are Netscape's Navigator, NCSA's Mosaic, and Microsoft's Internet Explorer. When you first launch a browser, your *home page* appears automatically. Your home page can be set to almost any page in the world, but typically it will be the main page for your college or university. In addition, you'll often hear the term *home page* referring to your own personal Web page or the main page of any Web site. For example, Microsoft's home page and the White House's home page are popular sites on the Web.

Moving around the Web is as easy as pointing and clicking. You place the pointer on a hyperlink, often an underlined word or expression on the screen, and then click. Figure 1.23 has several hyperlinks. You can tell you're on a hyperlink if the pointer changes to a hand that is extending a finger. Hyperlinks take you to pages at the current Web site or to pages at Web sites across the world.

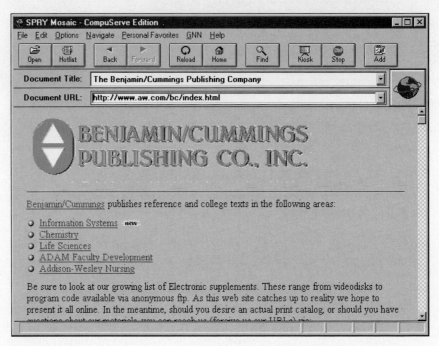

Figure 1.23

You can also go to a specific location if you know the *Uniform Resource Locator (URL)* or address for a page. For example, Benjamin/Cummings, the publisher of the module you are reading, has the URL http://www.aw.bc.com/bc/index.html. Web browsers display the current URL at the top of the screen, as shown in Figure 1.23. If you want to go to a different location, you would choose Open Location (or Open URL depending on which browser you are using) from the File menu and then type the URL.

Unfortunately, Works does not come with a Web browser. If you have access to the Web through your school's computer lab or through a company such as CompuServe or America Online, try the following steps.

1. Launch your Web browser. You will probably use Netscape, Mosaic, or Microsoft's Internet Explorer.

2. Choose Open Location or Open URL from the File menu.

3. Type **http://www.aw.com/bc/index.html** and then press (ENTER). The screen will look similar to Figure 1.23.

4. Click several of the hyperlinks.

5. When you reach a location you like, choose Print from the File menu to print it.

Operations Reference

FILE

Button	Menu Option	Keys	Description	Word Processing	Spreadsheet	Spreadsheet Chart	Database Form View	Database Form Design View	Database List View	Database Report View	Communications
	New	CTRL + O	Displays Task Launcher to access documents, templates, and TaskWizards.	●	●	●	●	●	●	●	●
	Open	CTRL + N	Opens an existing file.	●	●	●	●	●	●	●	●
	Close	CTRL + W	Closes the current file.	●	●	●	●	●	●	●	●
	Save	CTRL + S	Saves the current file.	●	●	●	●	●	●	●	●
	Save As...		Saves the current file with a new name.	●	●	●	●	●	●	●	●
	Page Setup...		Sets page size margins, and page-oriented options.	●	●	●	●	●	●	●	
	Print Preview		Previews the current file on screen before printing.	●	●	●	●	●	●	●	
	Print	CTRL + P	Prints the current file.	●	●	●	●	●	●	●	
	Send		Sends the document through electronic mail.	●	●	●	●	●	●	●	
	Exit Works		Exits Works.	●	●	●	●	●	●	●	●

EDIT

Button	Menu Option	Keys	Description	Word Processor	Spreadsheet	Spreadsheet Charting	Database Form View	Database List View	Database Form Design View	Database Reporting	Communications
	Undo/Redo	CTRL + Z	Reverses the last command.	●	●		●	●	●	●	
✂	Cut	CTRL + X	Cuts selected information and places it onto the clipboard.	●	●		●	●	●	●	
📋	Copy	CTRL + C	Copies a selection to the clipbroad.	●	●	●	●	●	●	●	●
	Cut Record		Places all the information in the displayed record onto the clipboard				●				
	Copy Record		Copies all the information of a record to a new location.				●				
	Copy Record Output		Copies output of a report for use in another Works tool or application.							●	
📋	Paste	CTRL + V	Pastes the contents of the clipboard to the current location.	●	●		●	●	●	●	●
	Paste Special...		Copies document formats or linked information to a new location in Works.	●	●		●		●		
	Paste Series...		Pastes a copied spreadsheet range into a chart as a category or value.			●					
	Clear	DEL	Deletes a selection in the current document.	●	●					●	
	Select Row/Select Record		Selects an entire row in a spreadsheet or database list or report.		●			●		●	
	Select Column/Select Field		Selects an entire column in a spreadsheet or database list or report.		●			●		●	
	Select All		Selects all data in the current document.	●	●		●	●		●	●
	Find...		Searches for a word or phrase.	●	●						

Button	Menu Option	Keys	Description	Word Processor	Spreadsheet	Spreadsheet Charting	Database Form View	Database List View	Database Form Design View	Database Reporting	Communications
	Replace...		Replaces one word or phrase with another.	•	•			•			
	Go To...	F5	Jumps to a specified bookmark, page, cell, record, or field.	•	•	•	•	•	•		
	Fill Right		Copies the left most cell(s) or entry(s) in a selection to the right across the selection.		•			•			
	Fill Down		Copies the tape cell(s) or entry(s) in a selection down the selection.		•			•			
	Fill Series...		Fills a series of dates or numbers in a spreadsheet or database List view.		•			•			
	Series...		Defines a selection as the unit of data in a spreadsheet Chart.			•					
	Titles...		Adds information to a chart to make it more readable.			•					
	Legend/Series Labels...		Adds or changes labels for a legend or series in a spreadsheet.			•					
	Data Labels...		Adds a label right next to the bar, line, or pie slice in a spreadsheet chart.			•					
	Position Selection		Positions an object that is linked to or embedded in a database form.						•		
	Links...		Establishes a link between a word processing and a database file.	•					•		
	Object		Allows an object in a word processing file or database form to be edited.	•					•		
	Field Name		Allows a field to be named or renamed.					•			
	Easy Text		Inserts easy text.	•							
	Bookmark		Inserts a bookmark.	•							

VIEW

Button	Menu Option	Keys	Description	Word Processor	Spreadsheet	Spreadsheet Charting	Database Form View	Database List View	Database Form Design View	Database Reporting	Communications
	Toolbar		Hides or shows the Toolbar.	●	●	●	●	●	●	●	●
	Zoom...		Places the current view in zoom display.	●	●	●	●	●	●	●	●
	Form	F3	Switches the database to Form view.				●	●	●	●	
	List	F3	Switches the database to List view.				●	●	●	●	
	Form Design		Switches to Form Design View.				●	●	●	●	
	Report...		Switches the database to Report view.				●	●	●		
	Normal		Switches to normal view.	●							
	Page Layout		Switches to page layout view.	●							
	Draft View		Displays all text in a single font and font size.	●							
	Wrap for Windows		Displays text in a word processing document to fit within the window.	●							
	All Characters		Displays all nonprinting as well as printing characters.	●							
	Ruler		Hides or shows the ruler.	●							
	Footnotes		Displays the Footnote editing window.	●							
	Chart...		Switches to Chart view.		●	●					
	Spreadsheet		Switches to Spreadsheet view.		●						
	Gridlines		Hides or shows grid lines.		●			●			
	Field Lines		Hides or shows field lines in a database form.						●		
	Format for Printer		Displays a database form as it will appear when printed.						●		

Button	Menu Option	Keys	Description	Word Processor	Spreadsheet	Spreadsheet Charting	Database Form View	Database List View	Database Form Design View	Database Reporting	Communications
	Hide Record		Hides highlighted records in a database.					●			
	Show All Records		Displays all records in a database.					●			
	Switch Hidden Records		Displays records that were previously hidden.					●			
	Formulas		Shows the formulas in a spreadsheet and not the resultant values.		●						
	Display as Printed...		Displays a spreadsheet chart as it will appear when printed.			●					
	Headers and Footers...		Accesses the Headers and Footers dialog box.	●		●	●	●	●	●	

INSERT

Button	Menu Option	Keys	Description	Word Processor	Spreadsheet	Spreadsheet Charting	Database Form View	Database List View	Database Form Design View	Database Reporting	Communications
	Page Break	CTRL + ENTER	Adds a page break at the insertion point.	●				●		●	
	Delete Page Break		Removes a page break.		●			●		●	
	Insert Row/Column		Inserts a row or column at the insertion point.		●					●	
	Delete Row/Column		Deletes the selected or active rows or columns.		●					●	
	Record		Inserts a record to the current database in Form view.								
	Record/Field		Adds a record or a field to a database in List view.					●			
	Delete Record		Deletes a record from a database in Form view.								
	Delete Record/Field		Deletes a record from a database in List view.					●			
	Function...		Automatically inserts a function and its arguments, in the formula bar.		●						
	Range Name...		Attaches a name to a selected range.		●						
	Special Character...		Adds a special character into a document.	●							
	Footnote...		Inserts a footnote at the current location.	●							
	Database Field...		Inserts a database field for a mail merge.								
	Field...		Inserts a field into a database in Form view.						●		
	Field Name...		Allows a field name to be changed or edited.							●	
	Field Entry...		Inserts a field entry into a database report.							●	
	Field Summary...		Designates a statistical summary to be printed at the end of a database report.							●	

Button	Menu Option	Keys	Description	Word Processor	Spreadsheet	Spreadsheet Charting	Database Form View	Database List View	Database Form Design View	Database Reporting	Communications
	Label...		Adds an information label to a database form.						●		
	Rectangle		Adds a rectangle to highlight information on a database form.						●		
	Delete Selection		Deletes the current data selection.								
	Chart...		Inserts a spreadsheet chart at the current location.	●					●		
	Spreadsheet/Table...		Inserts a spreadsheet or a table at the current location.	●					●		
	ClipArt...		Inserts a ClipArt object at the current location.	●					●		
	WordArt		Inserts a WordArt object at the current location.	●					●		
	Not-It...		Inserts a NoteIt note object at the current location.	●					●		
	Drawing...		Inserts a Microsoft Draw object at the current location.	●					●		
	Object...		Inserts objects of varying formats at the current location.	●					●		
	Page Number		Inserts page number.	●							
	Document Name		Inserts document name.	●							
	Date and Time		Inserts date or time.	●							
	Easy Text		Inserts easy text.	●							

FORMAT

Button	Menu Option	Keys	Description	Word Processor	Spreadsheet	Spreadsheet Charting	Database Form View	Database List View	Database Form Design View	Database Reporting	Communications
	Font and Style...		Changes the current font, font size, or font style.	●	●	●		●	●	●	
	Shading and Color...		Changes the shading or colors of a spreadsheet chart.			●					
	Paragraph...		Changes paragraph formats.	●							
	Tabs...		Changes tab settings.	●							
	Columns...		Changes the page layout to include the number of columns specified.	●							
	Picture/Object...		Changes the format of a picture or object.	●							
	Number...		Changes the format of numbers displayed in a spreadsheet.		●			●		●	
	Border...		Adds or changes the border of the current selection.	●	●	●		●	●	●	
	Alignment...		Changes the alignment of data in the current selection.		●			●	●	●	
	Patterns...		Changes the fill pattern of the current selection.	●	●			●		●	●
	Protection...		Changes the data protection settings.		●			●	●	●	
	AutoFormat...		Applies a predefined format to a spreadsheet table.		●						
	Set Print Area...		Sets the area of a spreadsheet to be printed.		●						
	Freeze Titles...		Freezes the row and column to the left of and about the current cell.		●						
	Row Height...		Adjusts the row height of the current selection.		●					●	
	Record Height...		Adjusts the row height of selected records in database List view.					●			

Button	Menu Option	Keys	Description	Word Processor	Spreadsheet	Spreadsheet Charting	Database Form View	Database List View	Database Form Design View	Database Reporting	Communications
	Column Width...		Adjusts the column width of the current selection.							●	
	Chart Type		Changes chart type.			●					
	Set Default Chart		Sets default chart to current one.			●					
	Horizontal (x) Axis...		Scales the horizontal-axis data in a spreadsheet chart.			●					
	Vertical (y) Axis...		Scales the vertical-axis data in a spreadsheet chart.			●					
	Right Vertical (y) Axis...		Formats the right vertical axis of a spreadsheet chart.			●					
	Two Vertical (y) Axes...		Adds a right vertical axis to a spreadsheet chart.			●					
	Mixed Line and Bar...		Creates a mixed line and bar chart from the current data selection.			●					
	3-D		Converts the current chart to a three-dimensional format.			●					
	Snap To Grid		Creates an invisible grid for aligning data elements in a database form.			●			●		
	Send To Back		Sends the current selection to the back layer.			●			●		
	Bring To Front		Brings the current selection to the front layer.			●			●		
	Field Size...		Changes the field size of a database in Form view.			●			●		
	Field Width...		Changes the field widths of a database in Form view.			●		●			
	Show Field Name		Toggles between showing and hiding the field names in a database form.						●		
	Shading		Applies shading to selection.					●	●	●	

Button	Menu Option	Keys	Description	Word Processor	Spreadsheet	Spreadsheet Charting	Database Form View	Database List View	Database Form Design View	Database Reporting	Communications
	Field		Applies format to selected field.					●	●		
	Easy Formats		Applies Easy Formats.	●							
	Borders and Shading		Applies borders to selection.	●							
	Bullets		Applies bullets to selection.	●							

TOOLS

Button	Menu Option	Keys	Description	Word Processor	Spreadsheet	Spreadsheet Charting	Database Form View	Database List View	Database Form Design View	Database Reporting	Communications
	Dial This Number		Dials a selected number from within a Works document.	●	●		●	●	●	●	
	Spelling...		Checks the spelling of the selection or document.	●	●		●	●		●	
	Thesaurus...		Provides a list of suggested synonyms.	●							
	Hyphenation...		Changes the hyphenation settings, if the hyphenation options are installed.	●							
	Word Count		Counts the number of words in the current document.	●							
	Envelopes and Labels...		Sets or changes the envelope or mailing label settings.	●				●			
	Paginate Now	F9	Repaginates the current document to reflect the most recent changes.	●							
	Sort...		Sorts spreadsheet row data.		●						
	Create New Chart...		Creates a new spreadsheet chart from the current data selection.		●	●					
	Rename Chart...		Renames the current chart.		●	●					
	Delete Chart...		Deletes the selected chart.		●	●					
	Duplicate Chart...		Creates a copy of the selected chart.		●	●					
	Recalculate Now...	F9	Recalculates a spreadsheet.		●						
	Filters		Creates, deletes, modifies, and applies filters.				●	●	●	●	

Button	Menu Option	Keys	Description	Word Processor	Spreadsheet	Spreadsheet Charting	Database Form View	Database List View	Database Form Design View	Database Reporting	Communications
	Report Creator		Creates a new database report.				●	●	●	●	
	Name Report...		Names the selected report.				●	●	●	●	
	Delete Report...		Deletes the selected report.				●	●	●	●	
	Duplicate Report...		Duplicates the selected report.				●	●	●	●	
	Customize Toolbar		Allows the user to customize the Standard Toolbar.	●	●	●	●	●	●	●	●
	Options...		Changes the Microsoft Works settings and startup options.	●	●	●	●	●	●	●	●
	Receive File...		Receives a file from another computer.								●
	Send File...		Sends a file to another computer.								●
	Capture Text...		Specifies the file settings for capturing text from another computer.								●
	Send Text...		Specifies the settings for sending text to another computer.								●
	Record Script...		Records a series of repetitive communication tasks for later use.								●
	Cancel Recording...		Cancels the recording of a script.								●
	Edit Script...		Edits a recorded script.								●
	Address Book		Opens Address Book.	●	●		●	●	●	●	●
	Lookup Referent		Searches reference title.	●							
	Form Letters		Creates a form letter.	●							
	Easy Calc				●						

SETTINGS

Button	Menu Option	Keys	Description	Word Processor	Spreadsheet	Spreadsheet Charting	Database Form View	Database List View	Database Form Design View	Database Reporting	Communications
	Phone...		Changes the phone settings.								●
	Communication...		Changes the current communication settings.								●
	Terminal...		Changes the terminal settings.								●
	Transfer...		Changes the settings for file transfers.								●
	Modem...		Changes the modem settings.								●

PHONE

Button	Menu Option	Keys	Description	Word Processor	Spreadsheet	Spreadsheet Charting	Database Form View	Database List View	Database Form Design View	Database Reporting	Communications
	Dial/Hangup		Dials a number or ends the current communication session.								●
	Easy Connect...		Connects to a predetermined phone number.								●
	Dial Again		Redials a number that was busy.								●
	Pause		Temporarily suspends the current communications session.								●
	Break		Sends a break signal to a remote computer.								●

Glossary

3-D bar chart   A bar chart that displays data in three dimensions.

absolute reference   A cell reference that does not adjust itself when copied. Contains a dollar signs ($) in front of the row number and/or the column letter. Examples: A1, $A1, and A$1.

active cell   The cell in a spreadsheet in which data will be entered, edited, or formatted. When you create a new spreadsheet, cell A1 is the active cell.

active window   The window in which you are currently working.

amortization schedule   A spreadsheet used to calculate loan repayment information.

analog signal   The signal that telephone lines carry, in which data is represented as sound.

application icon   An icon that represents a program that has been minimized.

application software   Software that helps solve a particular problem. Word processing software, electronic spreadsheets, and database management systems are all examples of application software. Windows and non-Windows applications are available.

application window   Contains a running application.

argument   A value contained within parentheses that is used by a function in the function's calculations.

ascending order   A sorting option that arranges values from lowest to highest.

B   *See* byte.

bar chart   A chart that uses side-by-side bars to display simple comparisons in data at different times or for different categories.

baud rate   The speed at which data is transmitted. The higher the baud rate, the faster the data travels.

bit   A binary digit, 0 or 1, that is the basic form of data representation. Bits represent electrical pulses: a pulse indicates a 1; the absence of a pulse indicates a 0.

bits per second (bps)   In the Communications tool, refers to the number of bits that can be transmitted in one second.

bold   A thick, heavy character style.

button   A part of the screen, on a Toolbar or in a dialog box, that allows you to choose and perform a frequently used action.

byte (B)   A group of 8 bits, roughly equivalent to a character.

calculated field   A field that uses numeric data within a record to determine a value.

case sensitive   A Works Help feature that gives the user help on the current task.

category label   A label displayed along the *x*-axis of a chart.

cell   The intersection of a column and a row in a spreadsheet.

cell reference   The column letter and row number of the active cell.

center tab   A tab stop used to align text in the center.

charting   A component of the Spreadsheet tool that is used to create a visual display of data.

check box   An area in a dialog box that can be used to toggle an option on and off.

checkmark   A mark next to an option in a menu that indicates the option is active.

click   To move a pointer to an object and then quickly press and release the left mouse button.

Clip Art Gallery   A feature that can be used to insert pre-drawn images into a document.

clipboard   The temporary storage location in memory that contains data to be copied.

column   The vertical sections of a spreadsheet. Works columns are labeled with letters.

command button   A button located within a dialog box; selecting it tells Works to immediately perform an action.

Communications tool   The Works tool that enables the computer to communicate, over telephone lines, with another computer.

context sensitive   A feature that enables Works to detect an operation in progress and give feedback applicable to that operation.

Control menu   Drops down from the Control-menu box. Enables you to control window operations, such as moving, sizing, and closing windows.

Control-menu box   Located in the upper-left corner of a window. When the Control-menu box is selected, a drop-down menu appears that lists commands for controlling a window.

Cue Cards   A Works feature that provides step-by-step instructions for completing commonly performed tasks. Cue Cards can be displayed on-screen or accessed at any time using the Help menu.

Currency format   Displays an amount in a cell with a set number of decimal places and inserts a dollar sign ($) before the number and inserts commas, if necessary.

data   Raw facts, figures, or letters that are processed by application software.

data bits   The number of bits, either 7 or 8, used to represent one character in data communications.

data label   A label placed above a data point in a chart to indicate the point's precise value.

data point   The exact point for a single numeric quantity in a chart.

data series   A group of related values in a chart.

database   A collection of highly structured data.

database management system (DBMS)   A program that enables you to manage databases by adding, editing, deleting, searching for, and sorting data. You can also summarize and print data.

database structure   Consists of the data fields; a database structure must be established before data can be entered into a database.

Database Tool   The Works tool used to manage large amounts of data. Data management includes sorting data, searching for data, editing data, creating reports, and printing data in a format of the users choice.

DBMS   See database management system.

decimal places   The number of places that follow a decimal point. The default number of decimal places for the Fixed, Currency, Comma, and Percent formats is two, but this can be adjusted from zero to seven.

decimal tab   A tab stop used to align the decimal point of a column of numbers.

default   The standard setting of a feature. For example, Works standard, or default, word processing font is Times New Roman.

default value   A value that will automatically appear in every record.

demodulate   To translate an analog signal into a digital signal by means of a modem.

descending order   A sorting option that arranges values from highest to lowest.

desktop   The screen background. In Windows the desktop is usually covered by one or more document windows.

dialog box   A rectangular box that either prompts you to provide data to complete a command or provides information, such as a warning or error message.

digital signal   The signal with which computers work, in which data is represented as 0s and 1s. Consists of electrical pulses that represent bits.

document   The letter, memo, report, or other textual item you are working on.

document window   Found inside an application window; contains a document.

double-click   To press and release the mouse button twice in quick succession.

download   To transfer data from a remote computer to a local computer.

drag-and-drop method   An alternative to using the Cut and Paste commands; used to move text to a new location. To use, select a section and use the mouse to move the selection to a new location by holding down the mouse button while moving the mouse and then releasing the mouse button when the insertion point is in the desired location.

drop-down menu   A menu that drops down from the menu bar. Lists a group of related commands.

edit   A feature found in all Work's tools that modifies existing text, numbers, or formulas.

Edit key   (F2) is called the Edit key. It allows the contents of a cell to be edited.

editing   The process of adding to, changing, or deleting the contents of a document or file.

ellipsis   Three dots in a row (...) following a command; indicates that additional information is needed to complete the command.

emulate   In the Communications tool, refers to a computer imitating or acting like a terminal.

end of document marker   A short horizontal line that marks the end of the document.

explode   To emphasize a slice in a pie chart by pulling the slice out of the whole pie.

field   A group of related characters in a database form, such as a person's last name. A field is made up of the field name and the field contents.

field contents   The characters, dates, or values entered in a field.

field name   The name assigned to a field.

file   A block of data or information that is known by a unique name.

file name   A name for a file. A filename can be up to eight characters long. At the end of the name of your choice, Works automatically adds a three-letter filename extension that indicates the document type: .WPS for a word processing document, .WKS for a spreadsheet, .WDB for a database, and .WCM for a communications document.

filter   Criteria that is used to define what data should be displayed from a database.

financial function   A function that serves as a shortcut to a complex financial operation.

find   In the Database tool, used to identify and display specific records.

font   The design of a character, including its typeface, size, position, and style.

footer   Text that appears in the bottom margin of each page of a document.

footnote   A reference, explanatory note, or comment placed at the bottom of a printed page.

form   A layout similar to a printed form or an index card that represents one record. A form is displayed as a single screen of information in Form view.

formatting   Setting the shape, style, and size of characters, paragraphs, and pages.

form design view   In the Database tool, used to arrange fields and labels in a form.

Form view   The Works default database view in which you create the database structure. Displays one record at a time for data entry.

formula   An equation used to create a new value from new and/or existing values. A formula always begins with an equal sign (=).

formula bar   A line near the top of the screen that displays the contents of the active cell.

forum   In an on-line information service, a group of users that exchange information of common interest.

freeze titles   To lock certain areas of a spreadsheet, such as titles or column headings, on-screen.

function   A built-in mathematical calculation that often serves as a shortcut to user-defined formulas. The SUM function, which adds a series of numbers, is an example of a commonly used function.

GoTo key   F5 is called the GoTo key. Pressing the GoTo key displays a dialog box in which you can specify a cell by entering a cell address and then pressing ENTER.

graphical user interface (GUI)   An easy-to-use, graphical-based work area.

grid lines   Horizontal or vertical lines that guide your eye across the chart and make it easier to determine data-point values.

group icon   Represents a group of program icons. Group icons resemble each other and can be distinguished by their labels.

group window   A window that appears when a group icon is opened. Represents the programs available.

GUI   *See* graphical user interface.

handshake   A simple set of rules that computers use to regulate data transmission.

hanging indentation   A paragraph format in which all but the first line of text is indented from the left.

hard return   The result of pressing ENTER at the end of a line to move the insertion point to the next line.

header   Text that appears in the top margin of each page of a document.

heading   A row label in a report. Prints at the top of each page of the report and is generally used for column headings.

Help index   A Works Help feature that can search for help on almost any Works-related topic.

home cell   The upper-left cell of a spreadsheet. Cell A1 is known as the home cell.

icon   A graphical representation of a Windows element.

indentation   The amount of space between page margins and paragraphs.

insertion point   A small, blinking vertical line that marks the position where text or other objects will be inserted in a document.

insert mode   A typing mode in which newly-typed text is inserted into the document. *See* typeover mode.

integrated software   All-in-one software that consists of a word processor, an electronic spreadsheet, a database management system, a charting tool, and a communications program.

intr Field name   In the Database tool's report view, used to place introductory text before groups of records.

italic   A character style in which characters slant to the right.

jump term   A highlighted term in the Help menu that, when selected, causes another screen with related definitions or topics to appear.

justified   To align text on the left and right edges of a document. Paragraphs in magazines, newspapers, and brochures are frequently justified.

key   A field that uniquely identifies each record in a database.

landscape orientation   Refers to the sideways postioning of a page during printing.

legend   A key at the bottom of a chart that serves to identify the *y*-axis data series.

left tab   A tab stop used to align text on the left.

line chart   A chart that uses lines to show trends or patterns over a set period of time.

line spacing   The amount of space between lines of text in a word processing document.

list box   Located within a dialog box, a list of choices from which you can choose only one.

List view   A Works database view that displays multiple records on-screen in a column and row format.

login   A formal procedure that allows you to use an ID number and a password to identify yourself to a computer and connect the computer you are using to a remote computer.

log out   The formal termination of a communications session with a remote computer.

logical function   A functions that returns one value if a comparison is true and another value if a comparison is false.

logical operator   An operator, such as #AND#, #OR#, or #NOT#, that is used to specify more than one condition in a field.

mail merge   The merging of a form letter with names and addresses. Used to produce mass mailings.

margin   The blank space surrounding text on a printed page.

Maximize button   Located at the right end of the title bar; used to return a minimized document to its maximized size.

menu   A list of commands.

menu bar   The list of menu names at the top of the Works screen, used to access commands.

Minimize button   Located at the right end of the title bar; used to minimize the active document or application to an icon at the bottom of the screen. You can use the Restore button or double-click the appropriate Toolbar button to restore the document to its original size.

mixed reference   A cell reference that contains an absolute reference to either the column or the row. Used when either the column or the row reference must remain absolute, such as A$1 or $A1.

modem   A piece of hardware that translates computer signals into a format that can travel over telephone lines (analog signals) and transmit data. Modem stands for MOdulator/DEModulator.

modulate   To translate a digital signal into an analog signal by means of a modem.

mouse   A hand-held pointing device whose movement on a flat surface causes a corresponding movement of a pointer on the screen.

multilevel sort   To sort by two or more fields.

operating system   A complex set of instructions that supervises and controls the operations of a computer.

operator   A symbol such as −, +, *, and / that is used in formulas.

option button   An area of a dialog box that provides several settings from which you can choose only one.

parity   An error-checking method used in data transmission.

pie chart   A chart that uses a pie shape and pie pieces to compare discrete values of a single data series in relation to the whole.

placeholder   A merge feature that consists of a field name from a database that marks the spot in a document where Works should insert an actual entry from the appropriate field in the database.

pointer   An on-screen symbol, usually an arrow, whose movement corresponds to the movement of a mouse or trackball. Used to select text, choose commands, and specify dialog box options.

points   The unit of measure used to describe character type sizes. When measured on a piece of paper, one point is 1/72 of an inch. Works has a default point size of 12.

port   A communications passage in and out of the computer. A computer may have more than one communications port.

portrait orientation   The vertical orientation for printing charts and text documents.

position   In the Font and Style dialog box, refers to the vertical position of text on a line. Can be either normal, superscript, or subscript.

portrait orientation   Refers to the standard or up-and-down positioning of a page during printing.

principal   The specific dollar amount of a loan.

program icon   An icon used to start an application.

Program Manager   A Windows feature that provides a quick way to start applications.

protocol   A set of rules followed by computers to check for and correct errors during data transmission.

query   A method of finding records that meet multiple conditions.

query expression   Also known as a query sentence. You build a query expression by selecting field names and relational or logical operators to design a query that lists records that meet two or more conditions.

Query view   A Works database view in which you specify conditions to find records.

random-access memory (RAM)   A temporary storage area for documents and programs.

range   A group of adjacent cells that you can work on as a whole. A range is referred to by its starting and ending points. For example, the range of cell A3 through cell D10 is referred to as A3:D10.

range name   A name given to a group of adjoining cells so the cells can be manipulated as a whole.

Record   A row label in a report containing data; prints once for each record until there are no more records or the page is full.

record   A group of fields that share a common element. A record is all the information in a database about a person, an event, or a product.

relational operator   An operator used in logical comparisons to indicate the equality or inequality of two values. Also used to find data in a database that falls within a range of values.

relative reference   A cell reference that, when copied, adjusts itself to reflect its new position.

report   A detailed display of database information that includes items such as titles, descriptive column headings, summaries, and so on. The information in the report can be sorted according to categories of the user's choice.

Report view   A Works database view that enables the user to design a report. Displays data in more detail than the list of records in List view.

Restore button   Used to return a window to its previous size.

right tab   A tab stop used to align text on the right.

row   The horizontal sections of a spreadsheet. Works rows are labeled with numbers.

row label   In Report view, one of four rows that indicates where Works will print different kinds of information.

ruler   A line at the top of the word processing window that can be displayed or hidden. The ruler is marked off in inches and can be used to display or control margin, indentation, and tab settings.

sans serif   A typeface without serifs, or delicate finishing strokes, at the ends of each character. Helvetica is one example.

screen font   One of the two types of Windows fonts. A screen font has a fixed range of point sizes and may or may not print as it appears on the screen. A screen font is designated in the Font and Style dialog box with an icon that looks like a printer.

scroll bar   The vertical and horizontal bars along the right and bottom edges of windows; used to scroll through a document. Also found on the right edge of list boxes.

scroll box   The box within the scroll bar that can be used to move to a specific location in a document.

search   A method of finding records that contain data that meets one condition.

select   The process of highlighting a word, sentence, paragraph, or block of data so the block can be moved, copied, deleted, or formatted as a whole. Used for applying character styles, formatting, and so on.

serif   A typeface with delicate finishing strokes at the ends of each character, such as Courier or Times.

size   In the Font and Style dialog box, refers to the height of characters.

soft return   The result of Works automatically moving the insertion point to the next line when the user is typing.

sort field   The field by which a database is sorted. Up to three sort fields can be sorted at one time.

sorting   To rearrange records in a database or rows in a spreadsheet in alphabetical, numerical, or chronological order.

spelling checker   A Works feature that checks a document for spelling mistakes. It can spell check as little as a single word or as much as an entire document.

spreadsheet   A grid of rows and columns into which one enters text, numeric values, and formulas to perform a variety of calculations. In most cases, a spreadsheet can also be called a worksheet.

Spreadsheet tool   The Works tool that creates spreadsheets and charts.

stacked-bar chart   A type of bar chart that uses stacked bars to show the relationship between individual values and the total.

status bar   A line at the bottom of the screen that displays information, such as the location of the insertion point in the file, the current character style, the setting of certain keys on the keyboard, and so on.

stop bit   The number of bits, either 1 or 2, used to delimit one binary word from another during data communications.

strikethrough   A character style that places a dash through each character, used to indicate that text is no longer needed in a document but has not yet been deleted.

style   The attributes of a character, including bold, italics, and underlining.

subscript   A character printed slightly below the normal level of a line of text; frequently used in math and science.

Summ Field Name   A row label in a report that summarizes groups of related records according to the contents of a particular field.

Summary   A row label in a report that summarizes the entire report. Calculates totals, averages, or other values for all the records in the database.

superscript   A character printed slightly above the normal level of a line of text; frequently used for footnote notations or exponents.

syntax   The order in which characters must be entered in a formula or function.

sysop   Abbreviation for *system operator*, which is a person who manages an information retrieval system.

tab   A set position to which the insertion point jumps when you press (TAB). Tabs align text more accurately than "eye-balling" the position or using spaces. Tabs can be left, right, center, or decimal aligned.

tab stop   A set position to which the insertion point jumps when "g" is pressed. Tab stops align text more accurately than "eye-balling" the position or using spaces. Tab stops can be left, right, center, or decimal aligned.

Task Launcher   A starting point for working with documents that enables the user to open a TaskWizard, an existing document, or any Works tool.

TaskWizard   Step-by-step instructions for creating common documents. For example, to create a resume, address book, or letterhead, run a TaskWizard and then Works lays out the document based upon input provided to the TaskWizard.

telecommunications   The merger of telephone communications and computers.

telecommuter   An employee who does his or her work on a personal computer away from the office and then sends information, via a modem and telephone lines, to the company's computer.

term   A fixed period for repaying a loan.

terminal   A keyboard and monitor that accesses a remote computer.

text box   Located within a dialog box, an area into which data is typed.

text label   In the Database tool's form design view, refers to descriptive text that aids a user to input data into a form.

Thesaurus   A Works feature that enables the user to look for synonyms for words to help avoid repetition or to select a more appropriate word. One can also use the Thesaurus to suggest synonyms for only a selected word or for the entire document.

Title   A row label in a report. Prints once at the beginning of each report and generally contains the report title.

title bar   The upper border of a window in which the document name or the application name is displayed.

toggle   An option or setting that can be turned on and off, or to turn an option on or off.

Toolbar   A bar of tools or buttons near the top of a Works screen that provides a quick way to accomplish common operations with the mouse.

trackball   A hand-held pointing device with an exposed ball on top. Moving the ball with your fingers causes a corresponding movement of a pointer on the screen.

TrueType font   One of the two types of Windows fonts. A TrueType font is scalable to any point size and appears the same on the screen as when printed. A TrueType font is designated in the Font and Style dialog box with a special *TT* symbol.

truncated   A number whose digits to the right of the decimal place have been dropped.

typeface   A collection of characters and symbols that have a unique design. Typefaces can be either serif or sans serif.

typeover mode   A typing mode in which newly-typed text replaces existing text. *See* insert mode.

underline   A character style in which a line appears under each character.

unfreeze titles   In the Spreadsheet tool, refers to unlocking text on the screen.

upload   To transfer data from a local computer to a remote computer.

what-if question   In the Spreadsheet tool, refers to the entering of sample data to predict what will happen under different scenarios.

window   A rectangular area on the desktop that contains a data file.

WordArt   A feature that creates fancy text which can be used for titles, logos, and elegant first letters.

Word Processing tool   The Works tool that enables you to create text documents.

word wrap   The Works word processing feature that automatically moves an entire word that extends beyond the right margin to the next line so the line of text never goes past the right margin.

worksheet   *See* Spreadsheet.

workspace   The large area of the Works screen below the Toolbar.

WorksWizards   A set of programs that perform several common Works tasks, such as creating form letters and creating mailing labels. A series of screens leads you through the process by asking specific questions and providing instructions at each step.

WYSIWYG   An acronym for "what you see is what you get." Refers to the fact that what you see on the screen is what you will see in the printed document.

x-axis   The horizontal axis on which categories appear across the bottom of a chart.

y-axis   The vertical axis that is automatically scaled to indicate amounts or values. Usually appears on the left side of a chart.

Index